D0622884

MASTERS AND JOURNEYMEN

Masters and Journeymen

A Prehistory of Industrial Relations 1717-1800

C. R. Dobson

CROOM HELM LONDON

ROWMAN AND LITTLEFIELD TOTOWA N.J.

© 1980 C.R. Dobson
Croom Helm Ltd, 2-10 St John's Road, London SW11

British Library Cataloguing in Publication Data

Dobson, C R
    Masters and journeymen. – (Croom Helm social
    history series).
    1.   Industrial relations – Great Britain –
    History – 18th century
    I.   Title
    331'.0941   HD8389
    ISBN 0-7099-0032-5

First published in the United States 1980 by
Rowman and Littlefield
81 Adams Drive
Totowa, New Jersey

ISBN 0-8476-6768-5

Printed in Great Britain by
Biddles Ltd, Guildford, Surrey

CONTENTS

TABLES

ACKNOWLEDGEMENTS

This book could not have been written without the help and goodwill of many people. I owe much to the knowledge and experience of librarians and administrative staff at several institutions, in particular the British Library, the Guildhall Library, the Institute of Historical Research, the British Library of Political and Economic Science, the Thames Polytechnic libraries and the Record Offices of the Corporation of London and the Greater London Council. I wish to thank Mr C.L. Wheble, historian of the lighterage trade, and Mr K.B. Reed, Deputy Director of Thames Polytechnic, for friendly encouragement, and my wife and children for their exceptional patience.

Much of the research was undertaken in the Graduate School of the University of Sussex, and I gratefully acknowledge the sustained interest of Lord Briggs (Professor Asa Briggs), Dr Colin Brooks, Professor J.F.C. Harrison, Professor E.P. Hennock, Miss Jennifer Platt, Dr Guy Routh and the members of the Graduate-Faculty seminar in Modern History. At various times, all were generous in advice and scholarly criticism, but I owe special debt to Dr Stephen Yeo for many stimulating discussions from the outset. For what follows, of course, the responsibility is mine alone.

C.R.D
Eltham

Every society constructs a legend of its own fortunes which
it keeps up to date and in which is hidden its own understanding of its politics; and the historical investigation of this
legend — not to expose its errors but to understand its
prejudices — must be a pre-eminent part of a political education.

Michael Oakeshott

When we strike, the masters cannot help themselves.

Witness, Old Bailey, 1765

This riot has the order and energy of a system.

Letter from North Shields, 1792

The laws do go but a very little way.

Edmund Burke

INTRODUCTION

The institutions of industrial relations are inseparable from their history. 'For better or worse the structure of present-day British trade unionism can be understood only in terms of its historical development', and this is equally so of employers' associations, collective bargaining and third-party mediation.[1] In Britain, both 'formal' and 'informal' systems of industrial relations are the outcome of a long and continuing evolution and, if in part regulated by rulebooks, written agreements and legislation, they remain in important respects elusive and ill defined. Many important rules governing employment relationships are to be found only in unwritten understandings, conventions, 'custom and practice'.[2] A system of industrial relations is a tradition of behaviour, and this book seeks the origins of the British tradition: not, it is argued, in the Industrial Revolution and the rise of the factory system, but in an earlier experience of conflict and conflict resolution between craftsmen or labourers and their employers.

The significance of pre-industrial experience is obscured not only by lack of documentary evidence, but also by preoccupation with technological change, economic growth and their social consequences. The problem of sources is real, but may be exaggerated. 'For the student of labour organization in the coal industry', noted Ashton and Sykes, 'the eighteenth century belongs, indeed, to pre-history'.[3] Cole and Postgate feared that the history of early trade unionism was 'one that can never be written', for the primary materials were 'partly deliberately concealed, partly naturally so'.[4] Yet the Webbs had described the west-country trade clubs in the woollen industry, their collaborator Frank Galton had begun to document the London tailors and George Unwin had traced the continuous history of the hatters' trade union to the seventeenth century.[5] Industrial and regional histories provide many, if scattered, references to eighteenth-century and earlier trade unionism.[6]

The Webbs have been charged with neglecting the eighteenth century, but they did nothing to foster the naïve, if widely held, belief that trade unions and industrial conflict originated in the concentration of industry early in the nineteenth.[7] On the contrary, they insisted 'that the earliest durable combinations of wage-earners in England precede the factory system by a whole century' and depicted trade unions 'springing, not from any particular institution, but from every opportunity for the

15

meeting together of wage-earners of the same occupation'.[8] The theory, common to Toynbee and Engels, of 'an irreconcilable antagonism of interest' between employer and worker under industrial capitalism, has been coupled with the myth of a pre-industrial golden age of harmonious working relationships.[9]

> 'We consider it a duty to keep our men', said one employer. 'Masters and men', said another, 'were in general so joined together in sentiment, and, if I may be permitted to use the term, in love to each other, that they did not wish to be separated if they could help it' .... Under such conditions the master busies himself with the welfare of the workman, and the education of his children; the workman eagerly promotes the interests of the master, and watches over the fortunes of the house. They are not two families but one.[10]

Nostalgia for supposed 'old bonds between employers and workmen' was shared by wage-earners whose traditional skills had been overtaken by new technology. Samuel Bamford pictured master and workman sitting down together to roast beef and dumplings, and afterwards 'with their ale and pipes, talking about whatever most concerned them'.[11] Gravenor Henson, the framework-knitters' leader, believed that 'if the masters and the men can be brought together there will be very little combination . . . it is only when they have been kept asunder that they have disagreed'; yet he also recalled an eighteenth-century history of strikes among tailors and silk weavers, and 'a system of extensive riot' against the high cost of provisions.[12] Modern research has amplified Henson's account, identifying the pre-industrial labour dispute not with the 'enlightened, orderly, bureaucratic' strike, but as a primitive mode of 'collective bargaining by riot'.[13]

In this model, peaceful conflict is abnormal. 'Acts of violence were the rule rather than the exception' and murderous affrays among coal-heavers were 'as typical as any of the eighteenth-century industrial dispute'.[14] Since trade unions were, it is argued, necessarily secret or disguised, and since under workshop production small groups of workers could not easily combine with others, neither orderly strikes nor peaceful petitioning could achieve their demands. 'The working-class was a crowd, not an army . . . . The workers could only fight by means of demonstration, shouting, cheering and catcalling, intimidation and violence.'[15]

Does this do justice to the level of organization achieved by the early trade unions? Contemporary employers believed otherwise. In

1810, the London master tailors complained of their journeymen's 'combination, subsisting for nearly a century, and ripened by experience', able to impose 'arbitrary and oppressive laws' upon the trade.[16] Fifty years earlier, the Privy Council heard how, on a Monday morning, journeymen cabinet-makers 'came in bodies to their respective Masters, and demanded the lessening of their daily hours of work, and raising the prices of their piecework; which, being refused, they immediately quitted their services'.[17] In 1777, the Middlesex magistrates proposed that masters and journeymen should 'amongst themselves, settle proper and reasonable wages', presupposing the existence of representative associations on both sides.[18] A few months before the first general Combination Act, a master printer wrote to the pressmen's secretary, 'in the hope that the difference, at present subsisting in the trade, may be brought to an amicable termination'.[19] At least in London, the elements of an industrial-relations system already existed.[20]

'Orderly and peaceful', 'intimidating and violent', are opposite ends of a spectrum; the pure form is rare at any time. The most violent or 'spontaneous' riot has some organization at its centre; even among 'moderate' or 'conservative' occupational groups, indiscipline and coercion may be peripheral to an orderly withdrawal of labour. In 1796, a journeyman printer in Chancery Lane fell out with his union committee.

He went to work about eight o'clock in the morning; about ten he heard the word, 'give attention', uttered among the printers. They formed a notice preparatory to hostility; something was immediately cast upon his head; and the whole company in the printing-room was in uproar against him, so that he was compelled to go down stairs as fast as he could, in the course of which he was much molested and assaulted. A heap of old letters from the composing-room was showered upon his head, after which followed a wet blanket. He made his escape from this fury into Mr Davis's private house, where he stood for two hours, being afraid to go out, there being a number of the men who had insulted him in waiting at the door.[21]

Henson related how weavers and woolcombers punished masters and journeymen paying and receiving low wages by riding them on the cool-staff, 'that is, seated astride a long-pole, mounted upon men's shoulders, and held up to the derision of the populace'.[22] Known as 'colting' in Dublin and 'stanging' on Tyneside, the rough horseplay differed in degree of violence from the armed battles of Spitalfields, and the ritual stoning to death of a Crown witness.[23] In the eighteenth century, the term 'riot' was applied indiscriminately to any unlawful assembly, whether or not accompanied by violence or disorder. When, in 1768, the 'riotous' merchant seamen marched through London to demand higher wages

> their behaviour was very orderly. Several great Persons took particular notice of them; and the Sailors, like honest, regular, loyal good subjects, gave three cheers, to God bless the King, and as they came on orderly, so in the same peaceable manner they marched off.[24]

There were, in fact, no 'typical' eighteenth-century labour disputes, but many forms of collective behaviour, varying with time, place, trade and occupation, or, as at the time of the Wilkes affair, the balance of political power in the wider society. The more spectacular manifestations are well documented in familiar sources, the others obscurely so. Following Dr Rudé's count of 'a dozen strikes . . . in Paris between 1720 and 1789, and in London perhaps a score',[25] the present study began as an attempt to enlarge the statistical coverage, and nearly 400 labour disputes were located in the British Isles between 1717 and 1800. These are tabulated in Chapter 1 by region, trade and principal issue. Chapter 2 examines some labour riots in provincial England, whereas Chapters 3 to 5 are concerned with associations of handicraft workmen in the London trades.

The rest of the book considers labour relations in a wider context. The role of magistrates as third-party mediators is discussed in Chapter 6, and the government's experience as an employer assessed in Chapter 7. Finally, the Combination Acts are related to problems of inflation and public order. If less than an exploration, this reconnaissance suggests some pathways, and a larger selection of documents will be published elsewhere.

1 DISPUTES AND DISTURBANCES

Eighteenth-century England was 'a land of hamlets and villages', the few towns being on or near the coast.[1] Security depended on the navy and prosperity on trade and navigation.

> Sea water flowed in our veins, our speech was salted with naval metaphors and similes: we knew the ropes, we quickly took our bearings, we got under way, we were seldom taken aback; things went swimmingly with us; if we found ourselves in deep water we tacked, veered or trimmed until all was plane sailing again; we worked like galley slaves, and if we chose to stop work we struck work as one might strike a mast or sail.[2]

Hence the term 'to strike' originated in May 1768, when merchant seamen 'unreefed the topsails, declaring that no ship should sail unless the merchants would consent to raise their wages', and, fired by their example, the journeymen hatters 'struck'.[3]

This is an attractive theory, but four years earlier the London tailors had 'struck (as they term it)', and in 1763 a hiring bond made at Newcastle required coal miners to 'continue at work, without striking, combining or absenting themselves'.[4] Seamen 'turned out' for pay increases, whereas those who most commonly 'struck' or 'struck off work' were landlubbers: staymakers, shoemakers, masons or house-carpenters.[5] Lacking the *mot juste* for 'a concerted refusal to work by employees till some grievance is remedied', their employers complained variously of 'riots', 'tumults', 'insurrection', 'mutiny', 'conspiracy', 'combination', or 'refractory behaviour', but by 1782 a minister was explaining to Parliament that, if house-carpenters were employed in the naval dockyards, 'all the shipwrights now employed would strike'.[6]

By whatever name, collective work stoppages were familiar at least a century earlier. Under the Protectorate the State Papers record disputes and disturbances, as does the journal of a Trowbridge clothier for 1677.

> Goeing forth he saw a great company of men ffollowing a ffidler and one of them made a kind of Proclamacon that 'whosoever was of their side should ffollow them'. Afterwards, hearing that they

were att an Alehouse neere the bridge he went thither with the Constables where he heard Aaron Atkins say he was the man who made the Proclamacon and that the intention thereof was to engage as many as he could for the raising of their wages sixpence per weeke and that Samuel Bowden (and others) affirmed the same and were with him in the streete upon the same designe, and Atkins said he had a sword and wished that he had had it with him.[7]

Being both their employer and Justice of the Peace, William Brewer had the ringleaders arrested and brought before him.[8] Such incidents marked the beginnings of a trade union movement in the west of England, based on journeymen's clubs in the wool-manufacturing towns. In imitation of their employers' chartered company, the clubs of weavers, woolcombers and labourers adopted a common seal, tip-staffs and colours, and raised a fund to enable members to leave their home towns when about to be prosecuted for combination. Certificates issued to such members setting off on tramp were mutually recognized by the west-country clubs, which in 1706 made a concerted attempt to enforce a closed shop,

> their Demands being, in effect, that no Master Weaver shall take a Prentice, without leave of the Confederacy, and the Apprentice to be inrolled in their Books; that the Master shall not employ a Journeyman, before he becomes one of the Bristol Confederacy, or brings a Certificate, that he is confederated at some other Place.[9]

The merchant clothiers complained to Parliament that in the course of their strikes at Bristol, Taunton and Tiverton the weavers had terrorized those wishing to work, had assaulted employers and magistrates, and rescued some of their number from the common gaol.[10]

In November 1717, troops and sailors were ordered to Devon to disperse a body of 900 weavers who were marching from town to town, cutting looms and breaking the masters' jars of oil. 'The price of wool having risen, the Master Weavers of the colour'd Serges (for which there is but a small Demand at present) cannot employ Journeymen to have Goods lie on their Hands, unless they will work for lower wages.'[11] In London, there were rumours of sedition but, had this been a political conspiracy, the leaders would not have escaped with gaol sentences of three to six months, fines from 30 to 70 nobles, and binding over to be of good behaviour for up to a year.[12]

In London itself, labour disputes began to be reported almost every year, 1720 marking the début of the formidable trade unions of tailors and curriers and the occasion for testing the indictment for conspiracy as a legal weapon against strikes.[13] In southern England and the west, the textile industry was disrupted over wage reductions and payment in 'truck'; after the worst disturbances seen in the south-west for forty years, an Act was passed against unlawful combinations of workmen in the woollen industry.[14] There were strikes of coal miners, in North Somerset and in 1731 on Tyneside. The London wheelwrights struck in 1734 for a wage increase and a reduction in the working day. There were riots in 1736 against the employment of Irishmen, who were accused of undercutting Spitalfields silk weavers, London building workers and Kentish farm labourers. Shipwrights in the Woolwich and Deptford navy yards struck in 1739 in defence of their prerogative of 'chips', and up to 1740 the other militant groups included the coopers of Cork, the bakers of Dublin, bargemen in Hertfordshire, nailmakers in Worcestershire, seamen at Southampton and keelmen on the Tyne. But more than a third of all reported disputes were of woolcombers, spinners and weavers in the depressed woollen manufactures. By 1743, the Devonshire weavers were 'up in arms, on account of their masters forcing them to take corn, bread, bacon, cheese, butter and other necessaries of life, in Truck, as it is call'd, for their labour'.[15]

The trucking system had been attacked in an *Essay on Riots*, but in a rejoinder it was suggested that the workers had brought it on themselves.

I have known very good manufacturers leave ready-money clothiers, without cause, to go to trucking masters. It's obvious from the public declarations of the clothiers, but 45 out of 50 abhor these mean practices. If they inform, they shall be unemploy'd, is their common excuse, How do they know this, when they never try'd in ten years past?[16]

From this year onwards, strikes or 'turn-outs' became common-place in London and the provinces, involving a great variety of occupations and raising many different issues. In 1744, London glaziers, tailors, and peruke makers demanded wage increases and a shorter working day, and were followed by wheelwrights, carmen, wharfingers' labourers, barbers, joiners and house-painters. In 1745 the bakers struck unsuccessfully to abolish Sunday baking, the barbers for abolition of deductions from their pay, and house-painters against the employment

Table 1.1: Reported Labour Disputes, by Region, British Isles, 1717-1800

Region	1717-40	1741-60	1761-80	1781-1800	Total
London	12	18	55	34	119
South-east	5	3	4	9	21
South	4	–	1	2	7
South-west	17	10	3	17	47
Eastern	6	3	3	12	24
Midlands	1	2	5	19	27
East and West Ridings	–	1	5	10	16
North-west	–	9	14	15	38
Northern	3	3	8	20	34
Wales	–	–	–	–	–
Scotland	–	2	8	8	18
Ireland	12	6	7	7	32
Total disputes, British Isles	60	57	113	153	383

Source: Burney collection, British Library (see Bibliography, Notes and References).

of non-freemen. Continuous association in these occupations is evident from their reappearance between 1750 and 1760 with farriers, wire-drawers, silversmiths and bookbinders.

Although the Webbs found 'scarcely a trace' of combinations in the building trades before the very end of the century, the carpenters, joiners, bricklayers and labourers in Manchester struck in July 1753 for a wage increase, rejecting conciliation by local magistrates.[17] In June 1776, 'a great number' of carpenters began to pull down the scaffolding before the new buildings in Brown's Gardens, St Giles's, and 3,000 assembled near Middlesex Hospital to demand an extra two shillings a week.[18] For several months, building work in central and east London was interrupted, and there were smaller 'wildcat' stoppages in the industry. When guardsmen were stationed at the doors of Westminster Abbey, to prevent sightseers hindering preparations for George III's coronation,

the workmen, finding that they were deprived of what they called their perquisites, by the soldiers taking the money of those that were let in, declared that they would work no longer unless they were paid double wages, which were ordered them till the coronation day.[19]

On the dismissal of their foreman, and his replacement by a Scotsman, craftsmen and labourers alike walked off the site of 'the new grand buildings in Durham-yard in the Strand'.[20] In 1765, two Irish labourers were imprisoned for riotous picketing at the new buildings in Theobald's Row, and there were similar incidents in Marylebone in 1775.[21]

The Webbs' omission is of theoretical interest, as it led them to associate trade union growth with blocked social mobility. Superior craftsmen tended to become employers, and 'the journeymen would possess the same prospects of economic advancement that hindered the growth of stable combinations in the ordinary handicrafts'.[22] As the capitalist builder or contractor began to supersede the small master, giving place to a hierarchy of hired workers, trade unions emerged, but until then any organizations of such craftsmen tended to become masters' guilds.[23] However valid this may have been for earlier centuries, we shall see that in eighteenth-century London, the clubs and houses of call for bricklayers, carpenters and masons functioned as associations of wage-earners, differing in no significant respect from those of other trades.[24]

Not all strikes were of unionized workers. The haymakers at Islington regularly exploited their bargaining power at harvest time. Success varied with the weather. In the great drought of 1763, when hay was selling at four pounds a load, 'they got a drum, and beat it through the town, and obliged all the other hay-makers to join them, which has done great injury to the farmers, who had a great deal of hay ready to carry in'.[25] Repeating the exercise in 1766, and refusing to work for under 1s 4d a day, they were suddenly deprived of employment by a heavy rainstorm; members of the Royal Exchange collected £11 to relieve their distress.[26] In 1774, the strike meeting became riotous and was dispersed by the magistrates, but the following year they

again struck from making hay, owing to their having but 1s. per day as wages; they all met in a lane near the Brill-house, Pancras; on which Mr. Roads, Farmer and Cowkeeper, rode thro', and informed them, that he and the rest of the Farmers would pay them 1s. 6d. per day; on which they all went to work, and were very well satisfied.[27]

Table 1.2: Reported Labour Disputes, by Occupations or Trades, British Isles, 1717-1800

Occupation/Trade	1717-40	1741-60	1761-80	1781-1800	Total
Farm workers and market gardeners	2	–	–	4	6
Harvesters	–	1	6	–	7
Coal miners	4	–	3	11	18
Nailmakers	2	1	–	1	4
Blacksmiths and farriers	1	1	–	–	2
Shipwrights, ropemakers and sailmakers	2	3	1	6	12
Millwrights	–	–	–	2	2
Wheelwrights	2	1	–	2	5
Woolcombers, weavers and spinners (wool)	21	15	7	21	64
Silk weavers	4	–	7	–	11
Hosiery (framework-knitters)	1	–	3	7	11
Other textile	3	3	3	7	16
Curriers	1	1	2	1	5
Other leather	–	–	1	–	1
Tailors and staymakers	5	7	10	5	27
Shoemakers	1	2	4	8	15
Hatters	–	–	4	3	7
Bakers (bread)	2	1	3	2	8
Sugar-bakers	–	–	1	–	1
Coopers	1	–	2	1	4
Papermakers	–	–	–	5	5
Printers and bookbinders	–	–	1	5	6
Cabinet- and chair-makers	1	1	4	2	8
Bricklayers, carpenters and building labourers	1	4	8	6	19
Stonemasons	–	1	2	1	4
House-painters	–	2	–	–	2
Canal builders (navigators)	–	–	2	1	3
Seamen and ships' carpenters	1	3	16	17	37

Bargemen and lightermen	3	—	2	1	6
Keelmen (coal trade)	1	1	2	6	10
Coal porters and carmen	—	1	3	3	7
Barbers and wig (peruke) makers	1	3	—	—	4
Other occupations and trades	—	5	16	25	46
Total, all trades and occupations	60	57	113	153	383

Source: Burney collection.

Mown grass, carried by the buyer, was selling in Kent at 25s a load and, made into hay, carted by the seller, at 36s.

However, the most consistently successful bargainers were those with a permanent base for continuous association. This was not necessarily the workplace, although there are references to 'shop committees' of shoemakers towards the end of the century, and the printers' 'chapel' can be traced to the seventeenth century and possibly earlier.[28] The rise of the British trade union movement is intimately linked with that of the public house. The three most conspicuously militant groups — woolcombers and weavers, merchant seamen and tailors — created their networks of committees and worked out their strategies over a tankard of porter in their 'house of call', or, in the case of seamen, 'the house of rendezvous'.[29]

The British seamen, 'the hearts of oak', enjoyed a distinctive status, if not always high wages and job security. 'This class of man', wrote a Londoner in 1747, 'are the source of the wealth and support of the freedom of Great Britain'.[30] Their demonstrations and petitions attracted widespread public support, and they were treated as a special case by Justices of the Peace. There was a remarkable exchange of civilities between the Sheriff of Bristol, Mr Williams, and the leaders of 500 sailors who were marching on the Council House to demand pay parity.

'My fellow-subjects, permit me to ask the reasons of your patrolling the streets with music and colours flying'. They gave for answer, 'To demand an advance of wages from the Merchants'. The Sheriff told them their manner of proceeding was very improper and illegal, but as he knew them to be a brave and generous set of men, he would be happy to do everything within his power to render them service and begged them to explain the extent of their wishes. Their reply was, 'To have the same wages as were paid their brethren at other ports'. The Sheriff said, 'Well, my honest lads, if this is the only cause of your assembling, let me request you to return in peace to your habitations, assuring you that I will interest myself with the Merchants to redress your complaint, by doing all in my power to compleat your wishes.' He accordingly applied to the Master of the Merchants-hall, and . . . they have had a meeting this day for that purpose, and very readily complied with the honest Tars' request.[31]

In the decade up to 1767, the average number of strikes per year was three for the British Isles, but less than two for London, the peak year being 1761, when, however, four of the five strikes were in the capital. In 1768 there was a dramatic outbreak of industrial unrest, coinciding with the Wilkes demonstrations, and sometimes confused with them.[32] The following year, there were ten disputes, but only two in London. Then followed a long period of relative industrial peace, but 1792 set a record for the century with 29 strikes, nearly all of them in the provinces. The peak year for London was 1777, and for the rest of the country, 1787. Curiously, London was virtually strike-free in 1780, the year of the Gordon riots, and in 1789-90 the events in France had no immediate impact, other than to increase the bargaining power of papermakers in Kent, Hertfordshire and Scotland.

Although the decade 1791-1800 accounts for nearly a third of all labour disputes reported in the entire century, these were nearly all in four years — 1791, 1792, 1793 and 1795 — the last being one of grave food shortages and riots in provincial England. In 1793 and 1795, there were attempts by farm workers in the Home Counties to raise their wages in a momentarily favourable bargaining situation, and these years mark the beginnings of agricultural trade unionism. Included in our list of disputes, although outside the scope of the present book, are five 'machine riots' (attempts to prevent the introduction of labour-saving machinery in the woollen and hosiery industries), and the naval mutiny of 1797, which in its early stages was a non-political movement for higher wages and better provisions.[33] The years of the two Combination Acts, 1799 and 1800, were comparatively quiet, but two strikes, of millwrights and bakers, were in politically sensitive areas. There was a concerted movement among shoemakers in Scotland and the north of England, which alarmed the authorities and possibly assisted the passage of the first Combination

Act.[34] The century ended with the second Combination Act, food riots and radical agitation in London, and a huge and largely successful strike of tailors.

If the number of disputes per occupation or industry is taken as a crude indicator of 'strike-proneness', the textile trades were foremost with nearly a third of the total. Next came the clothing trades and merchant shipping, each accounting for about a tenth. However, downward pressure on piece-rates, the main source of conflict in the wool trade early in the century, was not a principal issue outside the textile industries. Claims for wage increases to offset rising prices were almost universal from the 1760s onwards, frequently coupled with demands for a shorter working day. Disputes over perquisites were specific to a small number of occupations, but in the naval dockyards the question of 'chips' was the perennial bane of the Admiralty. If the spinning jenny and gig-mill posed the question of obsolescent skills, technical change as such was not a major source of conflict. On the other hand, labour costs and indiscipline may have prompted innovation, and, in turn, further strife, as in the Thames Valley.

We are here in the greatest confusion, for fear of the Bargemen. The late Act of Parliament for employing horses in the room of men, for drawing the craft up and down the river, has left many of them destitute of employment. They have got it into their heads that it was the Farmers round here that set the Act on foot, to employ their horses in those parts of the year they have the least use for them, and threaten to burn all our houses, barns &c., unless we get them employed as usual.[35]

As a Maidenhead resident, alarmed by the flames from nearby barns, observed at the time, 'on any alteration being made in any business, the Projectors (who always intend to benefit themselves) should be under obligations to provide for the sufferers; but too many of our Great Men have more regard to increase the bread of horses than that of men, as they gain more by the former than the latter'.[36] This view was widely held in the first half of the century and delayed, among other innovations, the introduction of wind-powered machinery to the timber trade.[37]

Perquisites and supplements, such as the carpenters' chips, the weavers' thrums, the iron hoops claimed by coopers and 'kettle-money' demanded by seamen, created issues at the boundary between lawful rights and 'custom and practice'. There was sufficient doubt in common

Table 1.3: Reported Labour Disputes, by Primary Issue as Stated, British Isles, 1717-1800

Type of Issue	1717-40	1741-60	1761-80	1781-1800	Total
Wages & hours					
Wage increase	16	25	62	87	190
Wage decrease	13	3	5	5	26
Perquisites & special payments	–	3	2	3	8
Hours of work	4	5	2	4	15
Other wage issue	10	9	9	6	34
Total wages/hours issues	43	45	80	105	273
Employment issues					
Employment of apprentices	3	3	2	5	13
Employment of other persons	5	2	6	7	20
Innovation and machinery	–	–	8	15	23
Imported goods and materials	3	1	1	–	5
Working arrangements	1	–	1	2	4
Total employment issues	12	6	18	29	65
Other issues					
Supervision & discipline	–	–	1	2	3
Unclassified	5	6	14	17	42
Total other issues	5	6	15	19	45
Total all issues	60	57	113	153	383

Source: Burney collection.

law as to what was a perquisite and what was embezzlement for special Acts of Parliament to be needed for the textile and clothing trades. In 1723, shoemakers and shopkeepers petitioned for relief against 'abuses committed by the journeymen they employ in making up their goods, by pawning and otherwise embezzling them'.[38] In 1749, a well-established practice among hatters was ended by an Act to prevent unlawful combinations of journeymen dyers and hotpressers and to provide for better payment of their wages: soon after its enactment, a 'notorious offender', Ann Edwards, was convicted of buying and receiving materials from a journeyman hatter, a 'crime of a most pernicious tendency' perpetrated over many years.[39] A bizarre case of large-scale theft came to light at Harbledown, near Canterbury, when a search of hop-workers' cottages led to the recovery of eleven cartloads of hop-poles. The employer declined to prosecute, and there was public comment on the need for regulation of the hop trade and the payment of proper wages.[40]

Whatever the importance of employment, disciplinary and other issues to particular groups at different times, the most important single source of industrial conflict was the money wage. In times of rising prices, most markedly in wartime, all workers with bargaining power made use of it, and for such periods it is meaningful to identify strike 'waves' and labour 'movements'. Above all, it was the great inflation of the 1790s that brought trade unionism to the centre of public debate, and created 'a general problem calling for a general solution'.[41]

2 CONFLICT AND COMMUNITY

From a statistical analysis of twentieth-century strikes, Kerr and Siegel found certain occupations to be consistently strike-prone, and explained this by the workers' location in the social structure.

The miners, sailors, the longshoremen, the loggers, and, to a much lesser extent, the textile workers form isolated masses, almost a 'race apart'. They live in their separate communities: the logging camp, the textile town. These communities have their own codes, myths, heroes and social standards. There are few neutrals in them to mediate the conflicts and dilute the mass.[1]

The 'isolated mass' hypothesis is also consistent with much of our data on eighteenth-century labour disputes. We have no evidence on loggers, but weavers held the record for the number of strikes, with seamen in second place. Riverside workers — coal heavers, bargemen, keelmen and lightermen — appear regularly in reports of strikes. The only other group with a comparable record of militancy were the highly organized London tailors, who fit awkwardly into an otherwise persuasive interpretation. The other characteristic of the eighteenth-century 'isolated mass' was its apparently high propensity to violence, so much so that Hobsbawm, Rudé and others saw 'collective bargaining by riot' as the distinguishing characteristic of the pre-industrial labour dispute. There were, however, regional differences: in the Wiltshire, Somerset and Devon woollen trade, disputes involved whole towns and villages, turning almost to civil warfare. A little way from the turbulent south-west, the contrast was marked. At Newbury in 1724 and Norwich in 1752, the journeymen weavers simply stopped work, and went into the fields as harvesters or labourers until agreement was reached with their employers.[2] Likewise at Alton, Hampshire, no rioting occurred, although a conspiracy was uncovered 'to break or cut off the Thumbs of some of the servants of the prosecutors who would not come into their Measures. The Defendants pretended they acted only as a Charitable Society.'[3]

Although the west-country riots were at first directed against master weavers, other groups became involved. When 500 weavers began breaking looms at Taunton, 'obliging the owners to bring small wood to set them on fire', local townspeople and tradesmen confronted them in equal numbers, and were joined by woolcombers who had been put out of work by the dispute. 'Whereupon a brisk engagement ensu'd and hundreds on both sides were down at once. Some had their Arms broke, others their Ribs, several their Skulls cleft, but very few kept their Heads whole, so that the Streets almost ran with blood.'[4] Many weavers were taken to the county gaol at Ilchester, but a year later combers and weavers were reconciled, joining together in procession to commemorate the Gunpowder Plot.[5]

The weavers of Bristol enjoyed a love-hate relationship with a prominent clothier, Mr Stephen Fetcham, and twice attempted to demolish his house. His neighbour, a Mr Edgar, had already suffered this fate, and Mr Fetcham appeased the crowd with concessions. Thereafter, he was dubbed 'the weavers' friend', and in September 1729, when another clothier decided 'to fall their wages 6d. a piece on their Snap Shalloons', Mr Fetcham 'stood by them, and said he would rather leave off his Trade than lower their Wages'.[6] Following his lead, most of the clothiers agreed to pay the full prices, and the dispute seemed over, but some days later, the weavers unexpectedly turned out for an increase of a shilling on a double piece.

> and would have had Mr Fetcham, who had been their Friend before, to be the first in thus raising their Price. But he refused it, telling them that as he would not fall their Wages, so he would not raise them.[7]

On the Monday morning, hundreds of weavers, summoned by the beating of frying pans, assembled at dawn and marched to his house, brushing aside a detachment of soldiers, whose instructions were to fire with powder only. From inside the house, Mr Fetcham and his family also opened fire, killing seven weavers and the sergeant in charge of the detachment. The regiment then intervened, but throughout the city great damage was done wherever the rioters found any of Mr Fetcham's work. The coroner recorded 'accidental death' on the sergeant, and *Defendendo* on the weavers. In June 1730, Mr Fetcham appeared before King's Bench to plead the Royal Pardon.

Such riots were not spontaneous, but carefully planned. A House of Commons committee had accumulated evidence of intimidation of employers by the clubs of workmen in the woollen manufacture. Mr Vowler, of Exeter, outlined their by-laws, and described the practice of 'coolstaffing': he had seen a master carried about on a coolstaff.

Mr William Pike affirmed that only fear of coolstaffing prevented his men from working at the usual wages. He favoured a Bill to prevent combinations of workmen and for the proper payment of their wages; he was prepared to pay his men in money if truck were abolished, and believed others would willingly do so if the law applied to them all.[8]

The committee reported on 9 March 1726, and a second reading to the Bill was immediately given.[9] There was no immediate reaction from the weavers, but in November they began a great protest march towards London, assembling near Bradford-on-Avon, and thence to Devizes, Melksham, Calne, Westbury, Shepton Mallet and Bruton. At Frome, they encountered two troops of dragoons, and retreated to Melksham, where the High Sheriff dispersed them by reading the Riot Act and warning them of the imminent arrival of more dragoons from Salisbury.[10] Thereafter, industrial unrest took a new form: clandestine groups of loom-cutters were formed. In Trowbridge, 'a great number of weavers, armed with great clubs, having high-crowned hats on and their faces sooted, came into Town one Day, broke into the workshops, and cut a great many fine Broad-Cloaths to pieces out of the looms and went off without being known'.[11] A year later, 500 weavers seized and burned 30 looms at Lawford's Gate, Bristol, and went on to do likewise at Chew Magna, Pensford and Keynsham, where they also pulled down a house.[12] These tactics failed, however, to check the steady downward pressure on prices and wages, and the weavers turned their attention from their immediate employers to the merchant clothiers. Industrial conflict became a war of country against town, of extra-mural wage-earners against the *bourgeoisie* within.

At midnight on 2 May 1738, 60 men of Colonel Mountague's regiment set off from Exeter in response to an express from the Mayor of Tiverton. The woolcombers in Uffculme, Collumpton, Bradninch and adjacent villages had sent 'Greetings, that they intended to come in a Body and pull down the Merchants' houses . . . they are not giving a Price for Goods to the Masters that employ'd them, sufficient for Masters to give Wages whereby a poor Man can live'.[13] The Mayor recruited a hundred special constables and, before the troops arrived, the decisive engagement had been fought on Lowman's Green: one man was killed and another had a fractured skull, but the combers entered the town and, to save their property, the merchants conceded higher prices. This success encouraged the Wiltshire clubs to make similar demands, and in November there was a rash of loom-cutting at Trowbridge, Hilprington and Studley. However, Mr Henry Coulthurst, an important merchant of Melksham, resisted a claim for a one-penny increase on the prevailing price of fourteen pence a yard. On Tuesday 28 November, a large group of weavers and shearmen entered the town and, to avoid further trouble, Coulthurst sent word that he would concede the penny. The men's leaders then raised their demands, first insisting on a note of hand for performance, and, after breaking into Coulthurst's dwelling-house,

> they returned into the Market-Place, and demanded first a Note sign'd by all the Clothiers in Melksham, that they would for ever forward give 15d. per Yard for Weaving, and 1s. for spooling. This done, they required a fifty pound Penalty to be inserted in the said Note. This comply'd with, they extorted a Bond of a thousand pounds Penalty to four of their Number for the abovesaid Consideration.[14]

During the night, one of the leaders, John Crabb, was seen entering a workshop through a broken window, and was arrested, brought before the Chippenham magistrates, and committed to the county gaol at Fisherton. A much larger crowd, put at 1,500, marched towards Melksham, demanding Crabb's release; the clothiers met them outside the town, and agreed to sign a letter to the justices, 'to beg the prisoner might not be committed'. Many of the crowd were determined to punish Coulthurst and, before long, poured into the town to demolish the remains of his house, workshops and fulling-mills: 'in all, nine Houses, besides the Mills'. Two local magistrates read the Riot Act, with little effect, and the crowd lingered in and around the town until Sunday night, when a detachment of foot-guards arrived. For their part in the riot — which all denied — three weavers were tried and hanged at Salisbury.[15]

After this explosion of violence, some clothiers moved from the strife-torn west country to less-developed regions to the north, and the next decade saw the steady decline of the west-country woollen trade. New centres of industry, but also of conflict, began to emerge: there were strikes at Kendal and Derby in 1760, at Carlisle in 1768, Aberdeen in 1769, Keighley in 1775 and Glasgow in 1787. After the commercial treaty with France in 1786, the export trade revived, but, whereas in the west, the 'old game' between masters and men revived, some regions enjoyed spectacular growth and prosperity. In an article on Paisley, William Carlile attributed the 'considerable revolution in the manufactures of Great Britain' to Arkwright's 'happy invention of machinery'.[16]

In the west country, another group of workers waged war on the City of Bristol. In 1727, the Kingswood coal miners resisted imports from the Forest of Dean to supply the glass industry. The Gloucester road was picketed, turnpikes and turnpike houses were demolished, and several boatloads of coal were sunk in the Avon.[17] In 1738, these actions were renewed in a strike over wage cuts. An old colliery had been reopened, and the tenants, finding it capable of improvement, offered to supply the glass-works, smithies and sugar houses at competitive prices. To remain in business, the other coal owners agreed to reduce wages from sixteen pence to a shilling a day, whereupon the miners struck.

And to prevent the bringing of Coal to Town, till such Time Matters were accommodated, have dispers'd themselves into several Parties, and stopp'd up the Communication of the Coal-Carriages and Horses; and as they are poor and not able to subsist without working, to supply their Necessities, forc'd a Collection on the Road, by obliging People to give them Money; and such as had Cheese or Bread, they took Care to lighten them of their Burthen, swearing that it was Bread they wanted.[18]

Some cases of gratuitous violence and drunkenness were reported. At Brislington, a crowd of miners, 'forc'd several of the civilis'd Colliers into their Service and violently beat those who refus'd; enter'd what Houses they pleas'd; ate and drank everything they could come at, without paying any Money; threw a great deal of Coal into the Pits; and burnt all the Oaken Poles used in propping up the Mine-Works'.[19] From there, they went on to Bristol,

some going through the Body of the City hallowing and shouting, others taking the Boat at the Temple-Backs, and pass'd without paying. All the Horses they met with laden, have been stopp'd, their Sacks cut, and the Coal thrown about the Highway and Streets, beating several Pack-Saddles to Pieces. Several Waggons full of Coal have also fallen a Sacrifice to their Rage, particularly one near Castle-Gate, the Wheels and Shafts of which they cut in pieces, and threw the Coal into the Street. Without Lawford's Gate they met with another Waggon, which they overset, wasted the Coals and would have destroy'd the Waggon, had it not been for the remonstrance of the Driver, who had formerly sav'd the life of one of the Colliers concern'd in destroying the Turnpikes, and giving them Half a Crown to drink. They were resolv'd to make an Example of one Roger Purnel, a Lighterman, who they oblig'd to leap overboard, and several swam after him across the River, but he made his escape.[20]

There were also complaints of highway robbery and, after the hold-up of the Bath coach on 12 October, the watch was doubled, super-numerary constables appointed and troops stationed in the Square under arms. The City Aldermen sent to the Forest of Dean for as many shiploads of coal as could be supplied immediately, but, after strong protests from owners of the Kingswood collieries, countermanded the message. After threats to fill in their pits, some proprietors hinted at compromise. Where men were still working, parties of strikers arrived to stop them up unless they came to the surface and joined them.[21]

In the night of 1 November, a strike leader, James Powell, was captured 'by stratagem' and taken to the county Bridewell. To prevent a rescue, a show of force was mounted outside the gaol and also the Lamb Inn, where the magistrates were meeting. By lunchtime, the whole of Brigadier Harrison's regiment had paraded conspicuously, 'every Soldier's Piece being loaded with a Brace of Balls'. Eighteen sentinels were posted inside the gaol and two outside. Next day, it became known that all the coal-works in Sir Isaac Newton's royalties had been stopped, four pits filled up at White Hill and five at Siston's Bottom, while Jeremy Ford, George Riddle, Charles Tippet, Henry Monk and Larry Price had suffered the loss of their carts, reels, hoses and other utensils.[22]

On 10 November, the justices without Lawford's Gate held a general meeting. The Grand Jury for Gloucester Division had indicted 36 colliers, and the necessary warrants were issued. James Powell and Samuel Willimot were already in Gloucester goal, under strong guard.[23] In the night of 15-16 November, a lock of the Avon navigation at Kelston was severely damaged, and a notice found beside it: 'This attempt is made by only three hundred Men, as the beginning of much greater Mischief that is intended against the said Navigation by as many Thousands, unless an immediate Stop is put to the sending of any more Coals by Water'.[24] Detachments of redcoats marched into Kingswood; as they approached, the women in the villages beat upon their frying pans. Two men were captured but the others fled.[25] The inconclusive struggle was, however, wearying to all sides, and troops, at first welcome, were expensive to the City. The Harris brothers, arrested at Kingswood, were released on bail, and in the New Year, work was resumed.[26]

Little more was heard of disputes at Kingswood until the end of the century; in 1792, there was an agreed settlement. 'The pit colliers of Kingswood, having in a large body peaceably required an increase of 4d. a day to their wages, making it equal to the pay of the Somerset colliers, his Grace of Beaufort interested himself in their behalf; and their request being complied with, they are returned peaceably to work.'[27]

Earlier, the miners of Timsbury and Paulton, North Somerset, had struck, and, accompanied by the High Sheriff, the colliery owners attended a meeting of four thousand men. On a promise of peace and good order, they agreed to raise the daily wages of haulers from fourteen pence to seventeen, and of miners from sixteen pence to eighteen. The same increase was agreed at Radstock.[28]

The Home Secretary received an anxious letter from Captain George Monro in Bristol, expressing surprise at the failure of the Gloucestershire magistrates or the Bristol Corporation to oppose 'this alarming combination'. He supposed some proprietors of the mines had connived as an excuse to raise the price of coals, but he pointed out the serious consequences for the 'very numerous and extensive glass houses, very large copper works, lead works, distilleries and other concerns that consume immense quantities of coal'.

One glass house will stop work this morning, and as the colliers will suffer no coal to be brought into the city, three more will stop on Monday should this combination continue. The house that will stop this morning employs near 200 people, and the glass business is so managed in this city that at least one half of these people, whether employed or not, receive wages nearly equal to at least £100 a week.[29]

At this point he broke off, having just heard of a march through Bristol of Gloucestershire colliers on their way to rally their comrades at Bedminster, Ashton and Nailsea. 'They behaved very orderly, but said they were determined to carry their point.' Then, after another interval, he concluded, 'On further inquiry, the advance is not so unreasonable as I at first thought it. I find the most they get, except they work extra hours, is only 10s. per week. The people in Bristol are in continual fear of their committing some excess in the city, but further than stopping the coals nothing of that kind has as yet happened.'[30]

Third-party mediation was often critical in transforming 'collective bargaining by riot' into an orderly settlement, a role usually performed by the Justices of the Peace. Occasionally, where power was evenly divided, the parties might negotiate directly, as at Ashfield, Derbyshire, in 1779. Delegates from Nottingham had visited the large hosiery manufactory of Unwins, to persuade the workmen to strike, but instead they reported the incident to the owner's son, who welcomed the diversion. He stationed armed men on roofs overlooking the village street, and lined the gutters with stones and bricks. As the public houses began to fill with strangers, young Unwin joined them, and asked their intentions. 'What was their design in assembling so many of them together? Was it to riot and commit disorders as at Nottingham, or were their intentions of the peaceable kind? If the former was their intention, he was prepared for them, and they might attack his property as soon as they wished.' At this point he called attention to his fire-power, and offered to 'shew them any civilities they were desirous of'. Negotiations then commenced. 'They wished, they said, to know his intentions with respect to a regulation of prices, which they hoped still to procure; this he agreed to put down in writing.'

> He then convinced them, by fair argument, that they had, in many particulars, respecting the disputes between the Masters and the Workmen, acted quite upon wrong principles, and that his only wish was to set them right, and shew them what was the true interest of trade in general, and of his neighbourhood in particular. Thus, with a little well-timed oratory, enforced by treating them with civility, and some liquor to drink, he turned the hearts of these very people, who were come out with a design to commit outrages, to declare themselves his friends, and ready to assist in opposing any thing riotous or disorderly that might happen in future in his neighbourhood. The mob dispersed the same evening without doing the least injury to any person whatever.[31]

There was an element of shrewd calculation in Unwin's conciliatory attitude. Even a peaceful withdrawal of labour was costly to capitalist hosiers, or to smaller employers who rented their frames. In more labour-intensive industries, with small overhead costs, the incentive to bargain was less evident.

3 THE HOUSE OF CALL

In the sixteenth and seventeenth centuries the population of London grew rapidly. In part this reflected the growth of overseas trade, but there was also a domestic aspect. 'For the City and its suburbs had a second function. Not only did they constitute a centre of production where substantial incomes were earned from industry and trade; they were also a centre of consumption where men expended the revenue which they had earned elsewhere.'[1] By the eighteenth century about one in six Englishmen and women lived in London or would do so at some time.[2] Most were drawn from the provinces or Ireland by London's wealth, freedom and anonymity, but employment and prosperity depended greatly on chance opportunities.

> Multitudes of people are brought to poverty and beggery because they do not timely meete with any one to Set and continue them at Worke. And at the same time, we likewise meete with multitudes of others, both Merchants and Shopkeepers of all Callings, that cannot furnish their Customers so cheape and speedily as were to be desired, because they cannot presently get Work-folk, or else not at such cheap rates as to make a benefit thereof.[3]

Private employment offices and hiring halls, such as Henry Robinson's office of 'Addresses and Encounters' and Evan James's 'Statute Hall', catered principally for domestic servants, shop assistants and clerks.[4] Artisans and craftsmen visited public houses recognized by their trade as 'houses of call', where the landlord kept lists of job-seeking customers. The house of call was the meeting-place for the box club

> for the relief and mutual support of the poor sort of artisans, during sickness or other incapacity, whereby they are rendered incapable of getting their bread. These clubs, erected by mutual consent, are supported by an amicable contribution of two, three or more pence per week by each member; who weekly met at a certain alehouse, where they spend two or three pence each; and wherein they have orders for their better regulation, and a strong box or chest, with divers locks, for the conservation of their books, cash, &c. The advantages arising to the several members of the respective clubs

are that every member, when sick or lame, whereby he's rendered incapable of working during his sickness or incapacity, receives a certain sum of money per week, provided his indisposition does not proceed from a venereal cause, in which case he is not entitled to any benefit from the society. And when any of the members die, there is not only a sum of money allowed by the society for the burying of such members but likewise the widows or nominees of such deceased members receive from the society the sum of five, ten or more pounds.[5]

On 'club night', when their wages were paid at the house, the members exchanged trade news, and arranged for the jobs notified to their landlord to be filled in rotation. Although the landlord was entrusted with the box, many clubs chose their own officers to keep the books, minutes and correspondence. To enforce 'fair' wages throughout the trade, networks of committees were established and discipline enforced: 'all persons that are detected of working, during the time of their being supported by the box, are immediately, upon conviction, expelled the club.'[6] These 'great and numerous societies' were tolerated 'as a very great ease to the several parishes of this City and Suburbs', but the ability of many of them to withhold labour except on their own terms was resented by employers, and frowned on by the courts.[7] 'Fair' wages and hours set by the tailors, curriers, wheelwrights, smiths and shoemakers were generally more favourable than those enforceable in the courts, where disputes turned on the 'usual' or 'customary' conditions for the trade.[8] For the masters in seasonal trades, these societies were a necessary evil, keeping together a pool of labour which could be drawn on to meet fluctuations in demand. In the tailoring trade, only the most skilled workman, the foreman cutter, enjoyed secure employment; he was an aristocrat beside

> the mere working Taylor; not one in ten of them know how to cut out a pair of Breeches; They are employed only to sew the Seam, to cast the Button Holes, and prepare the Work for the Finisher . . . They are as numerous as locusts, are out of business about three or four months in the year; and generally as poor as rats. The House of Call runs away with all their earnings, and keeps them constantly in debt and want.[9]

In or before 1700, five clubs of journeymen tailors confederated to form a trade union; by 1764, it was the most powerful in London, with

42 affiliated clubs, a delegate conference ('the House of Representatives') and an executive committee ('the Grand Committee for Management of the Town'). The sickness and unemployment funds were well managed, and in 1720 it claimed to have 'troubled no parish for above twenty years'.[10] The felt hatters, who struck over piecework prices in 1698, revived their union 70 years later, and by 1777 were regularly meeting in 'Congress'.[11] In 1744, a society of peruke makers announced

THAT on Thursday the 5th instant was held a General Meeting of the Journeymen of the Trade for Regulating their Working Hours; when was unanimously agreed between them, to leave off Work at Eight o'Clock, Winter and Summer; such Regulation to begin on Monday the 16th instant; together with several other Articles for the benefit of the Masters, their Customers, and the Journeymen in general too tedious here to mention; which Regulation will be fix'd up in Writing at the four Houses of Call for Peruke-Makers following, viz., the Three Crowns in the Old Jewry; the King's Head in Newport-Street; the Feathers in St Martins-Street, Leicester-Fields; and the Horse and Groom in Hedge-Lane.

Note, all Journeymen living with Persons who advertise selling of Perukes, and shall leave their Places before the 1st of August next, will be the first Persons provided for at each of the above Houses of Call, they conforming themselves to the above-mentioned agreement.

Those that work with Piece-Masters that work for Advertisers, will be deem'd as working with Advertisers.[12]

The Three Crowns, formerly known as the Globe and Sceptre, had a large room for meetings, and served as union headquarters. According to the official history of the London compositors, their members 'were summoned to hear Counsel's report (concerning apprenticeship limitations) at the Hole-in-the-Wall on the 1st October, 1787. This is the earliest evidence of the compositors meeting at that house.'[13] However, a society of freemen journeymen printers had its headquarters there as early as 1750, and campaigned against the employment of 'foreigners'. In 1763, it financed the successful defence of the *North Briton* compositors, who had been accused, with their employer, of printing a 'seditious libel'.[14] Carpenters and joiners had three houses of call in the City of London. Although City craftsmen were zealous in defence of their traditional rights, workmen in unincorporated trades used the house-of-call system, and were equally militant trade unionists.

All the societies were alert to potential threats to employment, and

adopted protectionist strategies. Ostensibly on behalf of women out-
workers, journeymen pipe-makers met at the Harrow, Southwark, to
resist

> that sort of pipes, call'd marked Pipes, distinguish'd by the King's
> Arms, Plume of Feathers, &c., and as many of our Masters (in a
> Manner for some sinister View) impose them upon the Publick
> Houses, and thereby a great many Women are in Want of Business
> that were always brought up to it; for by the aforesaid Pipes, two
> Women can do as much Work as would require four, because there
> is no smoothing or trimming in the Head of that sort of Pipes.

In the public interest, 'a plain, neat pipe' would be preferable, as 'the
mark'd pipes are subject to receive all manner of Dirt or Soil, from the
Use, or in the lying, and thereby very soon unfit for Service, by burning
red'.[15] Where 'unfair' competition came from foreigners, the societies
could expect help from the courts. In May 1772, the committee of the
Journeymen Cabinet Makers' Society complained to the Bow Street
magistrate, Sir John Fielding, that, under cover of diplomatic privilege, furniture was being systematically imported 'as would have
employed 400 journeymen many months to manufacture from raw
materials'. They were referred to Lord Rochford, 'but by no means
to offer any insult to the persons concerned in the importation'.
Several weeks later, Colonel Luttrell and customs officers raided two
warehouses in Soho, and seized several hundred chairs and sofas, 'near
a ton of curled hair, a large quantity of brass nails, a great number of
marble tables, some very rich slab frames, carved and gilt', all intended
for the Venetian Resident. The goods were auctioned for re-export.[16]

Journeymen, masters and shopkeepers were occasionally allies. In
October 1743, the Bakers' Company prosecuted several of their number
under an Act of 13 Charles II which forbade the exercise of trades or
callings on Sundays; the fines were distributed to the poor of the
parishes in which bread had been illegally baked and sold, and the Lord
Mayor issued a general warning to shopkeepers.[17] Soon after, victuallers
in the City held a series of meetings at the Black Swan Tavern, behind
the Royal Exchange, and in April the Company of Butchers, claiming
jurisdiction within two miles of the City, invoked the law against 'this
wicked custom' of Sunday trading, 'which is very notorious and
shameful to all good-meaning people'.[18] Master barbers prosecuted
their erring brethren, and a journeymen's 'Friendly Society of Peruke
Makers' joined the campaign. Clubs of journeymen bakers held several

Table 3.1: Reported Labour Disputes in London, 1718-1800

Year	Total Number	Incorporated Trades	Other Occupations
1718	1	Wheelwrights	
1720	2	Curriers	Tailors
1731	1		Cabinet-makers
1732	2	Clothworkers	Lightermen
1734	1	Wheelwrights	
1736	3	Shoemakers	Building labourers Silk weavers
1737	1		Tailors
1739	1		Silk weavers
1744	3	Glaziers Peruke makers	Tailors
1745	2	Bakers Wheelwrights	
1746	1		Carmen and wharfingers
1747	1	Barbers and peruke makers	
1749	2	Joiners Painters	
1750	2	Masons	Merchant seamen
1751	2		Tailors Seamen
1754	1	Painters	
1756	3	Barbers and wig-makers Farriers	Tailors and staymakers
1760	1	Curriers	
1761	4	Carpenters Silversmiths Gold and silver wire-drawers	Cabinet-makers
1762	2	Bakers	Silk weavers
1763	4	Silversmiths	Tailors Haymakers Silk weavers
1765	1		Building labourers
1766	2	Shoemakers	Haymakers

Table 3.1 (Cont'd)

Year	Total Number	Incorporated Trades	Other Occupations
1767	3	Bookbinders	Tailors Silk weavers
1768	11	Coopers Hatters Shoemakers	Tailors Coalheavers Glass grinders Lightermen Merchant seamen (2) Sawyers Silk weavers
1769	2	Carpenters, Brick- layers and masons	
1770	4	Hat dyers	Tailors Leather dressers Merchant seamen
1771	3		Tailors and staymakers Coalheavers Silk weavers
1772	2	Curriers	Merchant seamen
1773	1		Merchant seamen
1774	2		Haymakers Sugar-bakers
1775	3	Bricklayers	Haymakers Seamen
1776	4	Carpenters Masons	Sawyers Leather-breeches makers
1777	6	Carpenters Hatters Sword-hilt makers Shoemakers	Tailors Chair-carvers
1779	1		Coalheavers
1781	1	Wheelwrights	
1783	2	Hatters	Seamen
1785	2	Printers' compositors	Cabinet-makers
1786	2	Bookbinders Felt hatters	
1787	2	Carpenters and joiners	Cabinet-makers

Table 3.1 (Cont'd)

Year	Total Number	Incorporated Trades	Other Trades
1789	1	Gold and silver wire-drawers	
1791	1		Woolstaplers
1792	2	Curriers Shoemakers	
1793	6	Bakers Printers' pressmen Saddlers	Carmen and coal porters Lamplighters Ropemakers
1794	2	Bookbinders Saddlers	
1795	4		Tailors Coalheavers Millwrights Ship-riggers
1796	1	Bricklayers	
1798	4	Printers' pressmen Shoemakers	Coalheavers Sugar-bakers
1799	2	Bakers	Millwrights
1800	2		Tailors Cabinet-makers

Totals

Incorporated Trades	55
Other Trades, London	64
All London	119

meetings in July, and a notice purporting to come from shoeblacks applauded 'the laudable example of the Barbers, Grocers, Journeymen Bakers, Distillers'.[19]

The sabbatarian butchers successfully prosecuted over a hundred offenders, but their trade was deeply divided. On 14 August, their Company rescinded its earlier resolution and declared invalid the election of the Master and Court of Assistants. The journeymen bakers, on the advice of the Justices of the Peace, held a meeting at the Red Cow, St Clements, on 15 August 1745, but the campaign was stopped in its tracks by Lord Chief Justice Mansfield, who declared Sunday baking to be not merely a lawful, but an essential occupation.[20]

If campaigns on common issues momentarily united journeymen's clubs with their masters' associations, they were more often in conflict over wages and hours. On such occasions, masters formed anti-strike committees, which attempted to bring under their own control the houses of call and the friendly societies. In 1756, the master farriers of Westminster met at the King's Head, Great Rider Street, and promised that 'all honest industrious journeymen that continue to Work their Hours, shall have all due Encouragement, by applying as above'.[21] The same year, the master tailors invited 'sober and industrious journeymen that were willing to work the usual hours of the trade, to apply to the Bear and Ragged Staff in Leicester Fields'.[22] In other disputes, the Painter-Stainers' Company instructed the clerk to see that 'proper books were open at the Widow Minits at 2 the Sign of the Angel in Ironmonger Lane' and the master barbers and wig makers arranged similar facilities 'at the house of Mr Taylor, in Camomile Street, Bishopsgate'.[23] The most determined effort was made by 23 master tailors during a strike in 1764: they recognized nine independent houses of call, and through them recruited 800 strike-breakers from the provinces and 230 from the continent.[24] The magistrates had their own schemes for employment offices in Wapping and Rotherhithe, 'the better to prevent sailors from squandering away their money in those low places which generally go under the name of Houses of Call for Mariners'. Entrepreneurial magistrates ran employment agencies: the Fielding brothers and Saunders Welch promoted the Universal Register Office, and Alderman Beckford's agent managed a registration scheme for coalheavers.[25]

On the one hand, the box clubs were welcomed by London citizens as reducing the burden on the parishes.[26] On the other, their legal status was ambiguous. The early trade clubs were not 'disguised' friendly societies, but were identical with perfectly open box clubs. The 'box' was essential for continuous association, and the strict rules of the friendly society formed the basis of trade union discipline. To protect the benefit funds, special levies were often imposed to support members on strike or to defend arrested leaders, but the courts did not always recognize the distinction. In 1736, a society of silk weavers attempted to recover £30 loaned from the box to the landlord of their house of call; after argument by counsel, the Court of Exchequer ruled 'that they were not a legal society, whereby they may sue or be sued, that they ought to be discouraged, and that such clubs were beneath the dignity of the Court'.[27] Shortly afterwards, Lord Hardwicke attributed a riot in Spitalfields to 'that which often occasions oppression, I mean the unlawful and unjust Combination of Journeymen and

Labourers to keep up their wages'.[28] However, in 1753, a man was sentenced to death at Gloucester Assizes for stealing £40 from 'a box belonging to a society of plush weavers'.[29]

In wartime, trade unionism in London was strengthened by the reluctance of provincial journeymen to come within reach of the press-gang. During a strike in 1745, the master wheelwrights appointed seven alternative houses of call, and promised that 'if any such journeymen should happen to be imprest by coming to London, by their sending immediate Notice to any of the above places, proper Persons are appointed for their release'.[30] In retaliation, the box club at the Bowl and Pin, Thames Street, issued a warning to countrymen, for their security, to obtain prior guarantees and money to cover their travelling expenses.[31] During the same strike, the journeymen wheelwrights tried to outflank their employers by direct dealings with brewers, wharfingers, scavengers and carmen 'at very reasonable prices', promising that 'those gentlemen that are willing to encourage the journeymen wheelwrights will be firmly instructed in a proper manner how to buy timber at the best advantages'.[32] Such early experiments in co-operative production may have been widespread among artisans who owned their own tools and needed little capital; if so, their experience may have contributed as much as the moral fervour of Robert Owen to the rise of co-operative societies in the early nineteenth century, and to the strategy and tactics of the Grand National Consolidated Trade Union.[33]

4 THE RIGHTS OF CRAFTSMEN

If British trade unionism originated in the seventeenth and eighteenth centuries, 'the habit of acting together in certain ways, which we find' to characterize the journeymen of the eighteenth century, had been formed in a much earlier period'.[1] Independent fraternities of serving-men and journeymen were formed by saddlers and tailors in the four-teenth and fifteenth centuries, and the Webbs identified an embryo form of trade unionism among Wisbech shoemakers in 1538.[2] Under 'feigned cover of sanctity', the London saddlers combined in 1560 to raise their wages from forty shillings or 5 marks yearly to 10 or 12 marks or even ten pounds.

> The servingmen, according to an ordinance made among them-selves, would oftentimes cause the journeymen of the said masters to be summoned by a bedel, thereunto appointed, to attend at Vigils of the dead, who were members of the said Fraternity, and at making offerings for them on the morrow, under a certain penalty to be levied, whereby the said masters were very greatly aggrieved, and were injured through such absenting of themselves by the journeymen so leaving their labours and duties, against their wish.[3]

On 19 July 1560, six leaders of the fraternity applied for recognition to the Court of Aldermen and the Guild of Saddlers, but were told 'that in future they should have no fraternity, meetings, or covins, or other unlawful things, under a penalty'. Individuals could bring their grievances to the Mayor and Aldermen.[4]

However, by the eighteenth century, journeymen's clubs were recognized in some incorporated trades. In 1704, the Court of Assis-tants of the Curriers Company agreed 'that ye Stewarde of ye Journey-mens Club be summoned to show cause' for a complaint that a free-man had been refused work. The steward, Thomas Worsley, reported three cases where 'fforiners' from outside the city had been put to work in place of freemen, whereupon it was ordered

> that ye Beadle shall goe with any ffreeman that is out of worke to any of ye places where a fforiner is at worke & acquaint ye Master or Mistress that it is ordered by this Court that he or she turn away

ye fforiner & sett ye ffreemen to worke which if they disobey ye Master and Wardens are to take such ... with them as is provided against disobedient members by ye Orders of this Company.[5]

The degree of control exercised by a company depended on the wording of its charter and on the City of London by-laws (Acts of Common Council).[6] The bakers had authority to recommend prices and control quality, but for most companies the main function was to regulate the labour market. Masters and journeymen were required to become 'free of their Company' by serving an apprenticeship and there-after paying their quarterly dues. Although most companies lost much of their economic power in the eighteenth century, this was a slow process, and several remained active as employers' associations. Two important companies, the Carpenters and the Bricklayers, were weakened after the Great Fire of London, when the Rebuilding Act of 1667 transferred to King's Bench the authority to regulate prices, wages and the quality of building materials. After hearing witnesses and consulting interested parties, two judges were empowered to assess 'reasonable' prices, to be promulgated and enforced by the Lord Mayor. There was a similar procedure to prevent artificers, workmen or labourers, whether individually or in combination, from extorting 'unreasonable' wages.[7]

Although a temporary measure, limited to seven years, the Rebuilding Act had lasting consequences, for section 16 extended to all building workers the same right to work in London as freemen of their trades, 'any usage or custom of the City notwithstanding'. An official history of the Bricklayers' Company records the 'irony'

that an event which brought work for bricklayers and tilers on a scale never foreseen in dreams should entail disaster upon the Company which governed the craft. As a trade organization it never fully recovered. The very magnitude of the work open to the operative craftsmen was the Company's undoing; freemen brick-layers could never tackle the job alone.[8]

However, craftsmen in other trades resisted the encroachment of 'foreigners', and in 1712 an Act of Common Council gave them a 'speedy remedy' against masters who refused 'to take, employ or set on work, in their trades and occupations, the honest poor Citizens and Freemen of the same City, to the great Hindrance, Loss and Prejudice of the said poor Citizens and to the utter Undoing of a great Number of the said poor Handicraftsmen'.[9] Before long, the Act was being invoked during labour disputes to prevent the employment of black-legs. At a meeting in Blacksmith's Hall on 5 October 1717, four livery-men, Messrs Hall, Bourne, Harding and Roberts, complained of 'the grievances of the trade and irregularities of the journeymen but did not agree among themselves touching the causes of their complaint'.[10]

Earlier, 18 journeymen blacksmiths, on strike for a shorter working day, had prosecuted Mr Harding for employing a 'foreigner', and the Lord Mayor's court referred the dispute to the Company for concilia-tion. The Warden and Assistants 'declared their opinion that the em-ploying of Foreigners should not be countenanced and adjudging it not to be in their power to fix the wages and hours of journeymen's working, left it to the parties in difference to determine betwixt themselves'. Masters and journeymen failed to reach agreement, and on 14 November again attended the Court of Assistants.

And upon the Wardens interposition and advice the matters in difference seemed to be in a fair way of accommodation. But the Journeymen peremptorily insisting to work but from 6 in the morning to 7 in the evening and the Masters insisting on the evening hour to be still 8, the same occasioned the breaking up of the meeting without any final conclusions.[11]

The dispute was settled a fortnight later, when seven journeymen were reprimanded for failing to pay their quarterage to the Company. They promised to do so, but on condition that they worked 6 to 7 only, affirming that most master blacksmiths now acquiesced. The Company left the matter there, but a movement for the shorter working day became general throughout the London trades. In a dozen strikes between 1720 and 1750, journeymen's clubs and chartered companies polarized as trade unions and employers' associations. The Court of Aldermen continued to resist the importation of country journeymen but, in the wheelwrights' strike of 1718, permitted the employers to engage additional apprentices.[12] In 1724, members of the journeymen's club were excluded from the Court of Assistants of the Wheelwrights' Company. These measures having little effect, the masters, with finan-cial support from their companies, resorted to prosecution of strikers for conspiracy. In December 1720, six journeymen curriers were sentenced at the Old Bailey to three months' imprisonment and a fine of 20 marks each.[13] The Wheelwrights' Company sought the indict-ments of strikers at Middlesex Sessions in 1734, but these cases were removed by *certiorari* to the King's Bench and thereafter withdrawn.[14] Several companies remained aloof from trade disputes, and, as in the clothworkers' case in 1732, encouraged the masters to establish *ad hoc* committees.[15] In London and the provinces, masters and journeymen presented a common front against interlopers and 'tramps'; in 1739, master printers in the west of England gave notice that the name of any journeyman working with interlopers would be inserted in the London newspapers, so that he would be barred from every legitimate printing house in England.[16] A society was established in 1734, 'at the sign of the Three Tulips in Orchard Street, Westminster, in order for the raising Contributions towards a legal Proceeding against many Labourers and others, now exercising the Art and Mystery of Plaisterers'.[17] Some of these societies were encouraged, if not organized, by members of the legal profession. 'Why are there more grievances than when you resided in London?', wrote a London tradesman in 1750 to his brother. Deprived of opportunities for 'litigious and vexatious suits in matters of property',

> a certain set of men have turned their industry another way, and have made our by-laws . . . grievously oppressive . . . in which rights have been the pretence, the journeymen the tools, but iniquitous gain the real cause of the whole calamity.[18]

In twenty years, the condition of the City of London had been transformed: houses stood empty, rents had fallen and in some parts there was 'near desolation'. In contrast, trades and manufactures flourished in Blackfriars and the suburbs, creating a permanent shortage of manpower, 'for the men can at any time go out of the City for employ . . . but a Master cannot bring a foreigner in'.[19]

In the past, an employer had always been permitted to meet shortages of freemen by engaging temporary workmen, who were discharged 'when the hurry of business was over . . . and we very seldom heard of any prosecutions'. Now the laws were inflexible, professional troublemakers had encouraged combinations, taken men off the pursuit of industry, and made them 'disorderly and rude'. Masters had left the City and established workshops and manufactories in Southwark, Clerkenwell and Marylebone. Dyeing, clothworking and cabinet-making now thrived outside the scope of restrictive labour laws.[20]

A general confrontation was imminent between workmen free of the City and their masters, arising from a dispute between a liveryman of the Painter-Stainers' Company and a club of journeymen. Although house-painting had been a protected craft before the eighteenth century, new methods of mixing paint had eliminated much of the skill.

> ... by the help of a few printed Directions, a House may be painted by any common labourer at one Third of the Expence it would have cost before the mystery was made public ... it may be learned in a Month as will (sic) as in seven years .... The Numbers ... that pretend to this Branch have overstocked it: There is not Bread for one Third of them; and at all Times in the City of London and Suburbs, they are idle at least four or five Months in the Year.[21]

The Painter-Stainers' Company had ceased to exercise close regulation of the trade by 1749, when Mr Benjamin Cook, a liveryman, 'attended with a Letter he had received from Mr Joseph Rowe, another Livery Man signifying that he hoped Mr Cook and the Court of Assistants and others of the Company would join with him in the Defense he had begun against the Club of Journeymen Painters that will not work nor let others'.[22]

The club had lodged an information with the Chamberlain of London that Mr Rowe had employed a workman not free of the City, contrary to the by-law of 1712. The case came before the Lord Mayor's court on 5 December, and took many hours to hear. Leading masters in the trade affirmed that in summer it was impossible to carry out all the work without employing as many temporary workers as freemen, that no freemen was ever refused employment and that he could usually fix his own terms. The jury was divided, partly because one of their number, 'a Gentleman of large concerns in the Mercantile Trade, spoke and behaved with uncommon Zeal and Integrity'. At two in the afternoon, the jurymen went out, but twice returned without agreeing. As darkness fell, the Lord Mayor adjourned the hearing to six a.m., and ordered the jury to be confined to their room 'without fire, candle or any sustenance'. In the morning they returned a verdict for the journeymen.[23]

There was consternation throughout the incorporated trades, and employers demanded amendment of the law. Masters of various trades organized a general petition to the Court of Common Council, proposing a *noli prosequi* or licence to be granted to named persons who, although not free, were regularly earning their living at a trade or craft. The journeymen's clubs were bitterly attacked in the press.

What is still worse, even those Freemen who have been taken

Apprentices, and kindly brought up from the meanest Situations, and who are the most forward, and often Leaders in Combinations (many of them with low Minds and worse Hearts) are, according to the present System, MASTERS OF THE LIBERTIES OF LONDON; while the real Citizen, who bears the great Expence of Rent, Taxes, and the most burthensome Offices, must be in some sort subject to the Power and Insults of these Dictators, without being availed of his Privileges as a Citizen, or enjoying his natural Right as an Englishman.[24]

Journeymen from other trades, including carpenters, masons and the Fleet Street printers, rallied round the painters and organized a counter-petition. On 13 January 1750, journeymen printers free of the City were reminded that

a Society is already established, who *not only hitherto hath*, but (so far as may be consistent with *Honour* and *Integrity*) are determined to endeavour to *Support* your *Rights* and *Privileges*: As you cannot be *quite insensible* that these Affairs are attended with considerable Expence, any of you willing to contribute towards so *laudable* an Undertaking, are desired to send your Contributions to Mr William Philipbrown, at the Bell in Little Friday-Street, who is empowered to receive the same.[25]

Three weeks later, the printers were warned that their masters were trying to prove that there were insufficient freemen to do the business of the City.

You are therefore desired to leave your Names on a small piece of Paper sealed up, either at the Hole-in-the-Wall, in Fleet Street, or at the Bell in Little Friday-Street before Tomorrow Noon, in order to ascertain your Number as near as possible.

So many of you as are out of Work, are desired to write under your Names, *Unemployed*.

Those entitled by the late Act of Parliament, to write, *entitled by the Act*.

And those that have a Right to their Freedom and desirous of taking it up, by leaving their Indentures, or other proper Voucher, an Application will be made to the Chamberlain for Leave, without any Expence to the Person entitled.[26]

The Hole-in-the-Wall became the centre for trade unionism in the printing trade: compositors met there in 1787 and pressmen in 1839.[27] Three societies of carpenters and joiners similarly united in 1750, when freemen were called to be counted at the White Swan, Coleman Street, the White Hart, Gilspur Street, Pye Corner, and the Weavers' Arms, Grub Street.[28]

On 25 January 1750, the Court of Common Council considered the Petition of Citizens of London and Liverymen of their respective companies. As the document made clear, this was not merely a question of seasonal labour shortages; the authority of employers was at stake, challenged by the rise of organized labour.

> The exclusive Right of Exercising Handicraft and Retail Trades within this City and Liberties is a great and Valuable Franchise ... yet when this Right is perverted and made use of only to Indulge and promote a habit of Idleness, when it tends to Destroy Subordination, and to Raise an untractable Spirit in the lower Class of Freemen, it is no longer a Privilege, but a burthen to the Community, and a Snare to those unthinking individuals who are suffered to Abuse it.[29]

The petition showed that the majority of City journeymen supported the trade societies.

> ... the greatest part of the Free Journeymen presuming on this their exclusive Right are become Idle and Debauched, Negligent in their Callings, Exorbitant in their Demands, and Disrespectful to their Superiors, often entering into unlawful Combinations and busying themselves more to prevent others from Working than to procure or Deserve employment for themselves.[30]

The Masters tried persuasion and good usage to avoid a more powerful remedy, but to save themselves from ruin were obliged to propose a scheme which would in some degree encroach on the freemen's rights. In a second petition, it was argued that these rights were weighted unequally, since they constrained the master, but not the journeyman, who could go to work outside the City limits whenever he chose.[31]

Common Council then received the journeymen's petitions, which insisted that there was never a labour shortage, and that, at some times of the year, hundreds were unemployed. The journeymen masons pointed to the efficient rebuilding of Cornhill after the fire in 1748, and quoted statistics to show

> that the number of Free Master Masons . . . is not more than One
> and Twenty who upon an averidge in General do not Employ above
> three Journeymen each, when business is at its best, there are not
> more than about Eighty Journeymen Employed in the City, and the
> Number of the Journeymen in the said Trade is upwards of One
> hundred and twenty, so there are at all times Thirty and very often
> Forty Free Journeymen who for want of Employment in the City
> are Obliged to seek the same elsewhere.[32]

The journeymen published their complete case as a 31-page pamphlet,
which reaffirmed their rights and justified trade unionism. 'All our
advantage is, that none but Freemen shall work in the City.' Freemen
of every trade had, contrary to law, been refused employment; men of
'sense and sobriety' had 'in a thousand cases' been rejected by masters
when they had outsiders at work in their houses. Freemen had

> been months together out of employment, while they have seen
> Foreigners in possession of the most lucrative parts of every busi-
> ness; they have been deterred from summoning, for fear they should,
> by this means, find greater difficulties in procuring employment . . .
> This, Gentlemen, we have born with, because it was dangerous to
> complain . . . .[33]

The number of foreigners was now such that it would be impossible
to redress the evil by complaint to the Chamberlain's office. The only
remedy was to organize.

> It is a task above the strength of a few individuals, nor can it be
> accomplished without our uniting into great bodies, and unani-
> mously joining to seek redress. If a single Journeyman makes but an
> attempt of this kind, he is, as we have said, already in danger of
> being discovered, and consequently ruined.[34]

Nor was this only a trade matter; it concerned the whole nation.

> If ever England should be cursed with another invasion (which God
> prevent) in a time of danger, tumult and public discord, will the
> bank, or the treasures of the great mercantile companies be safer
> when the City shall be filled with French papists, than it would

when filled with its own loyal and faithful citizens? . . . . It is possible, at least, that an enemy may fill us with armed Veterans in the
guise of Journeymen, who may obtain licences to work at their
trades, and may have all the appearance of fawning slaves till the
signal be given for them to become our masters.[35]

Having heard all the petitions, Common Council appointed a committee to examine and report: there were six Aldermen and ten
commoners, with the *ex-officio* assistance of the Recorder, the
Chamberlain and the Common Serjeant.[36] A number of journeymen
attended the committee's first meeting, and a warning was given to
their spokesmen to ensure their good conduct. Large crowds waited
outside the second meeting, and there were complaints of insulting
behaviour by 'those very People who are a great cause of the Complaint, by not working themselves, not letting others do it in their
stead'. The trend of the committee's deliberations was clear from a
remark to the crowd by one member,

that there seemed to be nothing propos'd or ask'd by the Masters,
but a Redress of some particular Grievances, which could not
affect the Mens Privileges, but must be for the general good, and
what no reasonable Persons ought to object to.[37]

After some delays, the report was ready for Common Council on
20 May. It recommended that the Lord Mayor's court be empowered,
at its discretion, to approve an application from a master freeman to
employ a given number of non-freemen, under such restrictions as the
court might think necessary. No freeman should be penalized under
the Act of 1712 if he could prove that immediately before the hiring
he had genuinely tried and failed to recruit a free journeyman. The
Chamberlain pointed out that, although prosecutions had been formally in his name, he was not personally involved, nor did he benefit
in any way.[38] Common Council did not accept the report at once —
a majority seemed sympathetic to the journeymen — but instead asked
the committee to draft a new by-law, containing safeguards against
excessive hiring of non-freemen. It was not ready for approval until 22
November, and was restricted in scope to freeman masters who had
one apprentice or had employed one in the previous twelve months.
All employment of foreigners had to be registered with the City clerk,
on payment of a licence fee of 2s 6d. The registration book was to be
open at fixed times for inspection by any freeman of the City.[39]

The 1750 Act of Common Council gave employers only a limited defence against strikes and the closed shop. A more powerful sanction was to ease restrictions on Apprenticeship, which were within the discretion of the chartered companies. In 1760, the curriers received a complaint from three masters that their journeymen had fixed prices between 6s a dozen for 'great skins' and 10s for boot skins. When Mr Kitchin refused to pay, his journeymen left him, and their club began to advertise meetings to raise prices. Since the affair was of general concern, the Court of Assistants drew up a list of maximum prices and ordered 500 copies to be printed and circulated. The journeymen continued to insist on their own prices and, on 7 November, the court authorized liverymen to engage as many apprentices as they needed to complete their work, provided that no premiums were taken.[40]

This example was followed by the Worshipful Company of Gold and Silver Wire-drawers, whose profits were squeezed by 'rioting, drunkenness, debauchery, combinations and confederacies together'. In order to 'check, control or dissipate' the 'unwarrantable, unjust and illegal practices of the journeymen', they increased the permitted number of apprentices from two to three.[41] The Cordwainers' Company prosecuted journeymen for offences committed during trade disputes. In 1768, a reward was offered for the conviction of demonstrators 'at the houses of several Master Shoemakers in a very outrageous manner insisting on them to sign a paper agreing to raise their Wages and had broken the Windows of the Houses of sevl: Masters who had refused to comply with their Terms'. On the information of Peter Floret, a journeyman named William Ball was indicted, fined 3s 4d and sentenced to two years in Newgate. The Company instructed the clerk to apply through counsel for mitigation of the sentence to one year. Of two others indicted, one was acquitted, and the Company recorded on 3 November:

This day Mr Warne the person on whose Evidence Mark Gulliver a Journeyman Shoemaker was convicted as one of the Persons convicted in the late Riot applied for the Reward of Ten Guineas offered by this Co. in June last. And it appearing the £2: 12:6d had been paid by order of the Master & Wardens to 5 of the Lord Mayors Officers employed in apprehending Gulliver and Mr Warne being willing to accept Seven Guineas and a half in full of the said Reward This Court doth Order the same to be paid to him accordingly.[42]

In February 1792, prosecutions generated greater militancy. Mr Francis Bristowe, an export contractor, had singled out three shoemakers as leaders of a hundred strikers, whereupon a thousand shoemakers demonstrated outside Litchfield Street magistrates' court, and 170 additional warrants were issued. The Cordwainers' Company resolved that no journeyman in combination should be employed until good order was restored, but,

> feeling for the situation of such Journeymen as have been misguided or by threats Induced to leave their Work approve of the lenity and protection publickly offered to them by their Masters and as a further Inducement to put a stop to such Combination this Company will unite with the master Shoemakers in the City and Liberties of Westminster in endeavouring to procure a Mitigation of the Punishment of such of the Journeymen as have been convicted on the peaceable Return of the rest to their Employment.[43]

The Wheelwrights' and Curriers' companies were principally responsible for reviving the indictment for conspiracy to combine in the latter part of the eighteenth century. In 1781, the father of the Wheelwrights' Company was censured for breaking ranks and paying the wages demanded by his journeymen.

> Mr Warden Perryman informed the Court, that on or about Christmas last, the Journeymen in the trade made a general application to the Masters for advancing the prices of wages from fourteen shills. to eighteen shillings per sett for making Wheels, and the day men to be raised in proportion; on the Trade in general refusing to comply, the Journeymen one and all left work, proceeded to hold meetings and raised subscriptions for endeavouring to bring the Masters to comply with their demandes. These proceedings induced the Master, Mr Font, to apply for advice to the Bench of Justices, who were unanimous in the Opinion that such meetings & combinations were Illegal and that the Master might & indeed ought to indite (sic) them at the Sessions, on which Mr Font with the assistance of the Officers gott possession of their subscription book, and preferred a Bill of Inditement at Hickes Hall against six or eight of the principals which by the Grand Jury was returned a good Bill . . .[44]

Five years later, the Feltmakers' Company failed to break a strike by civil proceedings. Mr Richard Lake was awarded £100 plus costs against his journeyman, Andrew White, but 'he had reason to fear would not be attended with the desired effect so as to defeat and destroy such combination without the countenance, interference and support of this Company and in their corporate name and by their pecuniary assistance'.[45] A committee was appointed to consult the Recorder of London and Mr Serjeant Cross, and reported that 'the purport of their advice was for this Company to collect evidence of the combination of journeymen hat-makers and to proceed against the persons so offending by information or indictment in the Court of King's Bench'.[46] In the event, the case went no further than Clerkenwell sessions, having served its purpose: 'the prosecutions were withdrawn under the approbation of the Court, with proper acknowledgements and submission from the defendants, who promised never more to be guilty of the like conduct, and also to use their utmost endeavours to prevent others.'[47]

In a series of trials at King's Bench from 1788 onwards, Thomas Erskine appeared as counsel for journeymen carpenters, blacksmiths and shoemakers.[48] In 1793, however, his services were secured by the Curriers' Company and, deprived of their best advocate, the journeymen's committee capitulated.

> We, the Committee of Journeymen Curriers, whose Names are hereunto subscribed against whom Prosecutions have been commenced by the Company of Curriers of London, for having unlawfully conspired and Combined together to raise and advance the prices and Rates allowed to us and other Journeymen in the same Trade do hereby (in consideration of the Prosecutors having humanely consented to drop the said Prosecution) acknowledge and confess that we have been guilty of a very great Offence by such illegal conspiracy and Combination and are heartily sorry for the same And do hereby promise immediately to return to our respective Employments and not to offend again in like manner And we further agree immediately to enter into Recognizances for our good behaviour for six Months to be computed from this day dated the fifteenth day of February one thousand seven hundred and ninety three.[49]

This was an expensive victory for the Company, which was obliged to sell its stock and to meet the legal charges, paying £500 on account and the balance of £974 9s 11d over two years.[50] The journeymen reassembled three years later at the Pea-hen, Gray's Inn Road, reconstituted their union as a national Curriers' Tramp Society, and resolved that, from 1 September 1803, no person who had served his apprenticeship with a master 'having more than one apprentice besides himself' should be permitted to work in London. The Company urged masters to engage all the apprentices they could afford, and so preserve the 'proper subordination amongst workmen on which the success of all manufactures depended'.[51]

5　A PRE-INDUSTRIAL TRADE UNION

By general consent, the London society of journeymen tailors was the most militant and effective trade union in eighteenth-century England. When, in 1810, the master tailors denounced 'a combination, subsisting for nearly a century, and ripened by experience . . . an engine of oppression . . . imposing . . . arbitrary and oppressive laws on the trade', they did not exaggerate,[1] nor did Gravenor Henson:

> Upon the slightest signal, the tailors' shops were deserted, and a set of men, to the number of 30,000, arrayed themselves in divisions, led by committees formed from amongst themselves, upon any plan of annoyance deemed advisable, with a tact and determination which had been, with few exceptions, victorious.[2]

The tailors' union was not a craft society of the 'closed' type; a workman had only to prove his competence by working a 'stint' to be admitted to a house of call, for the system of apprenticeship regulated only a small minority.[3] Like its counterpart in Dublin, the London union was a response to the 'capitalist' workshop, the division of labour and seasonal fluctuations in employment.[4] In 1720, a House of Commons committee reported that the journeymen had 'entered into articles' for their own government; in Galton's words, 'they had already a code of rules, thus completing the idea of a formal organization'.[5] One rule forbade an 'honourable' man from seeking work in any other way than by entering his name in the society book, kept at the 'house'. A member refusing an offer of work could be fined or expelled, as could a bad workman for bringing discredit on the house.[6] Tailors were usually employed in 'squads' of six to ten men, headed by a 'captain': sharing his comrades' market situation, he was at once their foreman and shop steward, and from the captains came the core of union leaders.[7]

The London organization was formed about 1700 from five box clubs at White Hart Yard, Bedfordbury, Blackfriars, Billiter Lane and Southwark; by 1760, more than 40 clubs had joined the confederation.[8] Members worked only by the day and on the employers' premises, dubbing themselves 'Flints'. They were forbidden from taking work home, unlike the 'dishonourable' pieceworkers, or 'Dungs', and, in periods of slack trade, were required to share what little work there was.

> A young lad was playing about the front door of his dwelling, and all at once sees his father coming along the street. He rushes to the door, and calls out, 'Mother, mother, here's me father coming.' 'Is his damp-rag sticking out of his hat?', calls back the mother. 'It is', answers the boy. 'Lord have mercy', cries the poor woman, 'he's flinting it again. Sure I've had bad luck since I married a flint of a tailor, so I have . . . .'[9]

In the absence of statutory or collective wage-fixing machinery, the houses of call set their own 'fair' rate for labour. When, in 1720, several master tailors challenged the rate, there was a strike of the 'Flint' houses, followed by prosecutions and indictments for combination.[10] Two Acts to regulate wages in the London trade proved ineffective, and until 1834, when they attempted disastrously to convert their society into a 'Grand National Consolidated Trade Union' of all trades, the journeymen tailors were in almost continuous confrontation with their masters.[11]

John Fielding, the Bow Street stipendiary, outlined the structure and functioning of the tailors' union in 1764:

> they have formed themselves into a kind of republic and held illegal meetings at 42 different public houses commonly called houses of call and appointed from each of these houses two persons to represent the body and form the Grand Committee for the Management of the Town . . . which makes rules and orders for the direction of the Masters and the whole body of journeymen tailors. And whatever Master or journeymen refused to comply therewith the Master was not to have any men to do their business and the journeyman was fined at the will of the body of the journeymen and until he paid that fine and cleared his contempt the other journeymen would not suffer him to work for any master.[12]

The tailors had manoeuvred their employers into conflict with an Act of Parliament for regulating wages: 'for two years now last the combination of the journeymen has been so strong that they have exacted much greater wages from their Masters and have worked less hours than by law allowed.[13] The Act of 1721 'for regulating the journeymen tailors within the Weekly Bills of Mortality' resulted from the first major strike in the London trade. In 1720, the houses of call announced a reduction in the working day by one hour and a wage increase of 2s a week, on the grounds that 'they work for less Wages now than they have done for a considerable Time, and more Hours than they did before the pretended Agreement (to combine) is said to be made'.[14] Led by Mr Baldwin, of York Buildings, the masters formed a committee of resistance, designating alternative houses of call and establishing a sickness fund for journeymen who withdrew from the combination. An all-London strike followed and, on 9 August, the journeymen marched through the City to Merchant Taylors Hall, and sat down to a dinner of 'fifty-six legs of mutton, a hundred and twelve fowls and quantities of cabbage and cucumber'.[15]

The masters' committee sought strike-breakers from the country towns, and the society published warnings of 'more hands wanting in Town than can be brought to it upon any precarious encouragement whatever'.[16] Some country tailors followed the lead of London, and four were committed to Reading gaol.[17] Two of the masters' houses of call were closed: John Badger, landlord of the Black Boy, was denounced as an 'enemy of the trade' and visited by a deputation; and a crowd surrounded the Black Lion and began to demolish it. Three journeymen were charged with riot and assault, but proceedings against the union itself ran into difficulties. When 40 tailors were indicted at King's Bench for conspiracy, they counter-charged their masters with combining to reduce wages and were released on bail.[18]

The master tailors petitioned Parliament for an Act to clarify the law, to fix maximum wages for the trade and to enable the magistrates to make any necessary adjustments. The journeymen briefed counsel, at a reported cost of over £700, and nearly wrecked the Bill in the Lords, but it eventually reached the statute book on 7 June 1721. The strike continued in London and the home counties, several men now being prosecuted under the new Act. Men at Cambridge, who were outside its scope, were convicted 'not for refusing to work, but for conspiring . . . and a conspiracy of any kind is illegal, although the matter about which they conspired might have been lawful . . . if they had not conspired to do it'.[19]

The masters' committee also prosecuted four publicans for allowing strikers to use their houses, but they were eventually discharged by King's Bench.[20] The London magistrates committed several journeymen to prison until they agreed to work for the new statutory wages but, despite this legal activity, not all the masters supported the committee, some continuing to pay the 'customary' rates demanded by the union. In 1723, the committee's attorney, Mr Jones of Maiden Lane, offered a reward of £5 for information concerning master tailors who, to 'seduce and draw away the Servants or Journeymen of other Masters, have given or allow'd them greater Wages than is allowed by the Act'.[21] In 1727 several journeymen were committed to the house of correction for demanding 'exorbitant' wages, but by 1737 the statutory maximum of 1s 9½p was universally ignored, and the master tailors 'were in the greatest perplexity, the journeymen taylors refusing to work under a crown a day. Some have complied at four shillings, but the greatest number seem obstinately combined, and at present refuse to work under.'[22] These wages were higher than the society's published rates, which in 1743 they stated to be 2s 6d and the following year 2s 7½d.[23] After a dispute with an employer over the 'customary' price, the society served notice 'that the journeymen are resolv'd one and all, not to have their Price abated nor lower'd by any Master whatsoever'.[24]

There was again open conflict. The licensee of the Cock and Pye, Drury Lane, announced that his house would supply journeymen for 1s 8d per day, and the society ordered its members to move to other houses. Edward Ives, landlord of the Hand and Racket, Hedge Lane, then offered to supply 'good journeymen . . . according to Act of Parliament'. The union accused several masters of putting work out to be done by the piece to stallholders and 'People carrying on Trade in a Sales-Way in Monmouth-Street, Houndsditch, Rosemary-Lane, &c., to the Detriment of the capable Workmen'. The public was asked to avoid 'Stallmen and Women who work for the Saleshops, as such Work can't possibly do any Service, or be of Credit to the Wearer'. The staymakers likewise begged their customers, 'the Ladies . . . to consider what Risks theirs and their Children's Shapes' would incur at the hands of 'Country Lads . . . come to London, to circumvent experienced Workmen'. Country tailors and staymakers were warned that it would be 'most to their advantage' to stay out of London until the matter was settled, and some agreed to do so.

We, the Journeymen of the City of Canterbury and County of Kent, are absolutely determin'd to a Man, not to be decoy'd by (the Masters') Sugar-Plumb out of the wholsom Air, to work in their fulsome Garrets at any such Rate; and unless they can make better Proposals by their Advertisements, they will serve us only to save other Paper.[25]

A joint committee of master tailors and staymakers was formed at a meeting on 3 July 1744 at the Crown and Anchor Tavern in the Strand. General meetings were subsequently held throughout the summer at the Cross Keys Tavern, Covent Garden, the Strand Coffee House and the Ship Tavern, where it was resolved to 'concur in the measures already taken, in order to suppress the present unlawful combination of their journeymen'.[26] Five houses of call were designated for men 'willing to work for the wages as established by Law'.[27] The society, again appealed to country journeymen tailors.

> BROTHERS,
> This is to inform you, that the repeated Advertisements of the London Masters, is only an Allurement, contrary to Reason and Equity, because that Body is no more capable of protecting you from being Impress'd into his Majesty's Service, either by Land or Sea, than their Generosity is of supporting you . . . .[28]

They promised to inform customers whose clothes were put out 'in the same way as Soldiers Cloathes are undertaken' and instructed Londoners that

> they must not work with such Masters above named, under no less Penalty than being immediately expell'd all reasonable Communities, nor work on the same Shopboard with any Men from the Masters' advertis'd Houses, nor to the same Master or Mistress in any shops whatsoever, in regard to the Capacity of a Journeyman Taylor.[29]

Throughout August and September some 15,000 workers stayed out of the workshops. The landlord of one house advertised by the masters repudiated them the next day, and the other four had little to do. By September and October, the employers' committee was meeting almost daily, and appealed to the government for help. On 5 September, some strikers were impressed and taken to the Savoy barracks in the Strand.[30] A fortnight later, the Privy Council instructed magistrates to enforce the Act of 1721, and orders were issued to constables to suppress illegal meetings at alehouses and to prosecute the landlords. Threatened with the loss of their licences, many of them signed statements dissociating themselves from the strikers.[31] A special Petty Sessions for St George, Hanover Square, was held each Friday to receive information, not only against journeymen and publicans, but also against employers, and late in the year, after public warnings had been given, a small master, William Neal, was indicted at Middlesex Sessions for continuing to pay his journeymen 2s 6d per day. In December, two more masters were indicted for overpayment, but in one case the jury refused to convict.[32]

Journeymen were convicted at Middlesex and Guildhall Sessions, under the Tailors' Act, for leaving their employer's service before finishing work in hand. Their cases attracted some public sympathy, and the society made them the basis of appeal to Parliament. On 22 January 1745, a large number of journeymen went to the Commons and distributed printed copies of their case to the Members. They also handed in a petition drawing attention to the oppressive clauses of the Act and to

being deprived of the Liberty which all the rest of his Majesty's Subjects quietly enjoy, and which before the enacting of one particular Law, of a late Date, they humbly conceived must be acknowledged by their Birth-Right secured to them by Magna Carta, and the ancient Constitution of this Realm, which has always preserved a just and equitable Subordination, with respect to the Liberties of a free People.[33]

The petition remained on the table of the House, the trade gradually resumed its course, and for six years an uneasy truce was preserved. In July 1751, several masters complained to Middlesex Sessions that since the beginning of the year their journeymen had been exacting from them greater wages than they were legally permitted to pay. 'In order to prevent such Exactions for the future', the magistrates were asked 'to alter the Wages mentioned in the said Act, and to settle and ascertain the Wages of the Journeymen Taylors in such a manner as this Court shall think reasonable and just'. After hearing counsel for masters and journeymen, the Sessions fixed new rates of 2s 6d in summer and 2s in winter, plus three-halfpence 'breakfast money'.[34]

The society houses ignored the order, continuing to enforce the 'fair' rate, and, on conviction for refusing to work, two journeymen were imprisoned for six months.[35] These prosecutions were little more than symbolic, and many employers thought they would be no better off with their workmen in prison or on the high seas. Dissatisfied with lack of decisive action by the magistrates, some of the larger employers waited on the Duke of Newcastle, and on 16 October obtained a Privy Council order, instructing all justices to enforce the Act strictly and to prevent the intimidation of employers and non-union journeymen. The society men were

a numerous Body, and have committed many Riots, Tumults, and

Outrages; and some of them have sent Letters to the Master Taylors, threatening to murder them and fire their houses in case they would not comply with their illegal Demands, and have actually assaulted, beaten and abused some of them, to the great Terror of his Majesty's faithful and loyal Subjects.[36]

Henry Fielding committed some journeymen to Bridewell for leaving their masters' work unfinished, but he and other magistrates tried to appear impartial in the dispute itself. On 25 October, masters and journeymen were heard for four hours at Guildhall, the legal wages for the City were assessed as in Middlesex, but the working day was also reduced by an hour. The order was limited to one year, and when it lapsed many masters and journeymen thought it was still in force, for, in November 1752, the Lord Mayor and Sir William Calvert convicted three tailors

> for unlawfully departing from their Masters' Service at Seven o'Clock in the Evening, and refusing to work, according to the Statute, 'till Eight o'Clock. When those worthy Magistrates, out of their great Tenderness, from the Convicts Plea of the Ignorance of the Law, and from the Intercession of the Master Taylors themselves, were pleased, for this Time, to commit them to the House of Correction for twenty-four Hours only, but with a reasonable Admonition not to offend again, lest they should be adjudged to undergo the full statutable Punishment of two Months.[37]

At the next Quarter Sessions, the 1751 order was renewed, but the one-hour differential between the City and the rest of London created a new grievance. The Middlesex magistrates declined to order a seven o'clock finish, and the society men, encouraged by some masters, imposed it as 'customary'. Although a parliamentary committee had been studying the working of the 1721 Act, no time was available to amend it.[38]

In 1755, an attempt was made to split the union. On 21 July, an advertisement appeared in the *Public Advertiser* giving notice to master tailors of a new house of call at the Crown in Billiter Lane, and calling on journeymen join a new society.

> We are in no ways joined with Slatemen in Combination, neither are we forced by Articles to use any arbitrary Power nor Imposition in open Violation of the Law. We invite all Journeymen Taylors that

are in no Ways joined in any Combination with Slatemen, to meet their
Brethren at the above-mentioned House to-morrow July 22, to consult on Affairs of Importance.[39]

The *Public Advertiser* was the property of the blind stipendiary
magistrate, John Fielding, and was the successor to the *Covent Garden
Journal*, published by his brother Henry. It was one of several flourishing
enterprises, including an employment agency and a 'secret service'
fund, managed by the Fieldings from their house in Bow Street.[40]
During John Fielding's period of office, the paper was the semi-official
organ of the Bow Street court, and in its early years it waged a propa-
ganda war on highwaymen, forestallers, regraters and strikers. Later,
Fielding was to modify his attitude to industrial disputes.

In 1756, several advertisements appeared in the press, offering
clothes to the public at cut prices. The new 'advertising tailors' also
offered good wages and a short working day. Walter Butler, claiming
ten years' experience in Paris, offered a 25 per cent discount for 'ready
money only', adding, 'I will give the best wages to Journeymen now
going, to work from Six in the Morning till Seven at Night the Year
round.' Two houses of call, at Temple Bar and St Martin's Lane,
announced wages of sixteen shillings a week all year round, 'and no
objection to their leaving Work at Seven o'Clock'. This advertisement
added that there was 'at present a Dispute in the Taylors business with
respect to both Hours of Work and Wages'.[41] Soon after, a rejoinder
appeared in the *Public Advertiser*.

> Many Advertisements have lately made their Appearance, insinuately
> that the Master Taylors have proposed to allow their Men to leave
> Work at Seven o'Clock, and that they would employ none who have
> work'd for Persons who have, or do advertise to underwork the rest
> of the Trade. To convince the Nobility, Gentry, &c., that not one
> Master Taylor (a fair Trader) hath made such Proposals, we Work-
> men, the Journeymen in the City and Liberty of Westminster, have
> unanimously agreed, from no other Motive but the Public Good, not
> to work for any of those who daily lay Imputations on the Trade,
> by imposing bad Commodities and Workmanship on those who are
> trapped by the Snare called Cheapness.[42]

However 'unanimous' the agreement, a very large number of men
were successfully insisting on a shorter working day. On 2 August,
Fielding announced 'that divers Journeymen Taylors . . . have lately,

and do daily, refuse to work at the several Rates prescribed by the Justices' and that he had also received information 'that many unlawful Combinations have been entered into . . . to shorten the Number of Hours'. He ordered these unlawful practices to be ended at once, warned keepers of houses of call that their licences might not be renewed, and invited individual journeymen 'to lay their Complaints before me, at my House in Bow-Street', where they should be 'candidly and impartially heard'.[43]

A week later, a group of master tailors called a meeting of 'fair traders' at the Bedford Head Tavern, Covent Garden, 'then and there to certify their Resolution in a Body, of punishing all Journeymen who shall henceforth attempt to trample on the Laws made for the Benefit of their Trade, to John Fielding, Esq., who has kindly promised to attend the said Meeting and use his utmost Endeavour to redress the said Grievance'. No 'advertising tailors' would be admitted.[44] The meeting gave special attention to the houses of call.

Whereas several of the said publicans have since been with Mr Fielding, and declared that they did not know any Thing of the Laws relating to these Masters and their Journeymen . . . And as we are convinced by the Use our Journeymen made of the Leisure they now have, that their having another Hour to spend in an Alehouse cannot be of any Use to their Families, we think it our Duty to make them comply with the Law, which is as followeth.[45]

Summaries of the penalties under the Act of 7 Geo I were published in the *Public Advertiser* throughout August. On 1 September, the parish sessions for St Clement Danes and St Mary le Strand stopped the licences of all the tailors' houses of call and, on 23 September, 26 publicans signed a declaration that they would not in future 'suffer any Slate, Article or illegal Subscription' to be carried on.[46] The masters' committee stated that journeymen would only be engaged from houses the keepers of which signed the declaration. The Quarter Sessions solemnly warned journeymen, publicans and masters alike that the law would be strictly enforced, and there were a few exemplary convictions for leaving work unfinished, but the shift in power was negligible.[47] With the coming of spring, and the seasonal shortage of labour, large numbers of masters forgot their resolution, and quietly ignored the law.

John Fielding, who had upheld the letter of the law at the risk of unpopularity, gave these reasons for his failure.

The Master Taylors in this metropolis have repeatedly endeavoured to break and suppress the combinations of their journeymen to raise their wages, and lessen their hours of work, but have ever been defeated, notwithstanding the excellent provision of the above statute; and this has been in some measure due to the infidelity of the Masters themselves to each other; some of whom, taking advantage of the confusion, have collected together some of the journeymen, whose exorbitant demands they have complied with, while many other Masters have had a total stop put to their business, because they would not be guilty of a breach of so necessary a law; but the success of the journeymen in these disputes, and the sub-mission of their Masters, is chiefly owing to the custom the Masters have now got, of charging extra wages in their bills, by which means they relieve themselves, and the imposition is thrown entirely on the public, who can alone redress it, by throwing it back upon the Master Taylor, for whose benefit and security the Legislature has taken such pains as leaves him without room for complaint.[48]

By 1760, some journeymen were receiving a 'customary' wage of five shillings a day, and complaints were made of intimidation. Some irregular warfare went beyond the policy of the union, which in 1762 set a 'fair' rate of only three shillings. This decision was taken at a delegate conference of the 42 society houses, held at the Green Dragon, Fleet Street. Hours were not in dispute, as most masters were tolerating the seven o'clock finish. After reporting back to their houses, the delegates met again the following week at the Sun, Devereux Court, and thereafter weekly at different houses, to avoid interference from Fielding. The house of call chosen for each general meeting was desig-nated 'House of Representatives', and the representatives in turn elected a 'Committee for Management of the Town', commonly abbre-viated to 'the Town'.[49]

According to James Blood, a delegate to the House of Representa-tives, the masters were planning to lay off men in the winter to avoid paying the fair rate. The city houses raised a strike levy of six shillings per member, payable weekly or in a lump sum; the West End levied sixpence per week. The City men were also to contribute 18 shillings each to the defence of journeymen who were prosecuted, and the defendant's clubhouse was expected to raise a further six shillings per member. Journeymen refusing or failing to pay were disciplined.

If any member met with a refractory journeyman, he gave an account of him to the committee; then that was carried to the general committee. Each representative took his name to the respective clubs, and that man was not to be worked with. If the master insisted on keeping him, he was to lose all others. They that were agreeable to our rules we called *Flints*, and those that were not were called *Dungs* .... We looked upon it that Mr Dove, Mr Fell and Mr Mason, three masters, were stirring up strife against us: so we fixed upon them, that they should not be served. We insisted upon the men that worked for them to come away and leave them: it was a general resolution they should have no more men work for them. The master of the House of Call sends the men, and if he sent any there, the body of men in that house would be fined so much money for serving contrary to rule.[50]

A fortnight before Easter, 1763, representatives from the whole of London, including the suburbs, agreed to strike for the three shillings, but at the next meeting at the Queen's Arms, Newgate Street, the clubs were divided.

The city and the other end of the town did not agree: the city fell off from the agreement rather. Every house was not willing to strike; to other side Temple-Bar signalized themselves from this side; they said, if the city would not agree with them, they would strike on the Monday morning. They wanted to have 3 shillings and three halfpence a day; the city did not come to a resolution that day .... This division was on a Thursday night; but on the Sunday night we had a meeting among ourselves. On the Tuesday night the other end of the town struck; the city disagreed one among another.[51]

Blood, who represented the Hand and Sheers, Cloth Fair, worked to end the split, and a few days later, the city men came out as well.

On the Tuesday night, about 8 o'clock, came two men to us, and said, We hear the other Men have struck, and we are willing: they came from the Shepherd and Goat, Fleet-Ditch. They said, Let us go round and see if the others agree. I was chose out of my society to go to three more houses in the city. I went to the Ship in Lime-street, and the Crown in Duke's Place: we had word brought they were agreeable in Black Friars; there are two or three houses of call there. At the Ship in Lime-street I told them the resolution of our house, and that we had come to a resolution to strike: they were agreeable if the Crown in Duke's Place and two others would. I went to the Crown in Duke's Place on a club night, when the members were all present: they consented to it ... I went to the Faulcon in Duke's Place that was near it, and made the proposal to them, and they were agreeable; (our meetings were all on one night). I returned back to my society, and they sent about; they were all agreeable; every representative went to his own club, and every body were to strike in the morning. We did in general through the city all strike.[52]

For the moment, the masters gave way, but their committee prepared to counter-attack. In January 1764, they established a network of nine 'private' houses of call, delivered an ultimatum on the working day, and announced that they were 'united, and have unanimously agreed to support the private Houses of Call – and never more to call a Man from the public ones; it will be in vain for the Journeymen to stand out any longer against the Laws of their Country; if they do they will bring Poverty and Distress upon themselves and Families, and perhaps a more severe Punishment than they at present apprehend, for the Masters are determined to break the Combination'.[53] Within six weeks, the new houses claimed to have placed 800 tailors from the country and 230 Germans, French and Dutchmen, nearly all on piecework, but these were not enough to supply the whole trade nor to break the union, and it was necessary to warn that 'those Masters, who continue to employ the Journeymen in Combination, in contempt of the Law and other Masters of the Trade, will be prosecuted with the utmost severity'.[54]

On the night of 2 April, the chairman of the committee, Mr John Dove, took an unexpected initiative. At the head of a party of committeemen and loyal journeymen, he entered the Bull Head house of call, in Bread Street, within the City of London, seized 45 journeymen tailors and had them locked overnight in the Wood Street compter. In the morning, when the men were brought before the sitting Alderman, there was only time to examine five, who were finally discharged with a caution. By Tuesday morning, both masters' and journeymen's organizations had arranged for counsel, Mr Field, a judge of the Sheriff's court, appearing for the masters, and a Mr Cox for the defendants. The 40 prisoners then explained, at length, that they had only entered the Bull Head for the purpose of drinking with brother tradesmen, and the Alderman, finding that some of the prisoners were non-unionists, ordered all to be released and paid a guinea each by the prosecution for wrongful arrest and loss of working time. He also advised them to petition the next Quarter Sessions for enforcement of their 'customary' working hours.[55] Behind the scenes counsel had struck a bargain.

> On hearing Mr Field, in behalf of the Masters, and Mr Cox, in behalf of the Men, it appeared that the Men were not legally taken into Custody; whereupon a Proposal was made by the Men's Attorney, that all Proceedings on both Sides should be stopped, and the Men all discharged out of Court, upon their agreeing to conform to the Orders of Sessions till next General Quarter Sessions of the Peace; and that the Masters would join in petitioning the Court to reduce the last Hour of Work to Seven o'Clock; likewise, that the Masters would pay the Men for the Time they were in Custody, and pay the Fees and Expences of the Discharge. Which Proposal being agreed to by such of the Men as were present, they were all discharged out of Custody, and the whole 45 were also ordered to be discharged upon their conforming to the said Agreements. It is hoped this Agreement will be productive of a perfect Harmony between Masters and Men, which must be a Satisfaction to the Public in general . . .[56]

On Thursday, 39 men signed general releases, and were handed their guineas by Mr Ogle, attorney for the masters, on the understanding that proceedings on both sides were to stop. Six men did not sign; friends of two of them had obtained writs of *habeas corpus*, and they were discharged by Lord Chief Justice Mansfield. James Wesley and three others refused to sign the discharge or take the guinea, but announced their intention to bring a civil action against Mr Dove and three masters in the Court of Common Pleas. By early May, 21 actions had also been brought against the keeper of Wood Street compter.[57]

The General Quarter Sessions for the City and Middlesex simultaneously revoked their earlier decisions, fixing the hours of work throughout the metropolis as 6 a.m. to 7 p.m., with an hour for lunch, but the strike continued over the wages, and became more bitter, with several clashes between the 'Flints' and the new pieceworking 'Dungs'. In September, more than 6,000 journeymen were reported to have tramped from London, 'offering their services to every nobleman and gentlemen they can get to in the country'.[58] There were some secessions from the union, notably in Southwark, where there was discontent over the administration of the central strike fund. A dozen journeymen applied to the Court of Conscience at Guildhall for an order to refund their 12s subscription, and another hundred cases were said to be pending.[59] There were divisions among the masters also, and, in the first recorded conviction of employers for entering into a collective agreement, the principals of Andrew Regnier and Son and Messrs Barrett and Sanders were committed to the Gatehouse for 'consenting to, and being knowingly interested in, an agreement between them and their journeymen to advance their wages to 3s. a day, contrary to law'.[60] They were released after a week. For a similar offence, Justices Fielding and Spinnage committed another master to Clerkenwell Bridewell.[61]

Finally, the masters' association embarked on the expensive course of indicting 'the Town' committee for conspiracy. At the Old Bailey Sessions for Lent, 1765, John Cannon and Alexander Sparks were committed to Newgate for a year; William Milburn, John Marsham, Joseph Carrick and Robert Jones for six months; and Walter Berry and John Dobson for three months. Each was also fined one shilling and ordered to find security for his good behaviour for a further year.[62] James Wesley, however, succeeded in his action for false imprisonment, and was awarded £30 plus costs against Mr Dove and three other masters.[63]

The combination continued, and in 1767 journeymen were still being prosecuted for insisting on three shillings a day.[64] The society men continued to meet weekly on club night, while in the taverns their masters discussed the weakness of the laws, the state of trade and the Wilkes affair. Each side awaited the occasion for renewed hostilities.

This arrived with the events of May 1768.

6 THE MAGISTRATE AS MEDIATOR

Two years after his brush with the London tailors, John Fielding asked the Duke of Newcastle for a knighthood, drawing special attention to 'those bodies of journeymen of almost every trade whose combinations I have been industrious to break by the vigorous execution of penal laws'.[1] He eventually received both knighthood and secret funds from the Treasury, for the government recognized the importance of policing the newly built districts around Westminster.[2]

Fielding's remarkable colleague, Saunders Welch, attributed the growth of crime in the metropolis to 'the unlimited wandering of the poor of our own kingdom and the uncontrolled importation of Irish vagabonds'. He advocated a labour passport or certificate

> to prevent the servant or labourer from removing from their legal settlement, or other place of residence, without a certificate describing the name, age, stature, and person of the party, and that he or she have behaved with honesty and industry ... such certificate to be signed either by a magistrate, minister or churchwarden.[3]

Welch advised police constables to show 'temper and sobriety in the execution of your office ... Be not easily provoked by the ill-manners and scurrilous reflexions of those about you.'[4] In 1750, the Bow Street force comprised only six constables or 'thief-takers', later augmented by four 'Bow Street Runners'.[5] The magistrates were required to deal personally with riots and unlawful assemblies, relying on their moral authority and powers of persuasion.

> Whereas Information upon Oath has been made before us, that upwards of 700 printed Bills have been dispersed through the Bills of Mortality, inviting the Journeymen Barbers and Wigmakers to meet at the Half Way House leading to Hampstead on Monday next; the Purport of which Meeting being to unlawfully combine together to raise their Wages upon their Masters. Notice is hereby given, that we will put the Laws into Execution against any such Journeymen, who shall presume to assemble unlawfully for the Purpose above mentioned, either at the said House, or at any other House, and also represent to the Sessions the keepers of any Taverns or Alehouses

who shall presume to encourage such unlawful Meetings and Combinations, either of the Journeymen of the above Trades, or any other Trades whatever; and out of regard to the Public, it is hoped that if any such unlawful Meetings and Combinations should hereafter be attempted, that Notice will be sent by an anonymous Letter, directed to us, in Bow-street, Covent Garden. May 22, 1756.

JOHN FIELDING
SAUNDERS WELCH[6]

Saunders Welch rode out to Hampstead, where the barbers were meeting in the open air. They hotly denied any combination to raise wages, their case had been grossly misrepresented and all they asked of their masters was to end deductions from their wages of seven shillings a week 'for each journeyman's eatings of the Fragments and Refuse of their Tables'. Welch listened patiently, urged them to go home, and promised that he and Fielding would try to arrange matters to the satisfaction of all. The masters were invited to meet the magistrates at a mutually convenient time and place, but they were in no mood to compromise with 'a heedless Set of idle, disorderly, unthinking Journeymen ... who by their Behaviour, demonstrate they never will have Ambition enough to even hope of being any Thing more; therefore would, if possible, draw in the sober Part of the Men into their wild and incoherent Project'. Instead, the trade should discover the ringleaders, 'that they may be made useful by serving his Majesty' in the press-gang.[7]

Since Elizabethan times, local courts had acted both as industrial tribunals, handling complaints by individual workpeople, and as wages boards empowered by the Act of 5 Elizabeth to fix standard wages, which were maxima. Variations in these statutory rates were initiated by petition to the justices. In the City of London, guilds and companies sometimes agreed the wages and submitted them to the Lord Mayor's court for formal approval.[8] Sometimes the Lord Mayor was a reluctant arbitrator. In August 1732, two members of the Clothworkers' Company, Messrs George Davis and Benjamin Wilkinson, received anonymous letters signed 'Us, the Journeymen Cloth Workers of London', threatening to murder them or set fire to their houses if the wages were not increased. In September, spokesmen for the body of journeymen presented a petition to the Lord Mayor and Aldermen, who ruled that wages and hours should remain unchanged, but that overtime of 3d per hour should be paid for work outside the hours of 5 a.m. to 7 p.m., 'allowing two hours for breakfast and dinner'.[9]

This did not satisfy the journeymen, who drew up another petition.

On 2 October, the workshop of Mr Benjamin Barnes, of St Gregory Parish, St Paul's, was set on fire, with great loss and damage. A committee of masters headed by Barnes, Davis and Wilkinson offered a reward for information; other committee members were Thomas Hannam, William Farrer, William Cooper and Daniel Holbrow. A Royal Pardon was offered to the first conspirator to inform on his accomplices, but soon after the committee members received further threatening letters. The Lord Mayor's court washed its hands of the petition, redirecting it to the Clothworkers' Company, and after the Guildhall hearing a group of journeymen broke into William Farrer's house, warning that he would be the next to suffer.[10]

In the shires and the boroughs, the justices assessed wages intermittently, sometimes ritually renewing them 'as before', sometimes overlooking them altogether.[11] A strike or riot would remind them of this function, as at Ware, Hertfordshire, in August 1737.

> The Corn Factors there are in great distress for want of Men to work the Barges that bring the Corn from thence. It seems the Masters of those Barges have enter'd into an Agreement to reduce the Wages of the Men five Shillings in a Passage, and the Barge-men have also agreed not to work under the former Price, on which Account the Corn and other things have lain there several Days. Since this Dispute a Barge sank for want of proper Care, and the greatest part of what was on board was spoil'd before they could get People to take them out.[12]

When the malt-factors of Ware were returning from London, a band of 80 armed bargemen, their faces blacked to avoid recognition, were reported in the vicinity.[13] The dispute apparently began in the spring, when unusual publicity surrounded an adjourned General Quarter Sessions.[14]

After 'combinations and tumults' in November 1756, the Gloucestershire magistrate appeased the journeymen weavers by setting piece-rates for the woollen trade. There was an immediate outcry from the employers, who found the order impossible to implement because of the vast range of shapes in which broadcloth was made.[15] The weavers struck, and six companies of infantry, commanded by General Wolfe, were sent to keep order. Wolfe reported that 'those who are most oppressed have seized the tools, and broke the looms of others that would work if they could' and at one stage he feared they would 'force the magistrates to use our weapons against them'.[16] After petitions and counter-petitions to Parliament, a short Act repealed the wages section of the Weavers' Act 29 Geo.II, and provided that, irrespective of wage assessments, existing contracts between clothiers and weavers remained valid. The sections relating to truck were retained and a new clause required payment of wages within two days of completion of work, under penalty of forty shillings per offence.[17]

By mid-century, pay disputes were reaching the courts in growing numbers, the journeymen being encouraged to present petitions peacefully, but warned of severe penalties for taking industrial action. In May 1755, the Bristol magistrates announced their intention to put 'in strict execution' the laws against combinations of workmen,[18] but without help from the armed forces a magistrate and his tiny police force were powerless against a hostile crowd. In London, where the involvement of troops was politically sensitive, the City and stipendiary justices preferred the role of mediator between masters and men. Conciliation and arbitration were institutionalized in a tripartite system of industrial relations.[19]

Saunders Welch assumed this role with gusto, and he achieved a certain popularity. His daughter, wife of the painter Nollekens, enjoyed telling how her father had set forth alone into Cranbourn Alley for a noisy meeting of shoemakers. The journeymen had marched, 'with a drum beating before them, to several masters of that trade, in order to prosecute some people who work at the business, without a regular apprenticeship, and carry on the trade to the prejudice of those who have a right to it'.[20] Wages were also in dispute.

> Immediately her father made his appearance he was recognized, and his name shouted up and down the Alley, not with fear, but with a degree of exaltation. 'Well', said the ringleader, 'let us get him a beer-barrel and mount him', and when he was up, they one and all gave him three cheers, and cried 'Welch! Welch for ever!' In the mildest manner possible, Mr Welch assured them that he was glad to find they had conducted themselves quietly, and at the same time, in the most forcible terms, persuaded them to disperse, as their meetings were illegal. He also observed to the master shoemakers, who were listening to him from their first-floor windows, that as they had raised the prices of shoes on account of the increased value of provisions, they should consider that the families of their workmen had proportionate wants. The result was, that the spokesmen of the trade were called into the shops, and an additional allowance was agreed upon. The men then alternately carried Mr Welch to his office

in Litchfield Street, gave him three cheers more and set him down.[21]

John Fielding chose to play arbitrator in the cabinet-makers' strike of 1761, but the episode did less for his reputation. On Monday morning, 14 September, journeymen in the principal workshops presented to their employers a demand for a shorter working day and higher piece-rates. On being refused, they walked out. Most employers retaliated by discharging the strikers and the society men who refused to sign an 'agreement'. Although bedstead makers, sawyers, turners and porters remained at work, most of the cabinet- and chair-makers were either on strike or locked out. When nine employers conceded the men's demands, the others wavered between appeasement and intransigence, first offering the men 'protection and encouragement according to their merit', then petitioning the Crown for enforcement of the law. On 18 November, the masters met at the Crown and Anchor Tavern in the Strand, and 'unanimously' resolved

> That all Journeymen Cabinet and Chair-Makers, who are willing to come immediately to work on the usual terms of those Trades, shall be employed as formerly, and meet with every Encouragement due to their Merit. And those who do not return to work will be considered by the Masters as Persons bidding Defiance to the Order of the Lords of his Majesty's most Honourable Privy Council, and must blame themselves for the Consequences.[22]

The Privy Council had already instructed magistrates to suppress illegal meetings in public houses, and to prosecute the publicans when 'thought just and reasonable'. The magistrates' discretion was subject to their submitting 'an exact account of what they shall do . . . to one of His Majesty's principal Secretaries of State'.[23]

Fielding's first action was to announce willingness to hear both sides. The journeymen's case had been widely publicized, and public opinion, as reflected in the press, was sympathetic.

> We, as a free People, are determined to work no more for those Masters who will not agree to our reasonable Demand, altho' those Masters have declared, that several of their Customers will wait for the Completion of their Orders, which consequently can never be. Yet by the Masters here mentioned, and many others, who have agreed to our Request, the Nobility, Gentry, &c. may depend upon being properly supplied with Cabinet and Chair-Work, performed in

the best Manner . . .[24]

The Masters had reported, that granting the terms proposed by the men would raise the prices of work 15 per cent more . . . the journeymen say that their request, being granted, would not, by the merest calculation, amount to more than 3½, and which they offered to demonstrate to the public.[25]

What was the reason that the greatest part of the Journeymen was discharged? *Answer*: For refusing to sign an unjust and unreasonable proposal. What is the reason, that differences so often arise between Masters and Journeymen? *Answer*: By many Masters endeavouring to reduce the prices of workmanship, which frequently obliges them to make use of the most eligible methods of redress.[26]

The possibility of arbitration was canvassed early in November, probably at Fielding's instigation.

Justices of the peace have a right to interfere, upon complaint made to them on these occasions, and check oppression in the master, and idleness in the journeyman; but unfortunately for the latter, they seldom know anything of the redress provided by our excellent constitution; for which reason it were to be wished, that some of our great men would condescend to be their protectors. This is practiced in other countries.[27]

Two weeks later, the masters offered a return to work 'without signing any Article whatever; such Signing being proposed only to discover such as were misled by a too hasty Compliance with the Advice of a few inconsiderate Men'. They drew attention, however, to the Privy Council order, and on 11 December more than 30 journeymen were indicted at Middlesex Sessions for conspiracy and unlawful assembly.[28] In January the masters denied a report in the *Gazetteer* that the dispute had been settled in favour of the journeymen, and promised to prosecute the combination 'notwithstanding any vile Insinuations to the contrary'.[29] On the application of the prosecution, several indictments were removed by *certiorari* to King's Bench, where on 30 June 1762 all employers were forbidden

directly or indirectly to give to any Journeyman Cabinet or Chair-Makers any Benefit or Advantage, in respect of Time or Price, or other Allowance whatsoever, above the terms USUALLY given and allowed before the 14th Day of September last, when the Combination first broke out.[30]

A general meeting was held at the Crown and Anchor to enable masters not in court to acquiesce in this ambiguous ruling. The feelings of some towards Fielding may be gauged from a lampoon published a year later.

In the reign of King Edward the Third there was a great quarrel betwixt the Journeymen Cabinet-makers and their Masters, about wages. Justice should be blind and impartial, but we do not always find it so. The *Justiciarius Westmonasteriensis* was applied to on behalf of the Journeymen; the Advocate set forth the great hardships they had endured, the oppressions they had undergone, and the mischiefs that were meditating against them; but these arguments had little weight with impartial Justice; the said argument was, however, conclusive in their favour, for the Advocate begged Mr *Justiciarius* to accept of 60 rose nobles (twenty guineas of modern money) as a token of their respect; the upright Judge promised this countenance to their cause. Soon afterwards, came an Advocate from the Masters, and giving a like sum, received a like promise; but the Journeymen, who took care to keep proper emissaries about his Excellency's person, presently made a second application to him with 30 more nobles. This was driving the nail to the head, and it is almost unnecessary to observe that the Journeymen gained their cause. The manner in which this *Justiciarius* vindicated his conduct is whimsical enough; and, as most of our writers have omitted telling it, you are welcome to it from me. He observed, in the first place, that the Journeymen had right on their side, and that, before he received any present, his conscience prompted him to determine giving the cause in their favour; therefore the first present he received from them could not be called a bribe, as it had no influence over his opinion. As to the Masters, he said they were a parcel of rogues, and richly merited to lose the money for attempting to make him belye his conscience, but that he intended to *lay it out in private charities*. As to the last 30 nobles, he observed that every Labourer is worthy of his hire; that as men are more prone to evil than good he certainly merited them as a reward for his perseverance in the right way, his uprightness and his integrity; for, had he minded the Tempter at his left elbow, he might have given the cause in favour of the Masters. Thus did our ermined

Judge prove Corruption a Virtue. Thank God we have no such Judges now.[31]

Whatever irregularities may have occurred in the cabinet-makers' case, Sir John Fielding remained in office to deal with many more labour disputes.[32] His great test came with the political crisis of May 1768 when, in addition to the partisans and opponents of John Wilkes, very large bodies of workpeople seized the occasion to parade the streets of London in support of their pay demand.[33]

On an increasing scale, petitions to Westminster or to the King at Kensington Palace were escorted by processions, often many thousands strong. Processions of the unemployed silk weavers and their families were impressive but relatively peaceful, apart from peripheral activities of individuals and groups, but there was always a risk of clashes with the military. In 1765, an incipient riot near the home of the Duke of Bedford, who had vetoed the restriction of silk imports from France, was averted by the tact of a guards officer. He courteously explained to the crowd that 'he was under an indispensible duty of obeying orders, and hoped they would not press too much either his humanity or duty'.[34] There was some applause, and the silk weavers began their walk home to Spitalfields, pausing only to tear up the Duke's railings. From the East End of the town, however, came horrific reports of stabbings, shooting and grisly affrays attributed to a secret society of 'cutters', who broke into workshops and homes late at night to cut and destroy the silk being woven 'below price'. There were some conventional, but ineffective, trade societies of silk weavers, and the cutters tried to resist through terror the downward pressure on their piece-rates.[35]

Fearing a breakdown of authority, politicians among the 'King's friends' demanded the use of troops to disperse both the Wilkes rioters and the labour demonstrators. During an entirely peaceful march of merchant seamen on 11 May 1768, Lord Mansfield said that, unless something vigorous were done, there would be a revolution in ten days. The following week, when the London tailors petitioned noisily against a new Wages bill, Lord Barrington, Secretary for War, moved, to the embarrassment of other Ministers, that the King be empowered to employ the militia. Grenville supported this enlargement of the Crown's powers, but Sir George Savile and Lord Strange opposed, Lord North confessing that he did not know which way to vote. Barrington replied that he spoke in a personal capacity, and to triumphant Opposition cheers the matter was dropped.[36] Such pressures nevertheless compelled the Justices of the Peace to prove their ability to keep order. Fielding's objectives were to isolate the political agitation from the industrial movements, to keep all demonstrators away from Westminster and the royal palaces, and to remove the causes of discontent among four large labour groups: merchant seamen, coalheavers, tailors and silk weavers.

After pitched battles among coalheavers in Whitechapel, Aldermen Beckford and Shakespear brought the foremen of various gangs together on 29 April at the Angel and Crown. The Act for regulating their wages was read and explained, agreement was reached on an appropriate scale, and the foremen agreed to register their gangs with Beckford's deputy and agent, Mr Russell.[37]

Downstream off Deptford, the East India ships were about to sail. Coal ships were arriving from Newcastle, and in the public houses it was learned that after a great strike on the Tyne the sea-coal men had received a general pay increase. In the night of 5 May, parties of seamen assembled outside the 'houses of rendezvous', went aboard the East Indiamen and unreefed the topsails, declaring that no ship would sail until they too received an increase from the merchants. In the morning, boatloads of seamen boarded the ships at Wapping and the Tower, ships that had already sailed were pursued downstream to Blackwall, and placards were posted along the riverbank.[38] The strike spread to bargemen and lightermen: by Monday morning the movement of corn was at a standstill, little business was transacted at the Corn Exchange, and proprietors of coffee houses hastily removed their plate on the news that the seamen were marching on the City.

Processsions of sailors, 'with colours flying, drums beating and fifes playing' had been to St James's on Saturday with a petition to the King. On Monday, some of them pursued the monarch to the review on Wimbledon Common, while others went to the City, occupied the Royal Exchange, picketed the coffee houses, and carried placards reading 'MORE WAGES'.[39]

Just before dawn next day, Tuesday 10 May, a fleet of boats filled with scores of coalheavers appeared off Millbank, Westminster. After carefully inspecting the wharfs from the river, the men came ashore at the Horse Ferry, visited each wharf and public house in turn, and insisted that all men employed at coal wharfs should join them. Men still at home were knocked up and all carts in the streets, whether loaded with coal, flour or wood, were ordered back to their wharfs. Soon a procession of coalheavers was marching through the Strand, carrying a banner before them. They called at each wharf in turn until at Stepney Fields they were joined by many more, and marched on to the wharfs between Shadwell and Essex Stairs

> bearing with them a Writing, declaring their Resolution not to go to work till their Wages should be raised; the Masters of each Wharf having taken into Consideration the high Price of Provisions, agreed to advance their Wages, and signed their Names to the above Writing in Confirmation of their Consent.[40]

At the same time thousands of merchant seamen were assembling in Stepney Fields to approve wage demands and a petition to Parliament and to elect a committee to meet the merchants. A handful of the latter were discovered in the King's Arms, Cornhill, but they were unable to negotiate for the East India Company as a whole. On Wednesday, in the largest procession so far, 14,000 merchant seamen set off from Tower Hill to Westminster. Their 'adjutant' warned them to be orderly, and to throw away the hundreds of large sticks they had brought with them. All reports spoke of their discipline as they marched through the City and down the Strand.

> They were very orderly and regular in their proceedings, and had six flags in front, three in the center and two in the rear; and several ringleaders with boatswains' whistles interspersed throughout, which answered one another, and regulated the whole body.[41]

> A vast body of sailors attended the Houses, but in a modest manner, and desiring only to have their grievances considered, with promise of acquiescing to the determination of Parliament. They declared their attachment to the King, and meeting Wilkes's mob attacked and dispersed it. Yet notwithstanding this respectful behaviour, the Privy Council . . . issued out a proclamation against the sailors.[42]

The proclamation, signed that day by George III at St James's, referred to attempts 'to deter and intimidate the Civil Magistrates from doing their duty'. The Lord Mayor and other justices for London were now strictly required 'effectually to prevent and suppress all riots, tumults and unlawful assemblies' and the magistrates 'and all others acting in obedience to this our Command' might 'rely on our Royal Protection and support in so doing'.[43] Yet the magistrates viewed military protection and support as a mixed blessing. Already six people had been killed and fifteen injured in a clash between Wilkites and guardsmen, and

Fielding strove to avoid such a confrontation with labour demonstrators. On 12 May, before the sitting of Parliament, he awaited a procession of coalheavers and wharfingers as it approached Palace Yard 'with a flag flying, a Drum and two Violins',

> and upon going into the Midst of them, enquiring the Reason for their assembling, causing their Paper to be read by his Clerk, and reasoning with them on the Impropriety, at least, of their proceeding with a Flag, &c., they agreed to drop their Drum and Violins, and delivered their Flag to Sir John, at his Request, which he took with him into Guildhall, after first requesting them not to go through Old Palace Yard at all, but to go round through the Armoury, which they peaceably consented to, having, as they alleged, two or three more Masters to go to by the Water-side.[44]

In the City, where some employers had already signed the 'Writing', normal working was resumed, but some of the men felt doubts as to their masters' good faith and the enforceability of the agreement. In the evening of 11 May, a large deputation had been to the Mansion House to see the Lord Mayor. Harley admitted as many as his room would hold, explained his inability to fix their wages, and promised to support a petition for a new Act of Paliament. This was well received and the men departed peacefully. Two evenings later, Fielding held a meeting of masters and men at Bow Street, to work out an agreed procedure for settling the wages at Quarter Sessions.[45] Next day most of the Westminster coalheavers returned to work. A few merchants whose cargoes were deteriorating negotiated an agreement with the seamen's committee on 17 May, but most of the sailors and coalheavers in the Pool of London remained on strike, to be followed by hatters, glass grinders and coopers. All these disputes were disciplined and relatively peaceful, and Fielding may have been relaxing when, on 15 May, he received a warning from Lord Weymouth, Secretary of State, that 'the tailors intend to assemble tomorrow, and go round to the several masters in London to compel their journeymen to join them'.[46]

At least this was familiar ground, and early next morning Justices Fielding, Welch, Kelynge, Kynaston, Sayer, Read and Colonel Deane set off around the houses of call. They found them deserted, and learned that the tailors were all in Lincoln's Inn Fields preparing to march to Westminster. Fielding hastened to meet the men's committee, and convinced them of the risks they ran, but the crowd was already on the move, the justices and peace officers racing ahead to secure the steps of both Houses of Parliament. As the procession approached Middlesex Guildhall, peers and Members of Parliament were receiving confused and alarming reports: a 'tumultuous assembly' was at the door and 'the Riot Act had been read'. In fact, as with the coalheavers, Fielding and the constables had intercepted the procession, and persuaded many of the tailors inside Guildhall to agree to a solemn reading of their petition.[47] Six committeemen were then permitted to go to the Commons with the first part, which asked for the repeal of the Tailors' Acts. The second part, requesting an immediate wage increase, was referred to the London and Middlesex Quarter Sessions, which deferred a decision until October when, 'after a long and full hearing', it was dismissed 'on account of the prospect of the price of provisions lowering'.[48] Privately the tailors' demands were treated with contempt: 'They impudently set forth their inability to live on two shillings and sevenpence a day, when the common soldier lives for under sixpence.'[49]

Although the sailors from the coal ships had at first supported the coalheavers, they became impatient to return home and, seeing no end to the strike, began to unload the coal themselves. They were forcibly resisted by the coalheavers and, on 7 June, an attempt to seize a collier at Rotherhithe Stairs was repulsed by the crew, who were armed with cutlasses. Gangs of coalheavers ransacked houses in Wapping for all the weapons they could collect. Fearing mass bloodshed, the Tower magistrates reluctantly asked for military assistance, and five customhouse cutters were stationed off Limehouse, Ratcliff Cross and Wapping Stone-stairs to protect the shipping.[50] On 14 June, troops arrested 17 alleged 'White Boys', and the next day 20 coalheavers, chained in pairs, were marched through the City to Bow Street, followed by 15 more in three coaches. Two capital charges were brought: against four men for the murder of John Beatty, a seaman on the Whitby collier *Free Love*, and against three for shooting at John Green, a former coal undertaker, in his public house at Shadwell. Two other men were charged with riotous assembly and attempting to demolish a dwelling-house on the Ratcliff Highway.[51] Fielding issued a public denial of any massacre, and, after lengthy questioning, ordered the remaining prisoners to be released.[52] Two days later, he invited a number of coalheavers, each with between 12 and 30 years' employment in the trade, to state the men's grievances. A merchant with an interest in the coal ships arranged for the masters to pay the wages without deductions and, despite continued friction with the seamen, most of the gangs resumed work 'on reasonable terms'.[53]

Peace was still not restored to the East End. In the night of 26-27 June, bands of armed 'cutters' visited the homes and workshops of silk weavers employed by Mr John-Baptist Hebert, destroying all the silk they could find.[54] In July there were incipient food riots when great numbers of the weavers visited the pea and bean carts, 'but their intent being suspected, the pease and beans were sold at a very reasonable price'.[55] A few days later, a farmer was stopped by weavers at Bethnal Green, and ordered to sell his peas at sixpence a peck; the constables took two hours to disperse the crowd.[56]

On the initiative of Mr Lewis Chauvet, several master weavers formed a committee to draw up a piece-price-list, but they were unable to enforce it throughout the trade. The journeymen's clubs ordered a levy of sixpence a loom to support a strike against the throwsters; Chauvet told his pieceworkers to refuse to pay, and issued them with firearms. In August 1769, the cutters destroyed silk in over sixty looms, but the magistrates hesitated to ask for troops, and, throughout September, the cutters were almost unimpeded. At the end of the month, a large reward being posted, the residents of Hog Lane informed Fielding of the cutters' rendezvous. A handful of foot-guards raided the Dolphin public house and, in a short gun-battle, killed four weavers and took another four prisoner.[57]

More troops entered Spitalfields, engaging and killing five armed cutters. Following the arrest of its landlady, an alehouse in Vine Court was found to contain a huge quantity of firearms, and the East End publicans were summoned to Whitechapel Rotation Office for a solemn warning.[58] Simultaneously Chauvet's committee renewed its efforts to enforce a price-list, and Sheriffs Townsend and Sawbridge announced their 'readiness to answer for any consequences that may ensue from the hitherto supposed inefficiency of the Civil Power to quell riots'.[59] However, the troops remained.

At the Old Bailey, four cutters were found guilty on the capital charge of silk-cutting; John Doyle and John Valline were sentenced to death, but a technicality saved the other two. On 9 November, Townsend and Sawbridge received a royal warrant, ordering that, in place of Tyburn, the executions should be 'as near as convenient to Bethnal Green Church'.[60] They challenged its legality, but a conference of judges ruled that the King could order executions to take place anywhere, and the sheriffs were obliged to carry out the hangings in the midst of a large and hostile crowd. When the bodies had been hanging for half an hour, the weavers uprooted and carried the gallows to Mr Chauvet's house, where they broke the windows and damaged some furniture.[61]

Three more cutters were hanged in December, despite a campaign for clemency. Summoned by handbills to Moorfields, the silk weavers assembled to take their petition to the Queen's Palace. Sawbridge and the Lord Mayor went to Moorfields, to find a party of guards drawn up and, while the Lord Mayor politely refused the commanding officer permission to enter the City Liberties, the weavers reassembled in a field in the Kingsland Road. On the advice of Sawbridge, they appointed a committee of eight, and John Fielding met them near the Palace to divert the petition to the Secretary's office in Whitehall 'where proper care would be taken to deliver it to his Majesty'.[62]

The cutters were avenged in 1771, when a Crown witness, Daniel Clark, was pursued by a mob into Hare Street Field, next to a brickyard, where they

> stript him, tied his hands behind him, took him to a pond, threw him in, and then threw stones and brickbats at him for some time; then took him out, tied a cord around his neck, and threw him into the pond again, and then threw stones and brickbats at him till they beat out his brains.[63]

Two men were executed for this crime, in the same field. A vast crowd attended, but without disorder. The affair of the 'cutters' ended on 14 November 1771.

> Thursday last a large body of journeymen Weavers from Spitalfields attended at Justice Sherwood's, at Shadwell, to hear the determination of a complaint exhibited by one of the fraternity, against a Master Weaver, for refusing to pay the usual and accustomed price for work done; when, after a long and full hearing, at which Mr. Chauvet, and several other worthy and reputable Masters attended, the Justice was pleased to determine in favour of the journeymen, to the entire satisfaction of both parties. This, it is hoped, has put an end to a long dispute in that particular branch of business, and which formerly occasioned the unhappy disturbances in those parts. The decision the above Magistrate made, was chiefly owing to the candid and honest opinion then given, relative to that branch of the trade, by Mr. Chauvet, and the other worthy Masters then present, whose candour the journeymen then gratefully acknowledged.[64]

The chronic unemployment and depressed wages in the silk industry were commonly attributed to an excessive supply of labour.

Silks are more worn now than twenty years ago. Every servant hath one silk gown at least. Tradesmen's wives wear them every day ... The fundamental error is, the manufactory is overstocked with hands. More are employed in the trade than can be maintained by it. Confine the number of apprentices and persons to be employed to what is necessary, and the Weavers will neither want for work, nor their families food and raiment.[65]

In January 1773, moved by stories of hunger and personal tragedy in Spitalfields, the City merchants organized a distress fund. 'Thursday the widow of a Journeymen Weaver in Brick Lane, who died last week, and left her with five young children, and big with another hanged herself.'[66] The King gave £1,000 for distribution to needy families and a group of gentlemen organized daily breakfasts for over 800 women and children.[67] Spring brought no improvement, and agitators were feared to be inciting fresh violence. 'A person genteely dressed, who stiled himself a Peer, has gone for several days among the Weavers, advising them to go in a body to the King.'[68] Another well-dressed person promised employment in cutting a new canal at St Albans; scores of hungry weavers tramped to the site, to find they had been hoaxed and there were no jobs.[69] In April handbills announced a march from Moorfields to petition the King, but when Fielding and Lord Mayor Townsend went to the meeting-place they 'did not stay five minutes, as there was no occasion for their presence'.[70] Instead the City Marshal visited Spitalfields and persuaded the weavers to accept a plan for statutory wage regulation.[71]

The Bill enabling magistrates to regulate the wages and piece-prices of silk weavers in Spitalfields and within five miles of London was passed by Parliament with little opposition, receiving the Royal Assent on 1 July. A week later, John Fielding triumphantly reported its immediate enforcement by Middlesex Sessions.

The Wages were then settled by a numerous and unanimous Bench to the entire satisfaction of those Masters and Journeymen Weavers who appeared there on behalf of their respective bodies, and I sincerely hope that this step will prove a radical cure for all tumultuous Assemblies from that Quarter, so disrespectful to the King and so disagreeable to Government.[72]

The Spitalfields Act created a joint board or 'Union' of masters and journeymen to propose wages for enforcement by the Sessions, and it functioned successfully until 1824, when with other 'Combination Laws' the Act was repealed.[73]

Conciliation in industrial disputes was now a major part of a magistrate's duties. In 1769, a society of horsehair weavers tried to enforce a collective agreement by petition to Bow Street. The agreement, dating from 1765, provided for piece-prices ranging from 1s to 1s 6d per yard, which some masters had unilaterally reduced to 10d and 1s 1d. The journeymen invoked a forfeiture clause of £200 for each employer in breach of agreement, but the magistrates concluded that this could not be enforced at law. However, they agreed to write to the committee of manufacturers, then meeting at the King's Arms, asking them to 'kindly interpose in procuring these poor men such redress as they are entitled to'.[74] A master pipe-maker was brought before the Lord Mayor for refusing to pay his workmen a wage increase agreed by all other masters twelve months earlier. 'He was asked by my Lord, whether he had not advanced the price of pipes to the Publicans? He answered in the affirmative, on which he was severely reprimanded.'[75]

At Newcastle-upon-Tyne, where the Greenland Company took a firmer stand than the East India merchants, two strikers were sent to the house of correction for a month's hard labour, and William Guttery, the seamen's leader, was fined and sentenced to six months.[76] Even here, during one of the many strikes of keelmen,

> Mr. Alderman Mosley exerted himself in a very singular manner, by going down the river himself in different keels, time and after time, till he got them all to work, none of them attempting to insult him, though the standers-out would not suffer the keels to pass with such of their hands as were willing to work, till Mr. Mosley went down with them.[77]

In 1772, merchant seamen in the Thames again struck, owing 'to the captains of the Indiamen shipping foreigners, which the honest Johns took in the light of discouraging the trade of the kingdom, and therefore assembled at the India House, to expostulate *viva voce* with the Directors'.[78] John Sherwood and Burford Camper met the seamen on Tower Hill, reported their complaints to the Company, and received a written assurance that Britons would always receive preference. The issue persisted and a year later Sherwood had to dissuade the men from marching to St. James's to see the King.[79] Only twelve of the East Indiamen sailed, because, it was said, the overstocked warehouses held enough tea for seven years.[80]

With the help of the magistrates, master sugar-bakers and their men 'amicably adjusted' their differences at the Halfway House, Stepney Road,[81] but in the building trades, Sherwood ran into serious difficulties. In December 1775, the journeymen masons, having obtained a reading of their Company's charter, petitioned the Commons that their wages had last been adjusted 70 years earlier and that now there was no law empowering the magistrates to settle their wages. 'They therefore hope for the Interposition of the House in an augmentation of their Wages to 18s. per week, or such other Sum as the House shall think proper.'[82] The House declined to set up a committee, whereupon 200 masons struck, followed in June by more than 3,000 carpenters on building sites throughout London. The magistrates rescued a journeymen sawyer from a parade through Wapping (he was tied to a donkey, face to its tail, with a saw tied to his back and placarded 'WORKING BELOW PRICE'[83]) and, after other complaints of intimidation, Sherwood, Blackmore and Curtis went to Stepney Fields, where a large crowd had gathered.

The men drew up in a ring, and received the justices with great respect, acquainting them with their supposed grievances . . . On this Mr. Sherwood told them that if they would leave their case at his office, with any other plan for the redress of their grievances, he, with the other gentlemen, would do all that lay in their power to forward it; though he feared nothing less than a bill in parliament to regulate their wages would do, as in the case of the weavers.[84]

In the meantime, they should hold no more mass meetings, 'as they intended, notwithstanding their specific intentions, to many mischiefs through inconsiderate drinking, and insisted on their immediate dispersing; which they instantly complied with without the least indecent or irregular behaviour'.[85] When the strike continued throughout the summer, however, the magistrates declined to renew the licences of several publicans, and in October the press-gang visited the houses of call, taking away 150 carpenters.[86] Others left London for the provinces of Ireland, but there was a gradual return to work. In May 1777, 'a large body of journeymen carpenters assembled on Hampstead Heath and entered into a fresh combination against their masters'.[87]

During the building strike, a proposal was canvassed for 'the price of labour being proportioned to the necessities of life'. Under this 'practicable and eligible plan', a number of joint wages boards would be established for the whole of London. Previous attempts had failed for 'want of order and unanimity. . . . A sanction was wanting to oblige those who refused to agree to the advancement, and to prevent those who had agreed from revolting; a partial operation was the consequence; and though the good dispositions of some of the masters seemed to promise success, the ungenerous non-acquiescence of the others frustrated the design.'[88] The plan would do justice to the journeymen while protecting the interests of the masters, for 'there are many masters in some trades willing to advance the wages of the workmen, but as things now stand, cannot do it but at the hazard of their own welfare'. Under a procedural agreement ('a system of Articles') for each trade, the journeymen in every workshop would elect their 'deputy'. In turn, a parish meeting of deputies would choose from their number an 'agent'. Finally, the agents from the parishes would nominate the journeymen's side on a 'Special' or 'Grand' committee for the trade, negotiating with representative masters and independent members. 'The committee may consist of any number, provided there be an equality of masters and journeymen, with two Gentlemen, not of the calling or business.'[89]

This blueprint for a formal system of industrial relations was not then adopted, but the magistrates took a new initiative. On 28 October 1777, the Middlesex Sessions held a long and serious inquest into its own powers under various statutes, the occasion being a petition from the journeymen saddlers. The problem was whether, under the Acts of 5 Eliz. and 1 James I, the justices might settle the wages not only of labourers, but also of artificers and craftsmen. After argument by counsel and debate on the Bench, the justices voted 13 to 5 that they did indeed have 'an absolute jurisdiction', a decision of utmost consequence to society, going to the root of 'the tumultuous meetings of journeymen carpenters, smiths, farriers, cabinet-makers, shoemakers, &c'.

> For if the Masters and Journeymen would, amongst themselves, settle proper and reasonable wages, and leave that settlement to the judgment of the Court, to be established or altered as they in their wisdom should think proper, journeymen of all kinds must be inexcusable, and would be highly punishable if they take any steps to distress the trade to which they have been brought up, as they have so friendly a Court to apply to.[90]

By offering to enforce negotiated agreements throughout a trade, the magistrates sought to encourage and guide the growth of responsible organization on both sides, but they were on treacherous ground.

Already suspected of power seeking, they were subject to extravagant attacks. Three weeks before the Gordon riots, Edmund Burke described the Middlesex bench as 'a set of people of the lowest class, whom no Gentleman would sit down with in company or invite to his table; some were bankrupts, other carpenters and bricklayers, and these low people were not only to be entrusted with the care of our lives and fortunes, but to have the discretionary power to command the military'.[91] In practice, the justices rarely exceeded their powers, and if to the end of the century they cajoled and bullied masters and journeymen into compromise, they preferred to do so under clear statutory authority. In 1795 the members of Common Council sought the revival of the Coalheavers' Act, recording their thanks to the late Lord Mayor, Thomas Skinner,

> for his meritorious exertions to compose and adjust disputes between several Bodies of labouring Persons and their Employers, especially the Coal-porters, who, under his well-timed and prudent interference, were both industrious and content, which reflects lasting honour on his name, and constant lustre on his character.[92]

In a year notable for high prices in London and corn riots in the countryside, their gratitude was sincere, but the system was now under strain. 'After 1795, and still more after 1799, the additional cost of provisions became such as to oblige the labourer and mechanic, in self-defence, to stipulate a higher money payment for his services.'[93] In the context of war, manpower shortages, credit expansion and high government expenditure, the relations between wages and prices, labour and capital, became central issues in the new political economy.

7 THE STATE AS EMPLOYER

Before the rise of the factory system, the most important employer of labour was the government, and the largest units of industrial organization were the naval dockyards. There were considerable fluctuations both in the establishment and in the numbers employed; in peacetime, the four Kent yards had about 2,000 workmen on their books, of whom half were shipwrights, but this number was sometimes doubled in wartime or times of crisis. Similarly, the south coast yards at Plymouth and Portsmouth employed between one and two thousand shipwrights, sawyers, joiners, riggers and caulkers.

Table 7.1: Numbers Employed in Naval Dockyards, Thames and Medway

	1712	1754	1761	1783
Sheerness	162	276	455	450
Chatham	797	1,188	1,720	750
Deptford	647	801	1,074	550
Woolwich	511	698	1,080	600
Total	2,117	2,963	4,329	2,350

Sources: 1712, 1754, 1761: *Victoria County History, Kent*, vol. 2, pp. 367, 374. 1783 (establishment): *Lloyds Evening Post*, vol. 1, p. 478.

Visitors to naval and military establishments were usually impressed by their size and seeming efficiency. Defoe described Chatham arsenal as 'like a well-ordered city; and tho' you see the whole place as it were in the utmost hurry, yet you see no confusion, every man knows his own business'.[1] Members of Parliament were more critical, and debates on the Navy Debt focused on the use of manpower. In 1722, a group of Members tabled a motion regretting 'that in the Year 1720, 2,201 Men were Employed in the Yards more than in the Year 1714 and 2,627 Men more than in the Year 1698, and that the Wages of these Men have of late been greatly Encreas'd, both which for ought appear'd to us, are an Unaccountable Encrease of that Charge to the Publick'.[2] Sixty years later, Mr Minchin, MP, compared these yards unfavourably with private enterprise.

93

The manner in which the men were employed in the yards was absolutely scandalous; they were bound to work till twelve, and yet they always left off at half after eleven; and though the bell rang for them to begin again at one, he himself had often observed, that not a stroke of work ever was begun before three o'clock. At Deptford their negligence was scandalous; they never had more than one ship of the line and two frigates in dock; and yet in the private yards on the Thames there were actually eleven men of war now building; so that there was infinitely more work done in the private than in the royal yards.[3]

In their management styles, the dockyard superintendents ranged from indulgency to bureaucracy, appearing ill equipped to control large numbers of civilians. In 1721, 'complaint having been made that several of the workmen . . . very often leave their Business after they have answered to their Names, to the great Detriment of the Service', the officers were instructed to hold roll-calls at random, 'and to take Notice of those that shall be absent; who are to forfeit, for the first Default, one Day's Pay; for the second, Two; and on the third Default to have their Names laid before the Board'.[4] At other times, appeals were made to better nature.

Yesterday morning the artificers and workmen of the yard were mustered, when every person passed through the Commissioner's office as they were called over. Sir Charles Middleton in a very friendly manner admonished those who had been guilty of losing their time by neglect of duty, and recommended that they would in future act assiduously as the only way of meeting with encouragement.[5]

When employment was unstable and payment of wages inefficient and capricious, morale was inevitably poor. War brought feverish activity, high wages and overtime; peace meant immediate redundancy for all but the most skilled. In 1701 the shipwrights were 'working day and night to get the Fleet ready. There were near 700 men working in the Dock and Yard at Woolwich on Sunday last besides those at the several Yards at Chatham &c.'[6] At such times, the men were called on to work 'double tides', and could earn extra wages. By contrast, at Portsmouth in November 1727,

an order came to discharge several sorts of Artificers and Labourers

out of his Majesty's Yard here, which has put the whole in much
Disorder and Surprize, it happening so very unexpectedly; the
Number in all to be discharged is about 200, among whom, no
doubt, there are many having large families, who must greatly suffer,
having no Prospect at this dead Time in the Year where to earn
their Bread.[7]

Similarly, in 1774, 'upwards of 100 Artificers of his Majesty's Dockyard' at Plymouth 'were discharged on Thursday last; among whome
were eleven House Carpenters, several Joiners, Bricklayers and
Labourers, but only two Shipwrights'.[8] Four years later, 'the shipwrights and other artificers of this dockyard, are ordered to continue
working two tides a day extra, to give the greater dispatch to the ships
fitting out here for sea. Near 1,600 artificers and workmen are now
employed every day in this dockyard.'[9] The aristocracy of the yards,
the shipwrights, enjoyed virtually lifetime employment, but they saw
the influx of temporary workers, such as house carpenters, as a threat
to their status. One solution, advocated by a pamphleteer in 1762,
was to store ships' frames in magazines, keeping the carpenters con-
tinuously employed in peacetime and reducing the demand for additional labour in wartime.
Two other sources of indiscipline were identified.

The porter is allowed the privilege of keeping an open beer-house in
the middle of the yard, which serves as a lounging place for sots
and idle workmen. The worst workmen are noted for haunting it,
and on the other hand, it is the distinguishing character of the best
artists, that they almost never enter it.
The chips that fall from the axe are the perquisite of the Carpenters,
but this pretended privilege is shamefully abused by many workmen,
who make up their bundle of chips by cutting useful wood to pieces,
by which it may be easily demonstrated, that, in time of war, the
government loses more than 100,000 *l.* annually.[10]

The perquisite of 'chips' originated in the seventeenth century; in
Tudor times a 'chip-gatherer' was employed to collect waste wood and
sell the proceeds for the benefit of the Crown but, by 1634, the shipwrights and other workmen did so themselves, 'carrying chips out of
the yards three times a day . . . cutting up large timber to make chips
. . . and building huts for themselves in which to store their plunder'.[11]
In the reign of Charles I, a shipwright was apprehended loading into

a barge, 9,000 treenails up to two feet in length; he pleaded lawful privilege.[12] The Cromwell administration tried to buy out the custom, and appointed a committee of merchants to investigate. They recommended a wage increase of one penny a day to offset the cost of provisions, and a further twopence to the carpenters and caulkers, 'being able and deserving men', in return for giving up 'all Chips and former Perquisites whatsoever', but the men accepted the money and retained the practice.[13] This may have contributed to the financial problems of the Protectorate: in March 1657, the dockyard workmen were paid their wages to the preceding Christmas, their last punctual payment until the Restoration.[14] In 1675, when 256,000 treenails were reported missing from Woolwich, the Navy Board organized its own collection of chips, but soon abandoned the experiment as 'of great charge and little profit'. As well as costing up to ten shillings a day, the central collection point added to the existing fire hazards. In 1679, men found smoking were fined six days' pay, which could not be enforced as their wages were in arrears.[15] There was a dispute in 1702, when the Deptford and Woolwich men claimed the right to take out chips three times a day, and another in 1705 over both chips and mealtimes, the workmen downing tools and marching to the Admiralty.[16]

Without their chips, and 'greatly prejudiced by running scores with merciless chandlers and mealmen', the men would at times have been unable to make a living. In 1657, the Woolwich ropemakers petitioned that their wages were six months in arrears and later complained that this had risen to nine months.[17] In 1694 and 1696, the wages were said to be twelve months in arrears, and in 1710 the shipwrights and ropemakers refused to be paid in Exchequer bills.[18] When the wages began to be paid, there were still occasions for conflict.

> Up betimes and to my office; and at 9 o'clock (none of the rest going) I went alone to Deptford and there went on where they left last night to pay Woolwich Yard; and so at noon dined well ... After dinner to pay again and so till 9 at night — my great trouble being that I was forced to begin an ill practice of bringing down the wages of servants, for which people did curse me, which I do not love.[19]

In this manner, Pepys saved £100 on the previous quarter's pay, but, despite attempts at administrative reform, Albemarle complained that, on visiting Chatham in 1667, a roll-call produced less than a dozen of the 800 men shown on the books.[20] Seventeenth-century records constantly depict absenteeism, indiscipline and industrial conflict, ropemakers demanding parity with their London brethren, caulkers striking for the wages paid in merchant yards and the Deptford men for five days' holiday.[21] There was a five-day strike of ropemakers in October 1665, and after the Glorious Revolution they refused to take additional apprentices. Although eight ropemakers were impressed aboard ships at the Nore, their 400 comrades successfully struck for their return.[22] At Chatham in 1672, some shipwrights were put in the stocks for smoking amid shavings and chips in the cockpit of a man-of-war, but a whipping-post erected for future use was pulled down and thrown in the Medway.[23] The men made countercharges of maladministration: in 1717, the officer in charge of Woolwich ropeyard was accused of demanding 3s 6d from each man he engaged.[24]

In the eighteenth century, the chips and the payment system were the principal issues in dispute. In August 1729, a large number of ropemakers went to the Admiralty with a petition for arrears of wages to be paid; they had earlier been on strike over the employment of apprentices.[25] Ten years later, there were strikes over chips at Chatham and Portsmouth, which were quickly settled by negotiation.[26] When, at Woolwich, the newly appointed master joiner decided to abolish the chips without compensating wage increases, the carpenters and joiners stopped work, occupied the yard, and placed pickets, armed with axes, at the gates.[27] They dispersed on the arrival of a battalion of the First Regiment of Guards and a troop of the Earl of Pembroke's Regiment of Horse but, when the bell rang at six o'clock next morning, none of the workmen appeared. 'A man with a bell was sent about the Town to summon them, but to no purpose.'[28]

Deptford yard was also silent, but reopened next day when the differences were 'with Lenitives happily compos'd'.[29] The men were in a strong bargaining position, war with Spain having been declared on 23 October, and on 9 November, when some of the Navy Commissioners sailed to Woolwich in the Navy Barge, the differences 'proved of a knottier kind than was first imagined'.[30] By 14 November, matters were reported to be adjusted, and the artificers returned to work, but their leaders wisely absconded and a £20 reward was offered for their arrest.[31]

There were more strikes over chips in 1755 and 1757, the immediate cause being a regulation fixing the maximum as the amount that could be carried untied under one arm.[32] In June 1955, the Chatham men struck throughout June, and their leaders were sent to sea.[33] In April 1757, the Woolwich men complained of unjust dismissals, unpaid

overtime and lack of medical provisions, the yard management counter-
charging them with abusing their privileges. 'Under the denomination of
chips they take away large solid pieces of real use and value: loading themselves therewith three or four times a day, and secrete among them large
nails and pieces of iron, part of the King's Stores.'[34] The Navy Board
called a meeting of the workmen, but it was poorly attended, and the
blame was attributed to a combination. The presumed ringleaders were
impressed for sea service, and 400 guardsmen marched from St James's
Park to prevent any disturbance.[35] The privilege of chips was continued.

Shortly afterwards, a society of shipwrights came into existence,
not as a trade union, but as a retail co-operative society. It opened
a bakery at Chatham, a cornmill at Woolwich and a butcher's shop
in Church Street, Deptford.[36] The shops offered cheap provisions to
the local poor, undercutting the bakers by a penny per quartern loaf,
and in Deptford greatly reducing the cost of meat. The Chatham and
Kent bakers prosecuted the shipwrights, both for baking without having
served an apprenticeship to the trade and for selling bread below the
lawful price, but lost at Maidstone Assizes in July 1758 and at Quarter
Sessions the following April. The verdicts were followed by 'great
rejoicing' among shipwrights and townspeople and the Red Flag was
hoisted at Woolwich, but the following March, on a Sunday night, the
mill mysteriously burned down.[37]

The growing independence and confidence of the dockyard workers
was depicted in a dialogue purportedly between 'a Kentish freeholder'
and his officers during a parliamentary by-election.

> *Officer*: We are come, expecting your vote for Sir William, in the
> room of Mr. W----, made a Lord . . . The Government espouses Sir
> William, and you are a Freeholder.
>
> *Artificer*: I am so, but must think myself at liberty to vote as I
> please.
>
> *Officer*: As you please! Very fancy, truly; don't the Government
> employ and pay you?
>
> *Artificer*: Yes, and I honour the Government, know my business,
> and earn my pay with diligence and honesty.
>
> *Officer*: But are you not under their power, and obliged to do
> as they please?
>
> *Artificer*: Yes, as an Artificer, but not as a Freeholder . . . I am,
> as an Englishman, at liberty to chuse my representative.
>
> *Officer*: And the government to turn you out of your bread.
>
> *Artificer*: Not so, indeed. I do my duty as they expect, and this is

a case where they can have no just reason for resentment . . .

Officer: We did not expect this obstinacy; and to prevent its spreading, we will report it, so you have warning.

Artificer: I will be as early as I can in reporting it myself, and am glad, Gentlemen, this is all the ill report you can make of me.[38]

The artificers' self-confidence was strengthened by new-found job security; they knew that the government needed their skills and was alarmed by the activities of recruiting agents from Spain, France and the American colonies. In 1718, 1750 and 1765 legislation was passed to prevent free emigration of skilled artisans and trained operatives. Under the Act of 22 Geo.II, c.60, enticement of artificers was a crime punishable by a fine of £500 and twelve months' imprisonment per worker enticed; for the second or subsequent offence, the fine was £1,200.[39] Small groups of English shipwrights were employed in Spanish naval yards, as were Russians, Frenchmen and Danes in Holland, but their numbers were probably exaggerated. However, stories of high wages earned abroad stimulated greater expectations among the dockyard workers, and reports of the efficiency of continental yards obliged the Navy Board to examine its manpower policy. Greater security of employment was proposed and a pension of £20 a year would be paid to men who had served loyally for 30 years. Although benefiting only one man in fifty, the plan was well received when made known in October 1764.[40]

In March 1765, being reduced by loss of overtime to their basic wage of 12s 6d per week (a reduction of 7s 6d), men at the Thames and Medway yards petitioned for relief. They were promised more regular payment, as well as 7½d per day overtime in the summer months.[41] A report circulated that the perquisite of chips had been abolished, and that the men would receive a wage increase in lieu, but the news was premature.[42] In 1767, the idea was revived of recovering the cost of the wage increase from savings elsewhere. Once again, instead of cutting up waste wood for sale to the local 'chip-women', the workmen would take it to a central collection point for sale by public auction, and this would yield to the Navy Board £100,000 a year, twice the cost of the wage increase. There would consequently be fewer losses from embezzlement of iron and copper, and tighter security altogether, for the Navy Board disliked the presence of the chip-women in the yards, suspecting them of stealing more valuable materials.[43]

There followed a series of events, interpreted differently by the

Admiralty and the shipwrights, which culminated in a six-week strike at all the naval yards in the summer of 1775. According to Sir Hugh Palliser's *ex-post* explanation,

> this combination had been created by the wicked artifices of one Lee, a well-known agent of Congress, who had succeeded in his traitorous purposes, and by giving the workmen money, and supporting them while they absented themselves from the King's yard, got them over so entirely to his interest that [the] Government was under the necessity of abandoning their plan.[44]

However, the dispute originated well before 1773, the year when Alderman William Lee, a staunch supporter of the American colonists, first became privy to a movement among disaffected Woolwich shipwrights to induce them to emigrate.[45] It was in June 1770, with overtime again curtailed and the cost of living rising, that the shipwrights at Plymouth wrote to the other yards to organize another petition. Each yard appointed two delegates, who met in London as a committee on 16 July, and visited the Comptroller of the Navy, Mr Cockburn. He was sympathetic, warning them not to petition the King, but to address their request to the Admiralty and Navy Boards. They therefore petitioned the Boards on 20 July, but consideration was interrupted by the sudden death of Mr Cockburn and a serious fire at Portsmouth yard.[46]

The case for a wage increase was based on the cost of living ('the increase in the price of all necessities of life'), higher productivity ('the great improvements made in the business ... their genius in making such useful improvements') and relativities ('the advanced wages given to the meanest workmen in private yards'). William Shrubsole, an advocate for the Chatham men, published a pamphlet in support of their case.

> That the price of provisions have [sic] greatly increased within this twenty years, no person in his senses will deny; and increased, as most housekeepers find, in a most alarming manner. For it is truly alarming to a Man whose weekly pay does not exceed twelve shillings and sixpence, to find that this poor pittance has lost one third of its value in a few years ... It is true the Shipwrights wages were fixed by Parliament, and it is true that when they settled (above a century ago), they were a comfortable maintenance for a family; and even within our memories it was far from contemptible. But now it is

greatly diminished in value, and not worth half of what it was originally . . .

The great improvements made in their Business, with respect to Theory, Practice and Conversion, has advanced in gain to this Nation equal at least to the loss the Shipwrights have suffered in the diminished value of their pay; so that there is a balance in favour of government against those worthy servants, equal to their full pay; for had the price of provisions remained the same as when their wages were settled, the Shipwrights are justly entitled to an advance in their wages, as a premium for their Genius in making such useful improvements . . . the excellent Artist of the present Day, chuses his timber with a certain oeconomy, and saws and prepares it with the utmost precision, which is a prodigious saving to the government, both in the immediate price of timber and also in its conversion by the sawyers . . .

The common pay for a bare Day's work in private yards, has been 3s. 6d for many years, besides the allowance of their chips; which pay is above two thirds more than the Shipwrights receive in his Majesty's Dock-yards, and stay six or nine Months before they are paid, which greatly reduces their little wages . . . But this is comparing things with the least advantage to my clients, for altho the common Day pay in private yards is but 3s. 6d. yet the workmen in those yards generally work task or piece work, when they often double their Day pay, and hurt not themselves with their labour: whereas the dockyard Shipwright has no possible means to enhance his pay, if he is ever so willing . . .[47]

The new Comptroller, Sir Hugh Palliser, resisted the argument point by point.

Other Artificers in the dock-yards have the same right and necessity . . . the Army and Navy in general would also demand some advance of pay . . .

If there is such an advance of pay in private yards, and the Shipwrights are so much better off there, how comes it that so many make interest to get into the King's yard? . . .

. . . although the pay of the Shipwrights originally might be sufficient to bring up a family very comfortably, yet the present workmen are better off than the former, for it was useful to enter Workmen on an Emergency only, and discharge them when done with, and on some occasions they were obliged to impress Men for the yards and dismiss them again when their work was done. But now as the Shipwrights are in constant pay, they ought to rest well satisfied . . .

Appointments at present are very many and great, taxes are very heavy, it is a time of peace, means therefore should be contrived to pay off our national debt, and not to increase it.[48]

To circumvent these objections, Shrubsole himself, 'having seen original letters from the deputies of the committees of each Dock-yard on this very article', revived the question of the chips.

The sum of their requisitions is, that the government would be pleased to allow them 2s.6d. a day as a bare day's pay, and let them work extra as they do now in the summer season, to keep the Navy in repair; and they on their part will cheerfully give up the chips.

These are the conditions for which the deputies negotiated with the late comptroller, and which he was well pleased with, and said might be granted to them; and this, in short, instead of being an expence to government, will be a saving.[49]

The Admiralty responded positively to this reminder, but in 1771, when draft regulations had been prepared, serious industrial and political difficulties appeared. In August, it was reported that 'the workmen of his Majesty's yards are, in general dissatisfied with giving up their privilege of chips, in having their wages augmented from 2s.1d. to 2s.6d. per day, as a great many of them, it seems, make more of the wood they bring out, than what is equal to five pence a day'.[50] At the same time, Lords North and Sandwich informed King George III of their strong opposition to any wage increase, and a special meeting of the Privy Council was held.[51] In December, Lord Sandwich submitted to the Navy Board his own proposals 'for making considerable alterations in the manner of conducting business in His Majesty's dockyard'.[52]

For several months, nothing further was heard of these; then in August 1772, a new pension scheme was proposed.

By a late order, every shipwright bred in the King's yards, if disabled from working in any accident in his business, is to be allowed 20 *l.* a year. After 30 years labour, if feeble and of good character, the same. The joiners the same. The sail-makers and house-carpenters to have 17 *l.* The blacksmiths 11 *l.* and the labourers 11 *l.* a year;

all upon terms of good behaviour.[53]

A letter to the press from a Portsmouth shipwright gave the same details, and praised 'the goodness and sound judgment of the present First Lord of the Admiralty, who will ever be revered by the Artificers of the Royal Yards in general, for his goodness of heart, in causing the following regulations to be made'.[54] A month later, however, the 'order' was revoked.[55] There had been a bad harvest, food prices were rising steeply, and the government faced renewed demands for a wage increase. On 30 January 1773, there was an exchange in the Commons.

> *Gov. Pownall:* I just beg leave to ask one question, and that is, Whether the 48,000 [pounds] for repairs of the Dock-yards, is in contemplation for an increase to the wages of the Shipwrights, who are going to petition the House for that purpose?
> *Mr Buller*: Most certainly not, as their pay must be advanced by Parliament, and they are preparing a Petition.[56]

Meanwhile, the Admiralty had agreed to supply the dockyard workmen with provisions from store during 'the present scarcity'.[57] The petition was presented to the Commons on 3 March by Mr Mackworth, whereupon

> Lord North arose, and acquainted the House that he had no objection to the Petition being brought up, but that he had acquainted the Honourable Mover, as well as every other person who had applied to him for the same purpose, that he meant to give it the most strenuous opposition.[58]

The petition bore a remarkable similarity to the government's original plan, 'proposing to give up the perquisite of chips in lieu of a very trifling increase of wages'.[59] On 17 May, Mackworth and Whitworth moved unsuccessfully for a committee of enquiry but, for the government, Mr Buller stood firm, retorting that 'every argument operated more for a decrease rather than encrease of wages'.[60] Lord Sandwich was preparing another solution: task-work. His scheme, 'truly noble, profitable and salutary' to all parties, would yield a fully costed wage increase of fivepence a day to the shipwrights and threepence to the labourers or servants. Further economies would be made by withdrawing the underemployed labourers of the ships' carpenters, and redeploying them as servants to the shipwrights. Sandwich prepared the ground by holding a general inspection and shedding some surplus labour. 'Yesterday several Commissioners of the Navy came down here from London; they mustered up the people of the Dock-yard, and discharged upwards of 40, on account of their being absent.'[61]

The task-work system, borrowed from the merchant yards, became widely known by the end of December and final instructions were given at an Admiralty Board meeting on 17 January 1775. On 13 March, Sir Hugh Palliser went to Chatham with Sir John Williams, surveyor, and George Marsh, clerk of navy accounts, and gave instructions for 400 shipwrights to work by task and for those unable to do so to continue day-work. Next day he went on to Sheerness to make similar arrangements.[62]

Apologists for the Navy Board subsequently insisted that all the task-workers had volunteered, and that after a few weeks earnings had risen from 2s 1d per day to between 3s 8d and 4s 5d. According to 'a Friend to the Navy', task-work was abandoned at Chatham, Portsmouth, Plymouth and Woolwich as soon as objections were made; it was continued at Deptford, at the request of the shipwrights themselves, and at Sheerness, by agreement, until work in progress was completed.[63] The *Annual Register* also defended the government:

> having petitioned their superiors for redress, it was thought proper to pay them for the future, according to their earnings, as practiced in the merchants yards, just withholding the chips ... But this regulation putting it, so at least their advocates asserted, in the power of any petty officer to deprive them of the hard-earned reward of their labour ... numbers of them quitted the yards ... at a time the government stood most in need of their labour.[64]

The strikers' version was given in a handbill 'to the Gentlemen, Tradesmen, and Inhabitants of Gosport, Portsmouth and Portsmouth Common'.

> By order from the Hon. the Commissioners and principal Officers of his Majesty's Navy, directing the Shipwrights of his Majesty's Dockyard to perform a mode of work called Task; and conscious of themselves on the fullest conviction, it must occasion progressive suicide on our bodies, the destruction of our families, and the inhabitants in general. Another order is already enforced at Plymouth, whereby if any person from sickness or being wounded,

should be obliged to continue one month at home, be discharged. These with a daily increase of grievances, have united the Yards to apply for redress, but have received no satisfactory answer. We have, therefore, agreed not to enter the Yard till redressed. And it is humbly hoped the worthy inhabitants will assist in supporting us and the families till relief is obtained; when it is hoped we shall be enabled to shew our most grateful acknowledgments to each benefactor, with a return agreeable to his subscription.[65]

However, at Chatham, the payment system was not the immediate cause of the strike. According to a letter dated 17 May, 80 shipwrights building HMS *Formidable* had asked permission to work in the dinner break,

which was refused by their Officers, it being out of their power to grant them that favour. In consequence of the said denial, they assembled together in the afternoon, and forced themselves in a body out of the Yard-gate; this morning they came into the Yard, but would not work, and in the afternoon they staid away from the Yard.

In the afternoon another hundred shipwrights from the task gangs joined them, bringing the total to 180.[66]

The Navy Board was conciliatory, for the situation in America was deteriorating. Sir John Williams and George Marsh went to Chatham and persuaded the men to return, 'pretty well satisfied', on the understanding that in future they could work during dinner time, 'upon cases of necessity', but that at other times they must work the normal hours.[67] On 2 June, Sandwich and Palliser set sail from Woolwich for a special tour of the yards, having already dispatched orders to Portsmouth for six ships of the line to be fitted for immediate service. On 13 June, as the first reports of the battle of Lexington were arriving in London, Sandwich and his party disembarked at Portsmouth to inspect the Fleet. Next morning, nine gangs of shipwrights approached the commissioners to request redress of grievances and a wage increase. Told of the First Lord's sudden departure on important business in Town, the 400 men abandoned their work, and walked out of the yard. At a mass meeting, they elected a committee and resolved not to re-enter without a wage increase and abolition of task-work, on the grounds that they could not 'make above bare time, owing to a great deal of the timber being bad'.[68]

Meanwhile, Palliser continued to Plymouth to prepare for the official inspection. He found that on Monday evening, 19 June,

> all the Shipwrights on task-work belonging to this yard, declared to their Officers, in a very mild and peaceable manner, that they were determined not to strike a stroke more upon that plan, as it was impossible for them to subsist their families without their being paid for their labour. A number of them had been working many days, and had all their work condemned, owing to some defects in the timber.[69]

Like the Portsmouth men, 390 shipwrights had laid down their tools, held meetings in the fields and elected a committee. The rest of the shipwrights and caulkers were about to join them, and delegates had been dispatched to Portsmouth and Chatham. However, the Portsmouth men returned to work on 20 and 21 June, following the immediate discharge of their leaders 'never to enter a King's Yard again'.[70]

Lord Sandwich's vessel anchored off Plymouth on 27 June, and his first task was to dispatch a letter to the King.

PLYMOUTH, June 27, 1775

> Lord Sandwich has the honour to transmit to your Majesty the account of the proceedings in the Visitation at Portsmouth. Lord Sandwich is at this moment arrived in Plymouth Sound & has not yet been on shore, but he has seen the Commissioner Ourry who informs him that the men are in the same mutinous state as they were at Portsmouth; but as they had not heard that the others had returned to their duty, it is to be hoped they will soon be convinced of their error.[71]

Sandwich could not know that at this moment the Portsmouth shipwrights were again on strike. In the night of 26-27 June, the captains of all men-of-war there received orders from London to sail immediately for Spithead, there to be joined by HMS *Roebuck* and other capital ships from Chatham and Plymouth. In the morning, between 300 and 400 shipwrights stopped work, demanding that their wages be raised to 2s 6d per day.[72]

The committee of delegates met at Chatham, and prepared a petition to the King in the name of 'the United Shipwrights of his Majesty's several Dock-yards'. They drew his attention to the increased prices of necessities, and the erosion of their real wages. 'Your Majesty cannot, we humbly, conceive, be uninformed, that at the Time our Wages of two shillings and one penny per Day were established, the same was more adequate to our Subsistence than five Shillings per Day at present.' Ironically, their representations to the Admiralty and Navy Board had brought 'palliatives' that made their situation even worse. 'The Burthen of a Mode of Labour, called Task-work, lately imposed on us by the said Boards, though we hope without any design to injure us, has been found a Yoke on our Necks too heavy to be borne.' Unable to support their families on the present daily wage, they implored his Majesty to grant them 'the very modest Wages of two Shillings and Sixpence per Day'. Otherwise, 'though with inexpressible Regret', they would have to apply themselves to some other employment.[73]

After submitting the petition on 12 July, the delegates visited the Thames yards, hoping to spread the strike. They succeeded at Woolwich, but met opposition at Deptford. After a contentious meeting on 17 July, continuing until late at night, the Deptford men voted to remain at work, but rumours reached London that they were rioting and had set fire to timber and ships on the stocks. At daybreak, horse- and foot-guards arrived from Whitehall, and encamped on Blackheath. Troops were also sent to Woolwich, where to the great indignation of the inhabitants, they were billeted in the public houses.[74]

The same day, the Navy Board advertised for strike-breakers.

Navy Office, July 18, 1775

Whereas a considerable Number of Shipwrights of some of his Majesty's Yards have entered into a illegal Combination to distress the Public Service, by refusing to go on with the Works they had in Hand, unless they have an Encrease of Wages; this is to give Notice, that such able Shipwrights who do not exceed 35 years of Age, and produce their Indentures, will be received and entered at this Office ... and they will be allowed Conduct-Money, with the Carriage of their Chests of Tools, to either of the said yards.[75]

They were also assured of 'every kind of Protection and Encouragement'. Two days later, more than a hundred fresh hands went to work at Woolwich yard. 'They are all numbered, and have copper tickets, without which they cannot be admitted, as Centinels are placed at the Dock-gate.'[76] A King's cutter sailed from the Tower to Portsmouth with newly entered shipwrights on board; each received a naval seaman's bounty of 40s and was promised protection. At Plymouth a reward of £30 was offered for the discovery of those guilty of 'horsing on poles' workmen who remained in the yard and, after a clash at Woolwich, eight strikers were arrested and taken to the Admiralty for questioning by the law officers.[77]

The strike committee returned to Chatham, where at daily assemblies the men were informed of developments.

> They meet every morning, and sometimes twice a day, in Mr Louch's Cricketing Field, near this Town, at which place they transact all their business. They have appointed Mr Edward Randall, Shipwright, belonging to the Committee, to be their Chairman, he being a person of unexceptionable character, and a good orator. He reads them all the letters that come from the other yards, and gives them his opinion what is best to be done for the advantage of the community. He advises them to sobriety, and to act in a peaceable manner, as the only method of getting their grievances redressed.[78]

One suggestion, not acted upon, was to march to Deptford to persuade the workmen to reverse their decision.[79] Even at Chatham, the strike was less than complete and, as the weeks passed, unmarried men set out from all the naval yards to seek work with the merchants at London, Bristol and Liverpool.[80] Strikers were admitted to Plymouth yard to collect their tools, but at Portsmouth the commissioner limited them to two gangs at a time, and the rest went home.[81] Reports came of hunger among strikers' families at Plymouth, and of wives begging 'on their knees' for credit from unsympathetic Chatham bakers; but the strikers held out 'in hopes of government coming to terms, on account of the necessities of the service'.[82] News of the battle of Bunker's Hill reached London early in August, but the Fleet was not ready to sail; HMS *Roebuck* left Chatham, but had to put in at Sheerness to complete her fitting-out.[83] By now, the government was under pressure to treat the shipwrights' claim as a special case, 'which if granted would come to £16,250. If a single election has not often cost as much.'[84]

> The case of the discharged shipwrights deserves serious attention by people in power; all they ask is a small pittance of half a crown a day; and on their refusing to work at the present price, and showing some little resentment, bills of indictment are found against some of them. This dispute may be attended with very disagreeable consequences to this kingdom. It has been always our misfortune to neglect our navy in times of peace; and the bad encouragement given

to our artificers had put them to the cruel necessity of seeking their bread in a foreign state, when they have been denied it at home. And by our neglecting this useful set of men, France, Spain, &c. have given them the greatest encouragement; and there is not a doubt but some hundreds of them will, if this dispute is not soon terminated, leave this kingdom and enter into foreign service. If ever any maritime power (which is far from the improbable) equals us as a maritime power, then adieu to our trade, freedom, and everything dear to Englishmen.[85]

Reports of large-scale migration to French yards were exaggerated, although some men probably did go. (In 1781 there was 'an insurrection amongst the workmen in the dock-yards of Havre and St. Maloes, owing to their having some small perquisites of wood taken from them'.[86]) But Sandwich resisted all persuasion; his priority was to restore the authority of the Navy Board, and to re-engage the men only on his own terms. He was encouraged by division among the strikers; on 5 August, some of the Portsmouth men petitioned the commissioners for employment at the usual wages, and were turned away. This was to encourage the others, for on 12 August, Sandwich reported to the King: 'Twenty-one of the best men of the task-gangs are returned to their duty at Portsmouth, and we have no doubt but that as the knot is now broken the whole will shortly follow.'[87]

This time, his judgement was correct. As soon as the news reached Plymouth, morale collapsed, and petitions were sent hastily to the Navy Board applying for re-engagement. On 14 August, the strike came to an end.

Till then they used to meet regularly twice a Day, to consult on Matters, and receive the Report of their Committee, which they had chosen to correspond with the other Yards, and settle their Business in general; several of the single Men therefore this Day set out for London, Bristol, Liverpool and other Ports; those who have families remaining behind, are really in a very pitiable Situation, and I believe they are heartily sorry they ever quitted their Duty in the Yard. If the Measures of Government will admit it, I could wish they were received into Favour, as many of them seem to have a due sense of their Fault.[88]

At first, task-workers under 40 years of age were re-entered, but none of the day-workers nor the strike leaders, and for several days

400 Chatham men stood out against this condition.[89] Each day, groups of younger men were admitted to the yards, but the fate of older shipwrights was undecided until the end of September, when they were finally re-engaged. The Plymouth men were offered a last opportunity to accept task-work, which they unanimously refused.[90] Subsequently, they offered to give up the chips for an extra fivepence a day, but rejected the Navy Board's condition that 'the additional wages should be granted as an *extra* sum always to be entered separately on the pay books as in lieu of chips'.[91] At Woolwich, there was an orderly return to work, following agreement on monthly, instead of quarterly, payment of wages. On 18 August, the shipwrights 'assembled in a body, in a church yard, and being satisfied in respect to the terms which the Admiralty Board proposed, went into the Yard with drums beating and colours flying'.[92]

The strike settled, affairs of state could now proceed. On 23 August, George III signed a proclamation condemning the rebellious Americans. The sloop *Speedwell* arrived at Spithead to collect the shipwrights' wages and the *Arethusa* frigate sailed for the Downs. Great contracts were placed for wheat, peas and malt, and a huge quantity of biscuit was shipped at Deptford. Thirteen transports already lay between Woolwich and the Tower, 'loading with grape shot, howitzers, hand grenadoes, bomb-shells and other instruments of death, destined for the destruction of our brethren the Colonists'.[93] The crews demanded danger money, and the Guards were dispatched to Wapping, 'but the Tars having notice of their coming, retreated on board their ships'.[94] Notices were posted in the royal yards, warning of the penalties for emigration. On 27 August, a resident of Plymouth remarked on the new face of the town and its dockyard. Nothing, he wrote, could be a pleasanter sight than to see four or five hundred shipwrights parading through the streets, '... with their chips on their shoulders'.[95]

Appendix: House of Commons, Thursday 22 March 1781

Sir Hugh Palliser ... As soon as it was observed that France and Spain were arming, the number of our shipwrights was considerably encreased in all the dock-yards, and the next step was to procure yet a greater number; and this also was strenuously attempted, but without success, for the nation could not afford any great addition of these; therefore, as a substitute, it was resolved to increase the labour of the former complement in the yards, till one fourth more work should be done than before, by the same number of hands. This expedient would infallibly have succeeded, but for the interposition of the enemies to this country;

we know not whether they were foreign enemies or domestic; but our enemies, conscious that with a great navy we must be victorious, intervened, sowed dissentions among our workmen, and poisoned them against this new plan. Associations were then formed among them: petitions and remonstrances were sent up to the navy board; committees were appointed; and delegates and deputies were sent up to London, to treat with the navy board, in the nature of a Congress. (*A hearty laugh*.) He did assure the House, he was speaking serious truths, truths that had fallen within his own knowledge; for he had the honour to preside at the navy board at the time. As to the present state of the navy, he could not speak to it.

Mr. Burke said, he reprobated the little, insignificant, and contemptible endeavour of throwing obloquy on the associations, by this species of ridicule, and he pointed out the futility, or the criminality of the fact, if it was true as asserted. If it was true, it proved we had no government in this country, as that government was not able to maintain order and obedience even among the workmen of a dock-yard, but permitted every little combination of journeymen and apprentices to defeat the measures that were adopted for national salvation. The family compact took place in 1762, near twenty years ago, and the present administration had foreseen the evil of a war with France and Spain, but they were prevented from providing against it, by a combination of journeymen; such nonsense was at all times beneath his notice; but if Ministers dared to tell a British Parliament, that our misfortunes were all owing to a confederacy among the shipwrights, they were highly criminal. According to their idea, not America, not France and Spain, but a miserable committee of shipwrights had vanquished this country. If Ministry knew of it, why had they not applied to Parliament to enforce obedience? To acknowledge they knew of it, and yet to own that they had never applied to Parliament, was an admission of their guilt. The honourable Vice Admiral had thrown out something concerning associations, deputies, &c. He said, associations had been held, petitions presented, &c. the intent of which was to have an enquiry made into a seeming abuse in the expenditure of public money, and praying that it might not be lavished away in pensions, sinecures, &c. but appropriated for the services of the state. These petitions were disregarded, but those of men belonging to dock-yards could not be resisted, the Ministry was vanquished by them; the navy was in a state very inferior to what it ought to be; and the nation would probably feel the fatal consequences.[1]

8 THE PUBLIC INTEREST

In the second half of the eighteenth century, unemployment, poverty and rising prices became topics of everyday discussion. Demands for job creation and state intervention were as common as arguments for *laissez-faire* economic policies, and were justified on the grounds of social stability and public order.

> Find work for idle men, do any thing to employ them, go to any expence, no exertions can be too great. If ten or twenty thousand men are out of employment, yet willing and able to work, make some great roads, cut some convenient canals, erect some useful edifice, build some necessary bridges, invent some public works, establish some new manufactures, at all events set them to work. If the Statesman omits this, he deserves riots, and all their consequences.[1]

Comparisons were drawn with France, where in 1783 a general repair of roads was ordered, employing 15,000 discharged sailors and soldiers, and with Central Europe, where 2,000 soldiers and peasants were working on the great Roman road from Transylvania to Moldavia and Wallachia.[2]

The persistent rise in the cost of living affected all classes, but particularly town-dwellers.

> SIR, – I am the wife of a poor Journeyman, whose Wages are 19s. per week, which makes a great Sound, and I am well satisfied is as much as his honest Master can afford to give. We have five Children; my Husband gives me every Farthing of his Wages, every Saturday Night; he frequents no Alehouse, nor scarce goes in one from Year's End to another. I must now give an Account how I am straitened in keeping my Family, as Times now go, and for some Years have gone: We eat eight Quartern Loaves, and a Quartern of Flour, in a Week, two Pounds and a Half of Meat, at 4½d. and 5d. per Pound, comes to near 7s. more, for Small Beer 1s. 3d. Milk 8d. Coals and Candle 2s. Soap, Butter and Cheese 1s. 9d. Greens 7d. which make 19s. 4d per Week; so that what little I get myself is not sufficient to pay our unreasonable House-rent, and cloathe our Children from the Cold . . .[3]

Table 8.1: Estimated Annual Expenditure of a Journeyman's
Household (man, wife and six children), London, 1772

	£	s	d
Milk at 1d per day	1	10	5
Small beer at 1½d per day	2	5	7½
Candles at 1½d	2	5	7½
Coals at 3d	4	11	3
Tea and sugar at 6d	9	2	6
Butter and cheese at 6d	9	2	6
Bread at 1s	18	5	0
Meat for eight people at 1s	18	5	0
Soap, starch, blue etc. at 1d	1	10	5
Salt, vinegar, pepper, mustard, etc. at ½d		15	2½
Sand and small-coal at 2d per week		9	0
Vegetables of all kinds at 2d per day	3	0	10
House-rent and taxes	10	10	0
	81	13	4½

Source: *Lloyd's Evening Post*, 16-19 October 1772.

Families with higher incomes also felt themselves to be under pressure,
as is shown by the budget in Table 8.1. 'Suppose such a person having
such a family, does by great industry earn 30s weekly, there will be an
annual loss of £3 13s 4½d. But no allowance is hereby made for cloaths
or pocket money, not even the gratification of a single pot of porter
through the year is admitted. If so deplorable then be the situation
of a man who can get 30s. weekly, what must become of that family
the father of which cannot earn half the money?'[4] Here again, the
public interest required an interventionist policy. 'To keep provisions
at a moderate price is a matter deserving the most serious attention of
Government; for the dearness of provisions must enhance the price of
labour; and when labour is dear there must be a proportionate rise in
the price of manufactures; and if we cannot supply foreign markets
upon the same terms as other nations, our trade must be ruined.'[5]
Among many panaceas canvassed was a central body to review pay
relativities: 'Some proper persons should be appointed, by authority,
no way interested, but judges of the proportionable value of labour, in
the different branches of our manufactures, in order to settle their

prices.'[6] To some extent, deprivation was relative, and the more prosperous tradesmen and merchants were urged to refrain from ostentatious spending: 'be contented with villas something smaller, and keeping only one equipage each.'[7]

In London, much of the odium for high prices fell upon combinations of tradesmen and shopkeepers. Bakers, coal merchants and tallow-chandlers were particularly unpopular. In 1766, a crowd of journeymen bakers attacked a shop where bread was being sold at threepence per peck below the Assize price, and subsequently their employers were indicted for combining and conspiring to incite them.[8] In 1779, Parliament broke the monopoly of the Bakers' Company with a Bill to admit newcomers to the trade without serving a seven years' apprenticeship.[9] The following year, a Bill was proposed to enable the Court of Aldermen to fix the price of coals; on several occasions, high prices were blamed not on the coal 'vend' at Newcastle, but on an alleged combination in London.[10] The tallow-chandlers were said to combine both against the butchers, to keep their costs down, and against the public, to raise the price of candles.[11] Some competition was nevertheless possible: 'Whereas a certain set of ill-meaning Tallow-Chandlers have of late assembled themselves in Clubs and Meetings, in order to impose upon the Publick, by endeavouring to raise Candles to an exorbitant Price . . . This is to inform the Town that a considerable Number of Tallow-Chandlers of the honest and well-meaning Part of Trade are (notwithstanding the others' bad designs) resolved still to continue Candles at the present Price of 5s. 8d per dozen.'[12]

In provincial England and in Scotland, groups of workers took concerted action to enforce 'fair' prices of provisions. In 1769, the weavers of Paisley marched 'to the number of some thousands' to the Renfrewshire magistrates complaining that the stills, by consuming great quantities of grain, prevented the price from falling. On the advice of the bench, they resolved to refrain from buying or drinking whisky.[13] The corn riot was the most conspicuous expression of popular discontent in the eighteenth century, so much so that it has been postulated that whereas 'economic class-conflict in nineteenth-century England found its characteristic expression in the matter of wages, in eighteenth-century England the working people were most quickly influenced to action by rising prices'.[14] However, rising prices also led to wage claims in the eighteenth century, often justified by reference to high profits. In 1745, the London tailors published a detailed breakdown of their masters' costs, to demonstrate that a wage increase could be absorbed.[15] The saddlers did likewise in their submission to the Middlesex Sessions.[16] When there was little profit to squeeze, the journeymen changed their tactics. In 1796, a 'Humble Memorial' to the Painter-Stainers' Company proposed higher charges to the public, because 'their Masters could not increase their wages without an increase in the Prices of Painting'. The employers had sympathized with their case, but none would be first to raise prices. 'I am sensible of the Justice and necessity of increasing your Wages, but it cannot be done without advancing the Prices. I should be glad to hear a meeting of the Trade called and would attend it, but cannot think of being first to sign a requisition. The most respectable method would be for the Company to call a meeting.'[17] Wage claims were not incompatible, at least in the short run, with resistance to increases in food prices, and some occupational groups campaigned on both fronts simultaneously.[18]

The authorities responded with a variety of measures to curb prices: an Act of Charles II was invoked, giving the Lord Mayor of London power to fix the price of coals, the Royal Society of Arts planned to reduce fish prices by operating a direct carriage service from the ports, and cost-reducing innovations were encouraged.[19] All these initiatives encountered strong opposition from the interests concerned, particularly the chartered companies, but also from workmen who feared for their jobs, even when no immediate threat was apparent. In 1763, the RSA was urged to bring down the cost of timber by erecting a sawmill near London, 'by way of example' and 'employ men to saw timber by it at a reasonable price'.[20] After two or three years experience, the Society could dispose of it, 'for numbers will purchase it once established without molestation which is only to be apprehended for a few weeks at the beginning'.[21] Such a mill was built at Limehouse by Charles Dingley, and was attacked and slightly damaged by a crowd of sawyers in May 1768. On 6 May, Dingley received a letter warning him of a plan to pull down his mill, but his superintendent was unprepared for the scale of the attack.

> I met the mob of sawyers and other people pretty near the mill; I asked their demands, what they came there for; they told me the sawmill was at work when thousands of them were starving for want of bread; I then represented to them that the mill had done no kind of work that had injured them, or prevented their receiving any benefit; I desired to know which was the principal man to whom I might speak. I was showed one; I had some conversation with him,

and represented to him that it had not injured the sawyers; he said it possibly might be so, but it would hereafter if it had not, and they came with a resolution to pull it down, and it should come down.[22]

The crowd, led by a master sawyer named John Smith, cut the shafts of the sail, and destroyed the saws and frames. They also demolished a brick counting-house, but the damage seems not to have exceeded £200. In November, Smith was arrested in the Strand by a Bow Street Runner, and committed to prison.[23]

Some of the 'pre-Luddite' attacks on spinning jennies may have similarly been inspired by fear of competition, rather than by their effects on employment. In Somerset, the innovators held town meetings to persuade workpeople of the case for machinery, and a spinning jenny was installed at Shepton Mallet with the agreement of the men in return for a wage increase.

The destruction of this machine was apparently the work of outsiders from Frome and Warminster.[24] Although the journeymen's clubs petitioned against machinery, they reluctantly agreed to a trial period of two months, provided the clothier would 'work the Machines in their full capacity, by the most able workmen you can get, and to work them openly, subject to the inspection of two proper persons appointed by us, in order to give a creditable account of its utility which you have asserted, or that the dangerous consequences which we have apprehended, may evidently appear'.[25]

In years of bad harvests and high food prices, disturbances among farm workers could endanger supplies to the towns. In 1792, Justices of the Peace of counties adjoining London forestalled unrest by increasing the wages of day-labourers. On market day in Chelmsford, 20 October, the principal farmers of Essex agreed to increases of twopence per day, and were at once followed by Norfolk and the rest of East Anglia. A Cambridgeshire brewer, Mr Ives, offered to sell good wheat to his workmen at 5s per Winchester bushel, as did the farmers of Dorset and the Bishop of Durham.[26] In Sussex, however, discontent remained. 'When the use of the Winchester bushel was enforced here a few weeks ago, the Farmers appeared much displeased with the awkwardness of its shape and distinguished it by the name of the *flat* bushel. The Poor murmur at its shallow dimensions, which they say curtails them of their measure, without an adequate reduction of its price.'[27]

A club of labouring men, organized by a Mr Trigger, held meetings in the public house at Alfriston, near Lewes. They resolved not only to abolish the flat measure, and require the farmers to sell them wheat at 5s a bushel, but also to compel their masters to augment their wages.[28] When, on a Saturday night, their numbers increased from 30 to 300, the landlord, at the request of his neighbours, refused them admittance. The Court of Lieutenancy held the militia in readiness, and the inhabitants of Lewes were invited to declare their loyalty to the Crown, but, in the absence of their leader, only a handful of labourers attended the next meeting.[29] Similar clubs at Maldon, Ongar and Thaxted demanded minimum piecework earnings of 14s to 18s weekly, and at Sheering a guinea. Because of enlistment, there was a scarcity of labour, and successful bargains were possible at harvest time. At Thaxted, a strike was led by Isaac Seer, who was arrested while trying to extend it to outlying farms.[30] Labourers at Potton, Bedfordshire, were charged with riot, and James Gilbert was imprisoned for a year for inciting them to pull down the house of George Kitchen.[31] In 1795, farm workers at Monkton, near Pegwell Bay, demanded both higher wages and cheaper beans, threatening to strike against the inclusion of one-third barley-meal in their bread. After negotiations, they agreed 'to be served with wheat-meal at one shilling the gallon, as they had hitherto been accustomed to receive; to have beans for their hogs at three shillings the bushel; and an advance of their wages from one shilling and sixpence to two shillings a day'.[32]

In Norfolk, the clergy launched a movement to abolish the sale to labourers of flour below price and to introduce instead a statutory minimum wage. A meeting was held in a village church, Members of Parliament were approached and, in February 1796, Samuel Whitbread presented a Labourers' Wages Bill to the House of Commons. Under his Bill, magistrates would have been empowered to fix a minimum rate, 'that free scope might be given for strength, ingenuity and industry'. Fox supported him, but Pitt resisted. The Tailors' and Silk weavers' Acts were a bad precedent: 'they were enacted to guard the industry of the country from being checked by a general combination among labourers, and the bill now under consideration was introduced solely for the purpose of remedying the inconveniences which labourers sustain from the disproportion existing between the price of labour and the price of living'.[33] If, as Whitbread argued, labour's price should find its own level, there was no need to interfere. 'They should look to the instances where interference had shackled industry, and where the best intentions have often produced the most pernicious effects ... trade, industry and barter would always find their own level, and be impeded by regulation which violated their natural operation.'[34] The Bill was negatived.

London was vulnerable to interruptions in distribution. A strike of bargemen or lightermen could stop the supply of corn to the flour-mills or malt to the breweries. A dispute at any stage of the 'coal vend' had repercussions in the capital; during the Durham miners' strike of 1765, the price of coal reached 42s in the Pool.[35] Twenty years later, there was another serious crisis. The seamen and colliers of the Tyne struck in May, and two months later the ship owners increased the London price to 33s per chaldron. The coal merchants refused to buy and, for more than a fortnight, 200 coal ships rested at anchor in the Thames. Unemployed lightermen resolved to charter their own ships to bring the coal from Newcastle, and the Lord Mayor asked Pitt for a special Act 'to regulate the sale of coals whilst on shipping in the river'. On 29 July 1785, Court of Common Council resolved that 'whereas the Lord Mayor hath received information that contracts and combinations have been formed and entered into, to restrain and hinder the free selling, buying and unloading, navigating and disposing of coals, thereby to enhance the price', the Lord Mayor be asked 'to take immediately such measures as shall be found necessary to defeat and put an end to all such unlawful contracts and combinations'.[36]

The ship owners defended themselves as 'a body of men individually and collectively respectable, as valuable as the Corporation of London'. There was 'a combination to prevent the ship-owners from procuring the hard-earned bread which their industry demands'. Parliament remained in session into late July to pass the necessary legislation and, on 29 July, the water-bailiff ordered all ships in the river to unload without further delay, or to face prosecution for 'combinations to obstruct the sale of that necessary commodity and enhance the price thereof'.[37]

An equally necessary and politically sensitive commodity was the loaf of bread, and increases in its price had immediate repercussions. As *The Times* foresaw when, at Christmas 1800, the Lord Mayor permitted the quartern loaf to reach 1s 9d, there were also long-term effects.

The baneful effects arising from the present high price of provisions begin to be evident from the combinations which are arising in several branches of trade, as it will be a pretext for raising the price of wages, even where they have been considerably advanced within a few years; and make them permanent whenever the land is blessed with plenty, as it will be found extremely difficult afterwards to reduce them.[38]

Combinations, whether of masters or journeymen, to increase the cost of bread, were severely repressed by magistrates in all great cities. The Assize of Bread left narrow profit margins, and was a constant source of friction. When journeymen bakers pressed their masters for wage increases, the Lord Mayor could also use his discretion, under Act of Common Council, to issue temporary licences for the employment of non-freemen.[39]

Although an Act of Charles II, against profanation of the Sabbath, appeared to prohibit Sunday baking, Lord Chief Justice Mansfield had ruled otherwise.

Ist. That one Baker working on a Sunday would let fifty persons, servants and working people, go to church. 2nd. That the poor could not otherwise have a comfortable dinner on Sunday. 3rd. That as baking on Sunday could not require the attendance of so many men as on a week day, the journeymen by taking the labour in turns, would not find it so great a hardship as represented. That upon the whole baking on Sunday was a work of necessity and charity, and therefore included in the exception of the Act.[40]

In October 1793, the journeymen bakers announced that they would no longer work on Sundays, but would seek employment 'in any other business, rather than submit longer to the slavery of Sunday baking'. A few masters agreed to stop Sunday baking, and the rest were given notice of strike action from Saturday night, 2 November.[41] On Tuesday, 29 October, a deputation of six master bakers went to Downing Street, and asked Mr Pitt to intervene. Next day, leaders of the journeymen saw the Home Secretary, Henry Dundas, to ask for their case to be placed before the King in Privy Council. On Thursday, the Lord Mayor, several Aldermen and the Wardens of the Bakers' Company visited Dundas at his house in Somerset Place, and were promised the immediate attention of the government.[42]

The same day, the Lord Mayor explained to Court of Common Council that an amendment was necessary to the Act of 22 November 1750, to enable master bakers to replace strikers by journeymen from the country, and a temporary measure for the relief of bakers was immediately passed by the Court.[43] This was decisive, although the

journeymen immediately prosecuted some employers under the Act of
Charles II. Each master was fined 5 shillings, but a Mr Younger refused
to pay, and appealed to King's Bench.[44] Lord Chief Justice Kenyon
upheld Mansfield's dictum, and expressed a wish not to be troubled
again with such disputes. In this he was to be disappointed.

9 THE COMBINATION ACTS

Motives for the passage of the two general Acts of 1799 and 1800 'to prevent the unlawful combinations of workmen' have been traced to the fears of the political classes following the French Revolution, the substitution of *laissez-faire* economics for mercantilism, the common-law disapproval of combinations in restraint of trade, the subordination of the state to the interests of employers, the attempt to simplify legislation and improve administration, the extension of trade unionism to new occupational groups, and the generalization of private enactments for particular trades.[1]

The classical view of the Combination Acts as a radical departure was stated by the Webbs.

> There is a clear distinction ... between the various statutes which forbade combination prior to the end of the eighteenth century, and the general Combination Acts of 1799-1800. In the numerous earlier Acts ... it was assumed to be the business of Parliament and the law courts to regulate the conditions of labour; and ... although combinations to interfere with these statutory aims were obviously illegal, and were usually expressly prohibited, it was an incidental result that combinations formed to promote the objects of the legislation, however objectionable they might be to employers, were apparently not regarded as unlawful. Thus one of the earliest types of combination among journeymen — the society to enforce the law — seems always to be have been tacitly accepted as permissible.[2]

As Dorothy George first noted, the Webbs confused 'combination' with their own definition of 'trade union': a 'continuous association of wage-earners for the purpose of maintaining or improving the conditions of their working lives'.[3] This created an unnecessary difficulty: how to explain, given the 'severity' of the Combination Laws, the apparent toleration of unionized printers, coopers, framework-knitters, carpenters and tailors and the widespread joint regulation of piece-prices.[4] The Webbs' hypotheses — an inefficient police, the lack of a prosecuting agency and the apathy of employers — coexist uneasily with the popular image of a repressive class society.[5]

The Combination Acts did not forbid workmen from associating to improve wages and conditions of work, provided that they did so without industrial action, and it is incorrect to say that 'unlike legislation in the earlier paternalist tradition, they included no compensatory protective clause'.[6] On the contrary, they carried into the nineteenth century the eighteenth-century experience of mediation by the magistrates, and it was in the name of the new doctrines of *laissez-faire* and freedom of contract that they were repealed in 1824. Ironically, Francis Place is still honoured among 'makers of the labour movement', yet his aspiration was to see it wither away.[7]

The second Combination Act was an early attempt to bring British industrial relations within the scope of the law; it was 'the first of a long series of measures seeking to use direct sanctions in order to promote arbitration in labour disputes ... Somehow or other they all sought to promote conciliation and arbitration, they all sought to smooth the path of peaceful bargaining, to prevent or terminate stoppages — they were all, without any exception, complete failures.'[8] It may still be plausibly argued that the first Act, of 1799, was a product of political repression and economic exploitation. As Mr E.P. Thompson puts it, 'the aristocracy were interested in repressing the Jacobin "conspiracies" of the people, the manufacturers in defeating their "conspiracies" to increase wages: the Combination Acts served both purposes.'[9] Yet the link, if any, between the lower-middle-class corresponding societies and the trade societies of wage-earners was by no means self-evident, and before 1800 there is little to show that the authorities seriously suspected any. The reports of the Committee of Secrecy said nothing of combination of wage-earners, and the English 'Jacobins' were dealt with, not by the Combination Laws, but by the quite separate Corresponding Societies Act of 1799.[10]

If a disgruntled employer might 'scratch a trade unionist and find a Jacobin', half a century earlier he would have found a Jacobite. In 1750, some strikers at Newcastle, who had been drinking, proclaimed allegiance to the Pretender.[11] London journeymen were as hostile to the French Revolution as to that nation's manufactures, and during the Wilkes affair had proclaimed their devotion to the Crown noisily and extravagantly. So had the weavers of Paisley, in perhaps the only authentic 'political' strike of the eighteenth century.

A Silk Weaver in this Place, thinking to make some Advantage of the Madness of the Times, had invented a Pattern for his Handkerchiefs and Aprons of Silk Gauze, where, amongst small Flowers,

45 was wrought in large Figures, a Web of which, when finished, he sent to London for a Trial. It was quickly bought up, and his Correspondent wrote to him to send up a Dozen Pieces more, if he thought he could do it without giving Offence. On this he immediately employed a Number of Hands to finish the Commission, which being discovered, on Saturday a great Number of Journeymen Weavers assembled, and went in a body to the Magistrates, telling them not to be alarmed, as they were to make no Disturbance, but having been informed that several Men were employed in weaving Flags of Sedition, they were resolved to show their Loyalty, by putting a Stop to such Work, and desired that they would be pleased to order that no more of the seditious Pattern should be wrought, which the Magistrates thought it necessary to comply with, and promised to call the Manufacturer before them so soon as he returned to Town; but one of the Clippers with a Cap of the Pattern appearing at Church on Sunday, the Weavers again assembled on Monday to the Number of 1500, went to the Workhouse, and cut out of the Loom about a Yard, which was all that was wrought of it, and fixing it to the End of a Pole, along with the Clipper's Cap, they carried it in Procession, with Drums beating, and Music playing through the Streets to the Market-Place, and there set Fire to it, amidst the loud Huzzas of great Crouds of Spectators, who gave them Money to drink. The Healths of his Majesty, the Royal Family, and all loyal Subjects, and Confusion to all seditious Incendiaries, and their Adherents, were drank; after which they dispersed peaceably.[12]

Even when a corresponding society consisted largely of artisans and tradesmen, these were not necessarily trade unionists, nor typical of their fellow tailors, cabinet-makets, shoemakers or carpenters. In many cases they were small masters, rather than wage-earners. Until 1800, the government was concerned with agitation not within the trade unions but amongst the unorganized, unpredictable poor. The food riot rather than the strike was the principal danger to public order and internal security.[13]

All the same, it was the politicians ('the aristocracy') who brought in the first Combination Bill. Manufacturers seem to have had little say in the matter, having few voices in the unreformed Parliament, and Burdett, a disciple of Adam Smith, spoke against the Bill.[14] Pitt's draft closely followed the Papermakers' Act of 1796, which had been passed against the wishes of substantial interests in that industry.[15]

The claim by Wilberforce that 'a general disease requires a general remedy' found little echo with employers, whose labour problems were specific, and who were not in all cases opposed to trade unionism. No enduring association of workmen, militant or otherwise, could have long survived without at least *de facto* recognition by some masters, and it was as much to discourage 'rogue' employers – a Regnier, a Barrett or a Sanders – that the Tailors', Hatters' and Papermakers' Acts were sought by their competitors. Yet the more efficient manufacturers found such legislation irksome, and in 1796 the mid-Kent paper industry petitioned against the wage restrictions, which made it 'unsafe to give any Distinction of Reward as an Encouragement to superior skill or merit and by destroying all Emulation among the Workmen would, if suffered to pass into a Law, be productive of the most serious Inconvenience'.[16] In this industry, an employer even fomented a strike to ruin his rival. 'At a time when the plaintiff was in London, the defendant wrote to his journeymen, that the wages of the trade had lately advanced eighteen pence a week, and that if they stood out, they might have the same. The consequence was, that out of thirteen, eleven refused to work, and left his business without a moment's notice.'[17] The difficulty of enforcing anti-combination laws had already been demonstrated in the London tailoring trade.

The London Tailors' Act of 1768 imposed a penalty of up to two months' imprisonment on both a journeyman who demanded more than the legal maximum wage, and on an employer who paid it.[18] Under this provision, the Bow Street magistrates committed two master tailors to the Bridewell on 10 May 1769.[19] Two years later, the Lord Mayor found a master guilty, but gave him bail in order to appeal. To avoid hearing the appeal and many similar cases, the Quarter Sessions increased the legal rate to that already being paid, the Recorder explaining to the journeymen 'how ready the Court was to relieve every individual when the application was made with propriety and decency, but had they taken any unlawful method, by combining together and setting the laws at defiance, they might be assured the Court would have enforced the due performance of the law.[20]

Fielding followed precedent six years later, when a number of master tailors complained that the Act prevented them from paying the wages demanded by their journeymen, and that meanwhile the men were on strike. Sir John appealed for a return to work until the next Quarter Sessions, 'when the matter should be amicably settled between them and their employers'.[21] Some who ignored this offer were impressed and sent aboard a tender waiting at the Tower, and the society men retaliated by laying information against a large number of employers who until recently had been paying 'fair' rates, but were now resisting further increases. At Guildhall, on 20 and 24 April 1777, two employers were committed respectively to the county gaol and to the Wood Street compter. A week later, Alderman Lee, faced with a long list of charges, discovered a way out.

> The Alderman observed, that a Journeyman who took more wages than he had a right to demand, was punishable by the Act, as well as the Master; and asked a man if he would swear that he had received more wages than the Master had a right to give; but the man finding that if he did swear it, he should be committed to Bridewell for two months, and the Master for only 14 days, he refused to make an affidavit of the affair, upon which all the Master Taylors were dismissed.[22]

When next morning 'a great number of reputable Master Taylors' appeared at Bow Street, no witnesses came forward and all were discharged. The machinery of justice moved inexorably on, and attendance summonses were issued against the absent informers. Unable to trace one, the constable left the summons at his employer's workshop, and the society's attorney advised against answering it, since the service had not been at the journeyman's usual abode, namely where he slept. On being arrested, and brought into court, the witness was told either to answer the information or stand committed, whereupon counsel told him to say nothing and applied for *habeas corpus*.[23]

Other witnesses were persuaded to speak, and a series of convictions followed. On 9 July, two masters were sent to gaol for a month each, one successfully appealing to Quarter Sessions on the grounds that his journeyman had mistaken the date of the offence. On 23 October, a Mr Thomas, master tailor of York Buildings, was also convicted, but

> it appearing that this prosecution was set on foot because he would not continue giving more wages than allowed by law, the associating journeymen taylors threatening him with a prosecution in case of refusal, he thought it proper to abide the sentence of the Court, sooner than continue to pay the extra wages. This being proved, the sentence is mitigated to fourteen days, and a prosecution is carrying on against the journeymen Taylors for a combination.[24]

Mr Thomas gave notice of appeal; meanwhile Fielding was ruthlessly impartial. Sentencing another master to fourteen days, he advised him to summons the journeymen in retaliation, 'as the law inflicts an equal punishment on the receiver as well as the giver'.[25] The master tailors' committee petitioned Parliament urgently for an amending Bill, which was given a second reading on 3 April, but proceeded no further.[26]

Mr Thomas's appeal was heard on 24 April, and quickly turned to farce. Defence counsel, Mr Sylvester, asked for the written information to be produced, and when it could not be, asked for the conviction to be quashed, being similar to an indictment because taken under a penal statute. Prosecution distinguished between indictment and information, adding that the information might have been stolen or destroyed by a friend of the defendant. Sylvester retorted that it might have been destroyed by the prosecution on account of its insufficiency, and Sir John Fielding left the chair to side with the defence. Finally, by seven to two, the magistrates voted to quash the conviction.[27] Thereafter, little more was heard of the Tailors' Acts, and between 1777 and 1800, by repeated industrial action, the houses of call increased the going rate to thirty shillings a week.[28]

Not all anti-combination legislation was as ineffective, and there were other weapons to hand: prosecution for leaving work unfinished and the indictment for conspiracy. Although a powerful remedy, the indictment was costly, to be invoked only as a last resort, and Dowdell, who carefully searched the Middlesex Sessions for the early part of the century, was surprised at the small number of cases.[29] However, the records, if patchy and incomplete, do not support the Webbs' 'proof of the novelty of the workmen's combinations in the early part of the eighteenth century, that neither the employers nor the authorities thought at first of resorting to the very sufficient powers of the existing law against them'.[30] One of the earliest cases was brought by the Worshipful Company of Curriers, and tried at the Old Bailey on Thursday, 8 December 1720, when six journeymen were gaoled for three months and fined 20 marks each. Many journeymen tailors were indicted in 1721, but in the end the masters were obliged to seek an Act of Parliament. There were also indictments of 15 sailmakers, each of whom was fined one pound.[31] Fourteen years later, indictments of wheelwrights at Middlesex Sessions were removed by *certiorari* into King's Bench, and then withdrawn.[32]

For a quarter-century, the indictment was rarely brought, if at all, in labour disputes, but once revived it occurred more frequently. Twice, in 1765 and 1770, leaders of the London tailors were imprisoned for six months, but two-year sentences on bookbinders and printers were unexpected and disturbing to public opinion.[33] A petition to the

Table 9.1: Selected Indictments for Conspiracy Arising from Labour
Disputes, 1720-1800

Year	Court	Defendant(s)	Trade	Verdict/ Sentence
1720	OB	(6)	Curriers	3 months' gaol and 20 marks fine
1721	KB	(24)	Tailors	Discharged
1721	KB	Wise and others (Cambridge)	Tailors	Guilty (confirmed)
1725	Hants Assizes & KB	(8) (Alton, Hants)	Woolcombers	Damages and costs, total £80
1734	Middx Sessions	(9)	Wheelwrights	*Certiorari* withdrawn
1758	Lancs Assizes	(17) (Manchester)	Checkweavers	1s fine
1761	Middx Sessions & KB	'A number'	Cabinet-makers	Rule of court (bound over?)
1765	OB	Milburn, Marsham, Carrick, Jones	Tailors	6 months' gaol and 1s fine
1765	OB	Berry, Dobson	Tailors	3 months' gaol and 1s fine
1770	OB	Wm. Longland, Wm. Dixon	Tailors	6 months' gaol and 1s fine
		Js. Clifford, Wm. Bean, Cornelius Connor, Jas. Moley	Tailors	Acquitted
1772	OB	(10)	Curriers	Acquitted
1782	Middx Sessions	John Wilson, Jacob Freeman, Henry Hickson, Wm. Eldridge, Geo. Parry, James Eyres, 'Ar.' or 'John' Medley	Wheelwrights	Convicted; no record of sentence (prison?)

Year	Court	Defendant(s)	Trade	Verdict/Sentence
1782	Middx Court	Philip Holland	Wheelwright	Acquitted
1786	KB	Armstrong and 5 others	Bookbinders	2 years' gaol (released after 1 year)
1786	Middx Sessions		Felt hatters	Withdrawn after apology by defendants
1788	KB	'A number'	Carpenters	Indictment stood over: 'compromise'
1788	KB	Bunce and 4 others	Smiths	Postponed
1790	Herts Sessions	Thos. Arnold, John Corrall, Thos, Peacock, Wm. Maybank, Thos. Nash, John Davis, Jas. Harditch, Wm. Farr, John Wade, Thos. Adkins, Pardoe, Green (Hatfield, Herts)	Papermakers	Sent for trial
1791	KB	'A number' (Herts)	Cutlers	Rule granted (? on information, not indictment
1792	Notts Q. Sessions	(2)	Cordwainers	Guilty
1792	Middx, Surrey, London	Total not known	Curriers	True Bills found, but no further proceedings
1792	Bristol Assizes (Buller)	Wm. Russell and 5 others	Tailors	Guilty
1793	KB (Kenyon)	Cockburn and others	Saddlers	No judgement prayed by prosecution

Year	Court	Defendant(s)	Trade	Verdict/Sentence
1796	Herts Sessions	Thos. Brace, Henry Cleverly, Jonathan Clibbon, Isaac LeCourt, Andrew Newton, John Sherwood, Wm. Bateman, James Constable, Robert Cox, George Jeffries, Wm. Stamp, Wm. Wilkins, John Witnall (Ware, Herts)	Barge loaders	Removed by *certiorari*
1798	OB (Recorder)	Edward Atkinson, John Warwick, John Turk, Luke Ball, Nath. Lynham	Printers' pressmen	Guilty, 2 years' gaol
1798	KB (Kenyon)	Hammond, Webb	Shoemakers	Guilty; no sentence passed, all other indictments to stand over
1799	High Court, Edinburgh	(3)	Shoemakers	Guilty; 1 month gaol
1799	Newcastle Assizes	(49)	Shoemakers	22 guilty; recognizances for good behaviour
1799	High Court, Edinburgh	Js. Leishman, Wm. Hossack, Alex. Boyack, Alex. Marshal, Robert Oliver	Tailors	Indictment inaccurate
1800	KB Keynon, Grose)	Wm. Thompson Wm. Smith	Shoemakers	Guilty of perjury; 9 months' gaol

King, presented by Sheriff Bloxham, led to the release of the book-binders after one year in Newgate.[34] The conviction of the secretary and committee of the pressmen's society became a *cause celèbre*, and a transcript of the trial was reprinted and sold in aid of the prisoners.[35] In several cases, the prosecution asked not for punishment, merely for an end to a strike, whereupon the defendants were discharged with a warning. In 1758, during the great turn-out of 10,000 Lancashire check weavers, a Grand Jury found a true bill against 17 ringleaders, but added that 'as the punishment attending these offences is most justly severe, we wish rather to convince and amend than punish this ignorant and deluded multitude'.[36] The trial judge, Sir Michael Foster, fined the men one shilling each, advising them to 'go home and sin no more lest a worse thing happen to you'. He attacked the system of apprenticeship:

If none must employ, or be employed, in any branch of trade, but who have served a limited number of years to that branch, the particular trade will be lodged in a few hands, to the danger of the public, and the liberty of setting up trades, and the foundations of the present flourishing condition of Manchester will be destroyed. In the infancy of trade, the Act of Queen Elizabeth might be well calculated for public weal, but now when it is grown to that per-fection we see it, it might perhaps be of utility to have those laws repealed, as tending to cramp and tie down that knowledge it was first necessary to obtain by rule.[37]

In 1772, the London Curriers' Company prosecuted the committee of journeymen, with embarrassing consequences. After a seven-hour trial at the Old Bailey, the ten defendants were acquitted, and they at once brought actions for assault and false imprisonment against the Renter Warden and two constables.[38] The Companies of Wheelwrights and Feltmakers were more successful, in each case obtaining promises from the journeymen 'never more to be guilty of like conduct'; judge-ment was then respited.[39] There was a more complicated trial at King's Bench in 1786, when the master bookbinders, expecting an early return to work, asked for all but six strike leaders to be acquitted. Judge Buller commended their leniency but, the strike continuing, judgement was deferred. In November, the defence pleaded a mistrial: men named as ringleaders were 'the least offensive' of the prisoners. Judgement was again postponed, and by May 1787, when sentence was eventually passed, the masters had conceded a reduction in the working week.[40]

Eleven papermakers were indicted at Hertfordshire Quarter Sessions 'for conspiring against Thomas Vallance to raise wages 1s. a week', and in April 1791 some cutlers were also sent for trial.[41] Five years later, twelve workmen and labourers employed in the loading and unloading of malt from a barge belonging to Samuel Taylor were indicted on several counts:

(1) For conspiring to raise their wages . . . and unlawfully assembling . . . and compelling William Tomlin and Thomas Moss . . . to strike and leave unfinished their work . . .
(2) For being armed with offensive weapons, and assaulting William Tomlin and Thomas Moss . . . and for
(3) . . . obstructing John Jones and William Johnson, being on board of and navigating a barge at Reasons Lock and . . . throwing them out of the same barge . . . and riotously assembling to force the Bargemasters and Maltfactors of Ware to raise their Wages.[42]

Indictment (1) was removed to a higher court by *certiorari*, and the Sessions books reveal that, thereafter,

the public justice has lately been interrupted and the Execution thereof prevented by riots of Bargemen and others at the Town of Ware in this County, so that it became necessary for His Majesty's Justices of the Peace there attending in discharge of their duty to call in the aid of the Military Force then quartered there, as also the Yeomanry Cavalry of the County.[43]

In the last decade of the century, most trials at King's Bench for conspiracy to combine were presided over by Lord Kenyon, whose judgements revealed a paternalist sympathy for the poor, coupled with strong disapproval of 'forestalling' and 'regrating'. He disliked labour indiscipline, but considered that disputes between employers and workmen were best settled outside the courts.

He made this explicit in the Sunday baking trial. When the journeymen's counsel protested that his clients were 'in a worse position than African slaves', Kenyon interrupted 'that he was sorry to hear that any description of men in this country were in a situation that could warrant such a comparison, but as these men engaged by contract, it was in their own power to better their condition by making a proper agreement with their employers . . . a court of law was not at any rate a proper place for the redress of grievances'.[44]

In trade union cases, the defence could usually exploit the law's delays. Although a strike of 4,000 London carpenters and joiners began in July 1787, their leaders were not tried until 31 October 1788, by which time, as Thomas Erskine explained, the men had long since returned to work.

> He would therefore appeal to the wisdom and justice of the court, whether it would not be more conducive to the benefit of all parties to put a period to the prosecution by a friendly accommodation. If the Defendants were found guilty . . . the probable consequence would be a destructive discord where harmony ought to prevail.[45]

When the prosecution retorted that the men were still paying weekly contributions to their society, Erskine produced the rulebook, quoting at length from its 'very fair and honourable' provisions. This enabled the Lord Chief Justice to observe

> with respect to clubs, there were many of them instituted in a remote part of the kingdom, with which he was well acquainted, and when established with a design to afford mutual assistance to their members, in a season of need or distress, instead of being censurable, his Lordship conceived them to be very laudable.[46]

On the other hand, nothing could be more pernicious to trade and the public in general than conspiracies, and the legislature had shown wisdom in framing laws for their suppression. Counsel agreed that the indictment should stand over 'for the purpose of deliberating on a mode of compromise'.[47] Half a century later, a Mr Thomas Martin recalled how, 'about the year 1787, the master carpenters entered prosecutions against the men, and it ended with enormous expence, and they did not succeed at last, the men got their wages advanced'.[48]

A few days after the carpenters, five blacksmiths were brought for judgement. Mr Bearcroft stated that several others were still unlawfully assembled at the Newcastle-upon-Tyne public house in Carnaby Market, but Mr Erskine produced a sworn affidavit that the defendants, 'sensible of their being misled and willing to make every possible atonement for the pernicious errors into which they had fallen', had no connection with any illegal assemblies or combinations. Lord Kenyon told them that their offence, from its pernicious consequence, demanded exemplary punishment, but the court, 'desirous to afford them an opportunity of evincing the sincerity of their contrition', would postpone judgement.[49]

Four years later, in the journeymen saddlers' case, the prosecution called only one witness, since 'the object of this prosecution was to restore order and to conciliate masters and men together'.

He was authorised to say in the name of the masters, that if no new offence was committed, no judgement would be prayed. The learned judge observed that (the prosecutors) seemed to be actuated by a very proper spirit in wishing by admonition to bring the Defendants back to their duty, and not to inflict punishment unless it was absolutely necessary; the Prosecutors had acted like good Citizens, and he trusted that the lenity which had been shown the Defendants would not be thrown away upon them.[50]

In principle, the courts frowned on the unilateral use of collective power, whether by journeymen or masters, to impose charges in the terms of employment. In 1794, not only journeymen shoemakers were brought before the Mayor of Leicester for combining to procure an advance of wages and preventing or deterring other men from working, but also some masters were charged with countenancing and abetting them.[51] However, a body of employers claiming to be representative of their trade as a whole was not pursued as a conspiracy. In November 1795, a general meeting of master cart wheelwrights, at the George Inn, West Smithfield, unanimously agreed a list of piece-work prices 'as a sufficient payment for the work therein specified, and resolved that we will pay our several journeymen the said prices and no other'. The following 'Regulations' were also agreed.

Weekly Men to work from Six o'Clock in the Morning to Seven o'Clock in the Evening.

On Account of the Advance in the Bill of Prices, the Allowance heretofore made for Small Beer and Candles, will be discontinued in future.

Work not done to Satisfaction, the Master to stop for the deficiency as he shall judge right. If the Man thinks himself aggrieved, then to be referred to two Masters to decide.[52]

A similar decision was taken by master plasterers, convened to receive the report of their committee on 17 and 19 May 1796. They approved an eleven-page list of prices for measured work, and daily wages, 'winter and summer', of four shillings for plasterers, two shillings and ninepence for labourers, and one shilling and fourpence for boys.[53]

In these trades, the price-lists were enforced unilaterally, but in letterpress printing a measure of joint regulation was achieved. To avoid prosecution, the men's spokesmen were careful to present themselves as intermediaries rather than as strike leaders. In 1794, when the committee of printers' pressmen successfully proposed an all-London scale of piece-prices, they did so in order, they said, to end the disputes which 'continually arose in different houses'.[54] *De facto* collective bargaining had begun and, three years later, 'this suggested the idea, that a similar mode respecting Apprentices would be productive of the same happy effect'.[55] This initiative ended disastrously.

On 10 March 1797, the London master printers received five delegates from the pressmen's friendly society to discuss limitation of apprentices. Although in 1775 the Stationers' Company had ruled that, before engaging new apprentices, masters must send lists to the Company, the issue had become a battle-ground.

> ... the trade of printing in this metropolis has been interrupted from time to time by the journeymen printers in attempting to get their wages raised, which has been resisted, and with a good deal of effect by the master printers, who were obliged, on the occasion, to have recourse to their apprentices: therefore it was thought expedient by these journeymen printers that their masters should be prevented from taking more than a certain number of apprentices.[56]

The pressmen's committee proposed to limit apprentices to three for every seven presses, and in no case should they equal the journeymen in number. To allow time for the masters to consider this, the committee recommended a return to normal work for one month. When the trade rejected the restrictions, strikes broke out in several printing offices, and the master printers held the journeymen's secretary and committee responsible, although none of them were themselves on strike. After a lengthy and complex trial, the men were sentenced to two years' imprisonment for unlawful assembly and conspiracy and combination to

> unlawfully frame a certain order, rule and regulation to restrain and limit the number of Apprentices to be taken by the said Masters . . . and cause and procure to be conveyed and sent to divers journeymen and workmen . . . a recommendation to leave and abandon the

service of the said masters, by reason the masters would not comply with the said unlawful order.[57]

The main reason for refusing to accept the journeymen's proposals was the refusal or inability of the committee to call off a dispute with a Mr Davis. At the trial, the master printers insisted that they had negotiated in good faith, and had appealed to the law only as a last resort.

Q. You have stated a meeting in order to enter into a negotiation with the journeymen; is that the only meeting you have had in order to settle your differences?

A. No.

Q. Had you a meeting in the February preceding, at the Globe tavern?

A. We had.

Q. Had there been letters passed to the journeymen and the masters relative to the dispute prior to that?

A. I believe there were letters passed between the committee and a Mr Davis.

Q. Which was passed to the committee?

A. Yes, occasionally.

Q. How long before that meeting at the Globe had there been any communication and correspondence between the journeymen and masters?

A. Between the journeymen and Mr Davis.

Q. Was that correspondence regularly communicated to the committee?

A. Yes.

Q. How long had this correspondence being going on?

A. I suppose near two months.

Q. On both sides it was intended to communicate between you, in a friendly way, upon the subject of the dispute?

A. It was always the desire of the masters to do so.[58]

In the last common-law trial before the Combination Bill of 1799, two journeymen shoemakers, Hammond and Webb, were chosen from 'a great number' to appear before Lord Kenyon for conspiring to raise piece-prices throughout the metropolis by sixpence per pair. Detailed evidence was given of the organization of the eleven-week strike, and of the economic and technological influences on the outcome. 'For such purpose they held meetings, which are called *General Meetings* and also *Shop Meetings* . . . regularly and systematically organized, under rules and orders, made and agreed amongst themselves, and carried into effect by means of Committee-men, chosen for that purpose'.[59] Any shop on strike was to be isolated. 'Six persons from among the journeymen, who belonged to the men who had struck, were appointed to watch near the house of the Master's, to see that no work was carried out from his shop, and if they found any one coming out with any, they followed him, and by some means or another, prevented his working for that master.'[60]

The strike had its origins in the 'folly or ambition' of a few masters, who offered sixpence a pair more than others, in order to attract the best hands. 'Among these, the most forward was a Mr O'Shacknessy, an Irishman, who had frequently taken men away in this manner, for that if any other were to give 7s. a pair for making shoes, Mr O'Shacknessy would give 7s. 6d. for making them.' The pay structure was also disturbed by changes in fashion and in the content of the task. A Mr Hobby was responsible for

> the practice which first appeared of what are called 'right' and 'left', that is, making shoes to suit the right and left foot, according to the natural shape of the foot, upon a separate last for each. This was now become so customary in the fashionable circles of boot and shoe making that no man of fashion now wore any other sort of shoes and boots. This was at first more difficult than the common old way, and therefore Mr Hobby, and one or two more in the trade, voluntarily gave a higher price for making them than was usual in the trade; but . . . now it is indeed found that the rights and lefts are easier, instead of more difficult to make, insofar that the one may be left on the last to dry while the other is in the course of being made up.[61]

The consequent increase in the earnings of Mr Hobby's pieceworkers, while those of others remained unchanged, brought discontent to the trade and a demand for the general body of masters to follow suit. Profit margins were already narrow, and preserved at the customer's expense. 'Although there was more ingenuity at present requisite to make what is called a fine shoe or boot than formerly, yet they are not nearly so useful or durable as they formerly were; they are now made so very finely, that there was but little wear in them.'[62]

By the time of the trial, the strike had been over for a month, and Mr Erskine made his customary plea for masters and journeymen to continue harmoniously together.

> He could only repeat in the hearing of his clients, and he wished it
> to be reported to the public . . . that conspirators should find in
> him no advocate, and he hoped and trusted they would have no
> advocate at the Bar in any Court of Justice in this country . . .
> There must, however, be the same measure of justice held out to
> all. As the Journeymen were not permitted to *raise*, the Masters
> must not combine to *lower* the price of labour. The one might
> as soon be made the object of prosecution for conspiracy as the
> other; and if the Masters were prosecuted for any offence of that
> kind, the journeymen would find in him a willing and zealous
> advocate. But he hoped that the parties on both sides would now
> understand one another and also understand their own duty.[63]

In a long summing-up, Lord Kenyon said that punishments fell on
the few, but the example should operate on the many. Mr Erskine's
behaviour had been worthy of his great talents: 'he never made the
situation of the advocate a cloak for inflammatory harangues, to make
the populace discontented, and to endanger the condition of civil
society, by inducing the lower orders of it to throw off all notions of
obedience, and thereby throwing all the affairs of the world into
confusion'.[64] The defence having called no witnesses, the question
before the jury was not difficult, but was of immense importance
in its consequences.

> The number of journeymen in this trade in the metropolis had been
> stated at *thirty thousand*. This was itself a very considerable point
> . . . If the journeymen shoemakers were to succeed in their wishes
> . . . the precedent would extend directly to all mechanical trades,
> and not only to the mechanical trades but also to articles of imme-
> diate necessity to the sustenance of man. Suppose *butchers* were to
> combine to raise the price of *meat* and *farmers* the price of *corn*,
> (and they had as much right to do so as the *shoemakers*, for one
> combination to raise the price of any article might as well be carried
> on as another) . . . what would the shoemakers have gained to
> themselves or their families in point of comfort?
> . . . Very early in this century, there was another combination
> in the West of England which was suppressed by military force,
> but although the conspirators gave up their scheme almost imme-
> diately, yet the West of England had reason to lament the conspiracy;

the effects of it were, perhaps, felt there to this hour, for the shock it gave to trade was inconceivable to any but to tradesmen ... there were many who believed that much of the trade of the West of England fled upon that occasion to Yorkshire; he believed there were some intelligent tradesmen in Wiltshire who understood the matter pretty well.[65]

Finally, the Lord Chief Justice addressed himself to the conduct of the masters. 'If any of them were within hearing, they might profit by what he had to say.'

He admonished the Masters to be circumspect in their conduct, for most clear it was that they might also be indicted if they combined. The law of England held the balance even, upon the scale of Justice, between the rich and the poor. Those who were to administer that justice, from their feelings as men, which he hoped he should always carry about him, were naturally led to protect the lower orders of the community, and who, some of them, had perhaps no other protection than the Law. A feeling man, therefore, in administering the Law, would wish to protect the lower classes the more in a Court of Justice, from the reflection that they had no other place to look to for more protection: therefore let the lower classes of people feel, that if they behave uprightly, they may call upon Courts of Justice for protection whenever they are aggrieved, and they shall not call in vain ...[66]

There was little more to be said. For the masters, Mr Mingay explained that their only object was to end the conspiracy: the defendants had only to return to their duty, and work for the old wages, and everything would be at an end. Mr Gibbs, the prosecuting counsel, said that more handsome conduct on behalf of defendants he had never witnessed, than that of Mr Erskine. The jury found the men guilty, and on the understanding between counsel on both sides that nothing more should be done unless the journeymen combined again, the remaining indictments were ordered to stand over.[67]

Two other labour disputes were simmering in the capital. One group, the journeymen bakers, was very large; the other small, but strategically placed. They were the millwrights of London Bridge, whose employers contracted to maintain the machinery of the great cornmills in and around Tooley Street. Much of London's corn supply, shipped upstream from Kent, Essex and Suffolk, went through the mills, and a strike could deprive thousands of their daily bread. The millwrights had already tested their bargaining strength during the 'bread famine' of 1795.[68]

On 5 April 1799, the master millwrights presented a petition to the House of Commons, urgently praying for a private Act. They explained the delays and costs of indictment procedure, and asked for a Bill to prevent unlawful combination and to regulate the wages. The House agreed that the matter was urgent, and waived its rules to enable the petition to be read. A committee was set up under the chairmanship of Sir John Anderson who, only four days later, moved for leave to bring in a Bill to regulate the trade 'within certain limits'. At this stage Wilberforce made his famous suggestion that the Bill be given more extensive application, but the Speaker explained that this could not be founded on a report relating to a proposed private Bill.[69]

This was not the only case of combination before the House of Commons, and petitions for private Bills were now competing for time with government business. On 19 April, William Dundas asked leave to bring in a Bill to prevent combinations among coal miners in Scotland and to regulate their wages. Three days later, Sir John Stuart presented a petition from workers at several Scottish collieries, praying to be heard in person or through counsel against the proposal. They were ordered to be heard on the second reading the following Friday, but this debate was twice postponed, for the House was preoccupied with the Seditious Societies Bill and the suspension of *habeas corpus*. After brief discussion on 6 and 9 May, the Collieries Bill was given second and third readings.[70]

The Millwrights' Bill was given its first reading on 6 May and, after presentation of a journeymen's petition, its second on 9 May. The main debate, on 10 June, was on the third reading, which Sir Francis Burdett failed to postpone for three months. 'The wages of labour, as well as the prices of provisions, should be left to find their own level', and Parliament should not interfere. Sir John told him that he would have been of a different opinion with respect to the nature and extent of these combinations had he attended the committee. The business of millwrights would be at an end if the Bill did not pass. 'This was a business in which not the masters only, but the public at large, were materially interested. These men had impeded the commerce of the country by striking from their work.'[71]

All other speakers, including the Solicitor-General, supported the Bill, but agreed that a more general one was needed. On 17 June, Mr Pitt asked leave to introduce it, and next day the Secretary to the

Treasury included the general Combination Bill with miscellaneous others.[72] On 19 June the House gave an unopposed second reading to all of them. The trade unionists and their friends reacted slowly, and it was not until the third reading in the Lords on 9 July that Mr Gurney appeared as counsel for the journeymen. Lord Holland opposed the Bill as 'unjust' and 'oppressive'; he objected to the liability of 'any person' who aided or advised a journeyman to enter into a combination, and he moved an amendment to exclude persons who were not journeymen or workmen from any penalties.[73] Otherwise the opposition was muted, in contrast to 1795, when Sheridan had persuaded more than 60,000 journeymen to petition against the clauses in the Seditious Meetings Bill to restrict the size of meetings, which might have adversely affected the trade clubs.[74]

The reaction of English workers was also very different from that of the Irish, who had persuaded the Dublin parliament to abandon a general Combination Bill. In 1780, the Grand Committee of Trade was told that, although free trade with England had encouraged new manufactures, it had also created a labour shortage in the linen industry and obliged employers to raise wages by 50 per cent. The shortage was exacerbated by the journeymen's rules concerning apprenticeship and the employment of 'strangers' and by their refusal to work more than four days a week.[75]

On Saturday 3 June 1780, as Sir Lucius O'Brien was presenting an outline Combination Bill to the Irish House of Commons, the Gordon riots were breaking out in London.[76] Ten days later, several thousand journeymen artificers assembled in Phoenix Park, Dublin, to march to Parliament House with a petition against the Bill. 'Such a numerous meeting at this time, when the metropolis of our sister kingdom is convulsed with dangerous insurrections, was truly alarming.' The Volunteers assembled at the Royal Exchange and 'a thousand citizens in arms' prepared to support the civil power, but no riot or disturbance followed. Instead, the Lord Mayor authorized six of the demonstrators to enter the city with the petition, and the crowd dispersed.[77] The Bill passed, but combinations and strikes continued.

In 1792, another attempt was made to suppress Irish combinations, with similar consequences. The Dublin journeymen held an 'aggregate meeting' in Phoenix Park, and marched 'with wands in their hands' to the Commons. The Speaker came out, and was understood to promise that the Bill would not pass, but it went to a committee of the Lords, and 10,000 workmen again marched to Parliament. Under pressure, the Lord Chancellor repudiated the Bill, which required all journeymen seeking work to produce a certificate of discharge from their previous employers. 'The whole of this Bill is such a system of oppression and injustice as should not be countenanced in this House; it makes part of that system of vassalage which it has been attempted to build in this country, but the erection of which I trust your Lordships will ever oppose.' A motion that the chairman should leave the chair was carried *nemine differentiente*, and the Bill was lost.[78]

William Pitt's Combination Bill contained no such provision, nor did it create new offences, but codified and generalized existing legislation, including the much-criticized provision for hearings before a single magistrate.[79] Lord Holland's complaint that the Bill removed trial by jury was double-edged: trial by jury could lead to two years in gaol, summary conviction to three months at most. If the law was biased in the employer's favour, this was nothing new, and it was some months before labour protest began to be mobilized by Sheridan and his friends.

The master painters of London were the first to invoke the new Act as a remedy for 'inconveniences existing between the Masters and Journeymen as to their wages and conduct', resolving

(1) that fair, equitable and liberal wages as between Masters and Journeymen should be paid, namely, at the rate of one guinea per week for good and able workmen — a day's work being reckoned from 6 o'clock in the morning till 6 o'clock in the evening — and inferior workmen according to their abilities; (2) that the Act to prevent unlawful combinations of workmen be enforced; (3) that an abstract of such Act with the above resolutions be printed and delivered to the Masters and Journeymen and occupiers of houses of call for the trade for their full information.[80]

The Act received the Royal Assent on 12 July. Four days later, the Lord Mayor of London agreed to an application from the Bakers' Company to increase the price of bread to 10½d per quartern, consequent on the higher cost of flour. Soon after, about 50 journeymen bakers held a series of meetings at the Bell Tap alehouse in Wood Street, Cheapside, drew up a printed list of wage rates, resolved to strike unless conceded by the masters and, believing their meetings to be illegal in view of the numbers attending, decided to burn their minute book and records, but to keep a list of names on a single sheet of paper.[81]

On 1 October, the Master of the Worshipful Company of Bakers, Mr Loveland, called a special meeting of their Court. He explained that the Lord Mayor had informed him of a journeymen's combination to raise wages. Two men had confessed to their presence at the Wood Street meetings and on their information warrants under the Combination Act were issued for the arrest of six journeymen committee members. The Lord Mayor found the charges proved, and spoke of the dangers of such conspiracies in general, 'but most of all from a set of men whose abstaining from work must highly distress all orders and descriptions of people, and would ultimately lead to the disturbance of public tranquility'.[82] Under the Act he was empowered to commit them for three months, but he would allow appeals to Quarter Sessions, if they would find bail within an hour. Bail not being forthcoming, Walker and Ross, former committee chairmen, were sentenced to three months in Bridewell and Newgate respectively, but the others were discharged with a caution. On the same day a journeyman was committed for three months for trying to persuade another to attend an illegal meeting.[83]

Two days later, on Saturday 5 October, 900 journeymen bakers struck, and on Monday 400 more joined them. The quartern loaf rose to a shilling, a few days later to 1s 1d, and then, at weekly intervals to 1s 2½d, 1s 3d and 1s 3¼d. The bread shortage did not, as the Lord Mayor had feared, immediately disturb 'the public tranquility', but some anger followed the brewers' decision, against the wishes of the Prime Minister, to raise the price of porter to five shillings a barrel, and the publicans passed on the increase by a halfpenny per pot.[84] As the cost of living soared there was talk of reviving the committee, first established in the 1795 crisis, for the relief of the poor of London and Westminster, and a meeting was held on 6 December at the London Tavern.[85]

Magistrates were vigilant for unrest among the poor, and for the activities of agitators. An attempt by 'seditious emissaries' to stir up the weavers against the Combination Act was foiled by the acting magistrates of the Hundred of Salford, but the greater threat was the food riot, and the authorities cautiously manipulated the Assize of Bread and other price controls, treading a tight-rope between the producers and the poorer consumers. Their dilemma was that of the French revolutionaries in 1791-3, whose prices and wages freeze had appeased the restless poor, but had infuriated masters and journeymen alike. More logical than the English, the Jacobins suppressed both trade unions and employers' associations.[86]

In the north of England, journeymen were still brought before the Assize courts on indictment for conspiracy. On 1 August 1799, at

Newcastle, the 'long-depending cause' was tried between master and journeymen shoemakers. There were 49 defendants, of whom two had absconded, and 21 prosecution witnesses, but the judge was disinclined to hear them all. After the first witness, he concluded that the conspiracy 'was indeed of an alarming nature', directed the jury to find 22 defendants guilty, placed these on recognizances for their good behaviour, and threatened to send them to the King's Bench court if they ever combined again.[87]

From York, Mr Justice Laurence did send two shoemakers, Thompson and Smith, to Lord Kenyon for judgement. They had been members of the Friendly Society of Cordwainers of Hull, and, as usual, Mr Erskine pleaded that

> He had received from them the most solemn and sacred assurances of their contrition, and they were sensible of the enormity of their offence . . . This offence is extremely common in the Northern manufacturing parts of the kingdom . . . if this Society is still kept up . . . I should think my appearance here an act of ostentatious folly; but this Society is dissolved. These men have returned to work at the old wages, and they . . . have set a beneficial example to the Public.[88]

Kenyon asked whether the society were in fact dissolved, and Erskine quoted from the defendants' affidavits that it has been ended months before the trial. His Lordship then endorsed Mr Erskine's remarks: justice should be tempered with mercy,

> particularly in the cases of the lower orders of the people, who may not be so well acquainted with their duty; but we have shown so many instances of mercy that have not produced their effect, that we are very near the end of that line. However, I am still willing that mercy should not stop short in this case. Let their recognizances be taken up in a pretty large sum, that they will come up and receive the judgment of this court whenever they are called upon.

At this point, Mr Justice Grose intervened: 'In the affidavits of these defendants it is sworn that this Society was dissolved on the 27 February last. I should be glad if the prosecutor for the Crown would inquire into the truth of that.'[89] The Lord Chief Justice agreed, and ordered the men to appear again on the last day of term, but on 11 February he was not on the bench. It was Mr Justice Grose who heard a second affidavit, and told them

> that the Court, hoping that what had been suggested by them was
> true, that this abominable club ceased to exist, gave time to have
> that fact examined into ... it seemed that it still existed, and
> although there had been attempts to throw dust into the eyes of the
> Court ... it had proceeded in the most pernicious and abominable
> manner.

Taking into account 'the enormity of their offence', he sent them to
Newgate for nine months.[90] In this trial, six months after the first
Combination Act, the prosecution had referred to combinations in
almost all the great towns in the north of England, and hinted that
'these associations were easily convertible into every sort of political
mischief'.[91] This was the earliest reported suggestion of its kind. Two
other northern trade unionists were more fortunate: convicted under
the Combination Act, William Potter and William Lowe, hatters of
Stockport, were committed to Chester Castle for only a month.[92]

In the spring of 1800, there were widespread disturbances due to
rising prices: food riots at Stockport, Carlisle and Dorking, and on
7 March the King proclaimed a General Fast.[93] There were strikes of
master bakers against the Assize of Bread at Cork, Exeter, Nottingham
and Hinkley, where their windows were broken by crowds.[94] Grand
Juries at Warwick and York urged the cultivation of waste lands, and
called on the Board of Agriculture to consider a General Enclosure
Bill.[95] There were widespread complaints at the high price of coal, and
a Commons committee investigated the Newcastle 'vend'.[96] Whitbread
again attempted to introduce a Minimum Wage Bill, but achieved only
a first reading in the Commons.[97]

On 16 May, Erskine again addressed Lord Kenyon, this time in the
role of prosecutor. The defendant, Samuel Waddington, had harangued
planters and dealers at Worcester hop-market against selling at the
prevailing low prices, and the question was whether such a speech
constituted a misdemeanour. The Lord Chief Justice had no doubts,
and he took the opportunity to denounce Adam Smith's new economics.

> Mr Erskine, you need not answer it. I will not say positively what
> the effect may be, but this I know, that it is a question in which the
> country is mightily concerned ... It has been said that forestalling,
> regrating &c. are offences which people have no more reason to
> dread than witchcraft. It is easy for a man to write a treatise in his

closet. But if he would go to the distance of 200 miles from London, and see people at every avenue of a country-town buying-up butter, and all the necessities of life they can lay hold of, in order to prevent them from coming to market (which has happened to my knowledge), he would find that this is something more real and substantial than the crime of witchcraft. The country suffers most grievously.[98]

Kenyon granted a rule for Waddington to be tried at Worcester on 29 July. In August, he went on circuit, and opened Chelmsford Assizes with a charge to the Grand Jury to pay particular attention to the increasing offences of forestalling and regrating, should any cases come before them. He had just learned, with considerable pleasure, 'that a person, charged with numerous misdemeanours of the former description, had been convicted by the late assizes for Worcester, by a unanimous verdict of a most respectable jury of that county'.[99]

In this frame of mind, he proceeded to the trial of three farm labourers, indicted by Essex Quarter Sessions for insurrection and conspiracy. To compel the farmers of Dengie Hundred to raise their wages and supply them with cheaper provisions, they had organized a strike.

John Little was to be their Captain, and they were to carry a flag when their forces were strengthened by numbers; and their intention was to stop all the farmers' horses from ploughing, and make all the labourers in the county join them ... their very first measures would have tended, in a serious manner, to increase that scarcity and high price of corn and provisions, to remedy which was the pretence of this insurrection and conspiracy.[100]

Kenyon expressed horror at such behaviour, 'little short of raising troops and levying war against the King and government of the country ... many thousand lives have been sacrificed in riots and insurrections which had beginnings as small and leaders as insignificant as the present'.

The promoters and ringleaders of this conspiracy were not persons in distress and suffering particularly by the hardships of the times, but clearly they were persons of unquiet and evil-disposed minds ... not want, but wickedness and discontent prompted them to this insurrection. They were actually in the habit of earning from 18s. to 20s. per week, in the work of hoeing beans ... The cry of Scarcity was with them only an ostensible, and not a real cause ...

but they were sufficiently artful for them to know it to be a popular cry . . . if they had been suffered to proceed, scarcity and famine would have marked their footsteps, and the country would have become a prey to devastation.[101]

The prisoners were sentenced to twelve months in the county gaol, and entered in recognizances for seven years. *The Times* suggested that the case be printed and posted up in every parish, 'that the farmers' men might have the advantage of reading as well as communicating it to such of their companions who cannot read'.[102] But Kenyon was a tired man, and his social philosophy came under attack. In December, *The Times* reported his temporary absence from his duties and his 'state of health and of mind', brought on by the loss of one son and the illness of another.[103] Among his letters from friends and well-wishers was one from Erskine, urging him not to retire.[104] Waddington's counsel defended both his client and *The Wealth of Nations*; the House of Commons had repealed the laws relating to forestalling and regrating because, he said, by preventing the free trade in corn, they had been the means of raising the price. In asking the jury to forget the high price of provisions, and to rid themselves of outmoded prejudice, Mr Dauncey was addressing a wider public.

He adverted to what was said by his Friend respecting Dr Adam Smith, and observed that his speculations were not the subject of ridicule. But if names were to be referred to, and opinions were to be given on the subject, he might appeal to the opinions of the first two men in the country, Mr Pitt and Mr Fox, who though they disagreed in many things, yet they were both of opinion that the trade of this country would be injured by the destruction of these middlemen.[105]

In the course of the year 1800, the cost of provisions and public attitudes to combinations, whether of factors, manufacturers or workmen, fluctuated considerably. In February, Whitbread attempted to introduce another Minimum Wage Bill, and obtained a first reading, but the second reading was postponed for six months. Magistrates at Houghton-le-Spring heard a complaint by pitmen that the coal owners, having contracted to supply their rye-meal at eight shillings per boll, were now charging ten. The court ordered the corn to be supplied at the contract price, and advertised their decision: 'This is inserted with a view to show that it is always best for the pitmen to lay their complaints before the magistrates ... it being impossible for the magistrates to attend to them when in a state of riot.'[106] Workers at Portsmouth dockyard unanimously resolved to abstain from purchasing whenever the market price exceeded 9 pence per pound for butter, twopence per quart for milk and sixpence per gallon for potatoes. The miners at Chesterfield fixed their own purchase price-list for all food items. The citizens of Newbury held a town-meeting and agreed to boy-cott butter until the price came down to a shilling a pound, and, at Nottingham, representatives of townspeople and farmers negotiated an agreement fixing corn at £4 per quarter instead of £7.[107] London appeared quiet, but the horse-guards and City Light Horse stood by to quell any disturbances over food prices, and there was talk of em-ploying the fire brigade in their place, to minimize bloodshed.[108]

Led by Sheridan, the opponents of the Combination Act at last began their campaign. The Lord Mayor presented to the Commons a petition from the journeymen workmen of the Cities of London and Westminster, praying for repeal of the 'injurious, unjust and oppressive' law. Other petitions came from the journeymen coopers and ship-wrights of Lancaster, from 7,000 workmen in Bristol, 3,043 in Plymouth and 2,469 in Bath. The petition of the cotton and calico makers of Manchester, depicting the Act as 'so vague and indefinite as to interfere with and misconstrue the most private conversation into combination', was presented by Sir Francis Burdett Jones.[109] On 4 July, Colonel Gascoyne brought up a Bill 'to explain and amend the Workmen's Combination Act', which was given a first reading. In its final form, the amending Act retained the prohibition on 'contracts, covenants and agreements' between workmen for obtaining an advance of wages, but the hearing would now be by two magistrates. There was an additional clause.

XVIII. And whereas it will be a great convenience and advantage to masters and journeymen engaged in manufactures, that a cheap and summary mode be established for settling all disputes that may arise between them respecting wages and work, ... in all cases that shall or may arise within the part of Great Britain called England, where the masters and workmen cannot agree respecting the price or prices to be paid for work actually done in any manufacture, or any injury or damage done or alleged to have been done by the workmen to the work ... and in all cases of dispute or difference, touching any contract or agreement for work or wages between masters and workmen in any trade or manufacture, which cannot be otherwise mutually adjusted and settled by and between them, it shall and may be, and it is hereby declared to be lawful for such masters and workmen . . . or either of them to demand and have an arbitration or reference of such matter or matters in dispute; and each of them is hereby authorised and empowered forthwith to nominate and appoint an arbitrator for and on his respective part and behalf . . . and the award to be made . . . shall in all cases be final and conclusive between the parties . . .[110]

The Solicitor-General was unhappy at this clause: the journeymen might nominate an 'improper person . . . a sort of Solicitor-General in that trade, who would no doubt be paid and indemnified for his genius', but it was finally accepted.[111]

There was a fine summer and prospects of a good harvest. 'The farmers in general are in despair at the prodigious crops thoughout the Kingdom.'[112] For a short time, the price of the loaf came down three assizes to 1s 0½d, only to return to 1s 3d within a fortnight after an 'enormous' rise in the cost of flour. In September, when the Assize price reached 1s 4½d, the long-feared riot broke out at Mark Lane, in the City of London. The corn market was closed, and tumults lasted a week, until the Lord Mayor reduced the loaf by a farthing. In November, with prices again climbing, Burke's *Thoughts and Details of Scarcity* was published, the Committee on the High Price of Provisions issued its report and a proclamation urged economy in bread consumption. Unknown persons distributed handbills headed 'FAMINE', which called on tradesmen, artisans, journeymen and labourers to assemble on Kennington Common on Sunday 9 November to petition the King and Parliament for reduced food prices, higher wages or the means to emigrate.[113] On Sunday morning, a large force of cavalry, the Volunteer Corps and all available police constables moved on to the common, and the magistrates established themselves in the Horns Tavern, 'to partake of a good dinner'. Attracted by the display, a crowd of 400 gathered outside the tavern, and a magistrate, Mr Ford, came out and told them to disperse. There was a heavy shower of rain, but two men remained and were arrested for loitering: one, a journeyman named Harry Featherstone, 'was much intoxicated', but his companion, Dick Sewell, was a local master shoemaker and, according to Cobbett, 'a known Jacobin'.[114]

Just before Christmas, the price of bread jumped from 1s 7½d to 1s 9d. In the Commons debate on the high prices of provisions, the Prime Minister said 'he had a high opinion of the good sense of the people of this country, and he considered the patience which they manifested on the present occasion with pleasure and with pride, and if he might be allowed the expression, with gratitude'.[115] The first case under the new Combination Act was heard at Guildhall, when James Wilson and W. Wood, journeymen cabinet-makers, received two months in Bridewell for inciting workmen at Messrs Oakley, Shackleton and Evans to hold meetings for a new book of prices, to impose a fine of half a guinea on anyone introducing a new journeyman to the firm, and to collect subscriptions for men on strike under cover of a sick fund.[116] *The Times* devoted another leading article to the trade unions.

Conspiracies have been set on foot by Journeymen of various Trades, to enforce an augmentation of wages, which have been very properly resisted by the Masters, and repressed by the Magistrates. As the case of some of them is to be tried by Appeal at the Quarter Sessions, we shall abstain at present from any particular reflections. In general, however, we do not conceive the high price of provisions to fall with that degree of severity upon any of those classes of men, which (compared with the lower mechanic and the agricultural labourer) can authorise even complaint in their mouths. They do not certainly bear more than their share of the general pressure, and if every man who feels the burthen of these times is to revolt from his employment, and to discontinue his industry, society is disorganized at once. We trust the Journeymen, whose wages appear to be at least three times those of the laborious men who produce corn for them, will acknowledge their indiscretion, and return to work at once. Let them compare their lot with so many of their fellow-creatures, and then say whose wounds ought to be redressed first.[117]

As the century closed, the London journeymen tailors addressed themselves to their masters. 'Gentlemen', they began,

feeling along with the rest of the great body of the working part of community the extreme pressure of the times by the excessive price of every necessary article of life, have long waited with patient anxiety . . . and as a great majority of the principal Masters have, with a generosity that does them great honor, agreed to grant us an advance of wages, the Journeymen Taylors . . . are in hopes that the benevolent conduct of those Masters will be followed by Masters in general.[118]

A petition for amendment to the Tailors' Act was presented by the master tailors to the House of Commons. Thousands of journeymen tailors were on strike throughout London; the stalwart Flints were demanding thirty shillings, and were at last joined by the pieceworking Dungs, who aspired to 27s. As if the Combination Acts had never been, the masters appealed to the Home Secretary to invoke the traditional remedies, and

> order and direct the magistrates in their respective divisions to summon before them the landlords of the different houses of call and admonish and forewarn them against suffering these Societies upon pain of forfeiting their licences, or that your Grace will adopt such measures for their suppressing as to your Grace shall seem expedient.[119]

A strike of tailors presented no threat to London's essential supplies, to the nation's commerce, nor to public order. His Grace read through the Humble Memorial, then wrote a short note which he attached to it: 'I do not know, that as Secretary of State, I have any right to interfere that every magistrate does not possess equally with me.'[120]

10 EPILOGUE: A CONSERVATIVE INTERPRETATION OF LABOUR HISTORY

The study of labour history has for generations been an essential element in trade union education, but in recent years has attracted a much wider public. The 'lessons of history' are drawn upon not only to explain the development of modern society, but also to justify the behaviour of groups within it. Contemporary ideologies influence the selection and presentation of historical evidence. Strikes and industrial disputes are studied in the context of class and class conflict; trade unions are identified as a challenge to capitalist enterprise and, ultimately, therefore, as in opposition to the whole associated system of social, legal and political relationships.

Closely related to this perspective is another: of trade unionism as a response to the process of industrialization. Economic and social historiography makes much of the concept of 'industrial revolutions' in Britain, Europe and America in the course of the nineteenth century. In this model, trade unions were the workers' defences against the evils flowing from division of labour, powered machinery, the factory system, large-scale business organization, exploitation and bureaucracy. The Industrial Revolution in Britain is commonly the point of departure for trade union histories, as is the French Revolution for parallel studies of working-class political organization. Whilst it would be absurd to ignore the economic and social consequences of widespread technological change, it is possible to exaggerate the contribution of the factory system to the rise of the trade union movement. As late as the 1860s and 1870s, unionized workers were mostly to be found outside factory employment, and it was

> the members of the 'trades' — carpenters and bricklayers, printers and bookbinders, engineers and shoemakers — who took the lead in the establishment of a national congress of the unions, which met annually from 1868; and it need not surprise us that this was not called a labour congress but rather a trades' congress . . . under which name it has ever since been known.[1]

All these trades had traditions of union organization going back far beyond the industrial and political 'revolutions' of the eighteenth and nineteenth centuries, and in some cases continuities can be traced to Stuart or even Tudor times. Whereas in France similar continuities were interrupted by the Revolution of 1789, no such break occurred in Britain. The Combination Acts of 1799 and 1800 had little effect on the evolution of trade unionism, and had become superfluous long before their repeal in 1824. Early unions in America closely resembled those of Britain in membership, structure, policy and growth, and the craft tradition persisted long after the rise of mass production.[2]

The present pattern of British trade unionism and industrial relations can only be understood in a very long temporal perspective. Industrial attitudes and experience which are commonly attributed to modern technology (alienation, impersonality, monotony, fragmentation of work) were equally present in the pre-industrial workplace. Romantic nostalgia for the 'harmonious' work relationships of the domestic and workshop system is largely founded on a myth. Personal relationships may have been closer, but they were far from conflict-free, and the rise of the factory and bureaucratic organization may in fact have improved them. At all times, the realities of economic life have obliged masters and men to associate to protect their group interests; if, in eighteenth-century England, the emergence of interest-groups was resented as 'combination' against the public interest, their survival and growth was inevitable in an open, relatively tolerant society.

Strikes, restrictive practices, autocratic management and obstinate labour are in an old tradition, part of our national heritage. Few features of modern industrial disputes cannot be traced to pre-industrial times. Most institutions and procedures to handle and channel industrial conflict – collective agreements, compulsory arbitration, productivity bargaining, prices and incomes policies – were rehearsed in the reign of George III: only the terminology remained to be invented. The assumptions and values of an eighteenth-century system of labour relations persist in a 'post-industrial' age, supposedly regulated by science, rationality, planning, management-by-objectives and programmed decision making; yet, every day, reason fights a losing battle with tradition, as 'scientific' management stumbles over 'irrational' custom and practice.

How could such a system have survived for more than two centuries? In part because of an essential continuity in economic, technological and political change. In part because a tradition of behaviour is indestructible. 'Nothing that ever belonged to it is completely lost; we are always swerving back to recover and make topical out of even its remotest moments; and nothing remains for long unmodified.'[3]

Institutions of industrial relations have adjusted to social change, if slowly and reluctantly. 'A viable system of collective bargaining takes many years to develop. It requires the establishment of attitudes of mutual forbearance, and the realization by employers that they are playing a game rather than the extinction of their opponents.'[4] Irrespective of ideology or wider aspiration, the trade unionist's role is equally constrained by the immediate interests and pressures of his fellow-members: to preserve jobs, to protect status, to improve wages, to defend differentials, to challenge arbitrary or incompetent management, and to raise the quality of working life. It is a pragmatic role, drawing upon precedent, experience and habit, an unending exercise in negotiation and compromise, and as necessary as it is conservative.

APPENDIX: A LIST OF LABOUR DISPUTES, 1717-1800

Year	Trade or occupation	Place(s)	Principal issue(s)
1717	Woollen weaving	Tiverton Taunton Collumpton	Wage reduction, imports
1718	Coachbuilding (wheel-wrights)	London	Wages and hours of work
1720	Leather dressing (curriers)	London	Wage increase
1720	Tailoring	London	Wages and hours of work
1721	Tailoring	Windsor	Wage increase
1721	Tailoring	Cambridge	Wage increase
1721	Woollen weaving	Taunton	Wage increase
1723	Serge weaving	Crediton	Wage increase
1724	Woollen weaving	Newbury	Wage reduction
1724	Bay making	Colchester	Wage reduction
1724	Woollen weaving and combing	Bradninch Collumpton Uffculm Cullumstock	Wage increase
1725	Bay making	Colchester	Wage reduction
1725	Woolcombing	Alton	Apprenticeship
1725	Woollen weaving	Taunton	Wage reduction
1726	Woollen weaving	Wiltshire Somerset	Combination Bill
1726	Woollen weaving	Bristol	Arrest of workman
1727	Woollen weaving	Wiltshire	Combination Bill
1727	Coal mining	Bristol	Coal imports, turnpikes
1728	Peruke making	Dublin	Apprenticeship
1728	Tailoring	Dublin	Apprenticeship
1728	Woollen weaving	Bristol	Wage reduction
1729	Naval dockyard (rope-makers and sailmakers)	Woolwich	Arrears of wages, apprenticeship
1729	Woollen weaving	Bristol	Piecework prices

Year	Trade or occupation	Place(s)	Principal issue(s)
1730	Weaving	Braintree	Imported yarn
1730		Coggeshall	(Irish)
1731	Cabinet- and chair-making	London	Hours of work
1731	Bargemen	Reading	Wage increase
1731	Coal mining	Newcastle-upon-Tyne	Increased size of coal baskets
1731	Smiths	Dublin	Employment 'below price'
1731	Hosiery	Dublin	Employment 'below price'
1731	Narrow weaving	Dublin	Employment 'below price'
1731	Linen weaving	Dublin	Wage increase
1731	Silk handkerchief weaving	Dublin	Wage increase
1731	Woollen weaving	Bristol	Wage reduction
1732	Lighterage (Trinity House)	Port of London	Ballast regulations
1732	Nailmaking	Dublin	Employment 'under price'
1732	Cooperage	Cork	Wage increase
1732	Clothworking	City of London	Wages and hours of work
1733	Woollen weaving	Bristol	Employment 'under price'
1733	Baking (masters and journeymen)	Dublin	Assize of Bread
1734	Coachbuilding (wheel-wrights)	London	Wage increase and reduction of hours of work
1734	Weaving	Dublin	Imported cloth
1736	Building (labourers)	Shoreditch	Employment of Irishmen
1736	Silk weaving	Spitalfields	Employment of Irishmen
1736	Farming and market gardening	Dartford	Employment of Irishmen
1736	Farming (labourers)	Essex	Employment of Irishmen
1736	Shoemaking	Shoreditch	Employment of Irishmen
1736	Baking	Dublin	Assize of Bread

Year	Trade or occupation	Place(s)	Principal issue(s)
1737	Tailoring	London and Westminster	Wage increase
1737	Bargemen	Hertfordshire	Wage reduction
1738	Woolcombing	Tiverton	Wage reduction
1738	Woollen weaving	Collumpton	Payment in truck
1738	Woollen weaving	Melksham	Payment in truck
1738	Coal mining	Kingswood Bristol	Wage reduction
1738	Nailmaking	Halesowen	Guarantee of piece-prices
1738	Coal trade (keelmen)	Newcastle-upon-Tyne	Wage increase
1738	Coal mining	Croxdale, Newcastle	Wage reduction
1739	Silk weaving	Spitalfields	Wage reduction
1739	Naval dockyards (ship-wrights, carpenters and smiths)	Chatham Woolwich Deptford	Wage increase and perquisites ('chips')
1739	Merchant shipping	Southampton	Wage increase
1740	Web spinning	Bocking, Essex	Wage reduction
1741	Woollen weaving	Bradford-on-Avon Trowbridge	—
1743	Woollen weaving	Bradninch	Payment in truck
1743	Broadcloth weaving	Leeds	Wage increase
1744	Glazings	London	Wage increase and hours of work
1744	Nailmaking	Walsall	Wage increase
1744	Tailoring	London and Westminster	Wage increase
1744	Peruke making	Holborn and Westminster	Working hours
1745	Baking	City of London	Sunday baking
1745	Coachbuilding (wheelwrights)	Holborn Westminster Southwark	Wage increase
1746	Coal trade (carmen and wharfingers' labourers)	Westminster	Wage increase

Year	Trade or occupation	Place(s)	Principal issue(s)
1746	Merchant shipping	Bristol	Wage increase
1747	Woolcombing	Norwich	Apprenticeship
1747	Barbers and peruke makers	City of London	Board wages
1747	Weaving	Dublin	Wage increase
1748	Tailoring	Edinburgh	–
1749	Joinery	London	Wage increase
1749	Farming (reapers)	Tranent	Wage increase
1749	House-painting	City of London	Employment of non-freeman
1750	Merchant shipping (East India Company)	London	Wage increase
1750	Woollen weaving	Dublin	Wage increase
1750	Building (masons)	London	–
1750	Woolcombing and weaving	Tiverton	Imported worsted (Irish)
1750	Woollen weaving	Trowbridge Melksham Bradford-on-Avon	–
1750	Coal trade (keelmen)	Newcastle-upon-Tyne	Increased work-load
1751	Tailoring	Dublin	Wage increase
1751	Tailoring	Westminster	Wage increase and shorter working day
1751	Royal Navy	London	Bounty money
1752	Woollen weaving	Bradford-on-Avon	–
1752	Woolcombing	Norwich	Wage reduction
1752	Velvet weaving	Cork	Employment of apprentices
1752	Timber (sawyers)	Bristol	Employment 'below price'
1752	Woolcombing	Tiverton	Limitation of apprentices by journeymen's society
1753	Building (carpenters, joiners, bricklayers)	Manchester	Wage increase

Year	Trade or occupation	Place(s)	Principal issue(s)
1754	House-painting	London	Wage increase
1754	Tailoring	Dublin	Wage increase and shorter working day
1754	Weaving	Paisley	Wage reduction
1755	Unspecified workmen	Bristol	Wage increase
1755	Naval dockyard (shipwrights)	Chatham	Perquisite of 'chips'
1756	Tailoring and staymaking	London	Wage increase and reduction in hours of work
1756	Tailoring	Liverpool	Wage increase
1756	Barbers and wig makers	London	Deductions for board; board wages
1756	Shoemaking	Liverpool	Wage reduction
1756	Farriery	London	Hours of work
1756	Shoemaking	Chester	Wage parity
1756	Woollen weaving	Stroud	Wage assessment by magistrates
1756	Pewter and copperware	Liverpool	Employment of 'interlopers'
1757	Naval dockyard (carpenters and shipwrights)	Woolwich	Perquisite of 'chips'
1757	Pottery	Liverpool	Employment 'below price'
1758	Check weaving	Manchester Salford Rusholme Pendleton	Wage increase
1758	Naval dockyard (shipwrights)	Deptford	
1758	Baize weaving	Braintree	Withdrawal of perquisite of 'thrums'
1759	Shearing	Dublin	Wage increase
1760	Weaving	Kendal	Wage increase
1760	Check making	Wigan	Hours of work
1760	Leather dressing (curriers)	London	Wage increase
1760	Woolcombing	Derby	Wage increase

Year	Trade or occupation	Place(s)	Principal issue(s)
1760	Cabinet-making	Liverpool Manchester	Hours of work
1761	Gold and silver wire-drawing	City of London	Wage increase; apprenticeship
1761	Carpentry (stands for coronation ceremony)	Westminster Abbey	Withdrawal of perquisite of 'entrance fees' from members of the public
1761	Cabinet-making	Holborn and Westminster	Wage increase and shorter working day
1761	Cabinet-making	Manchester	Employment of non-unionist
1761	Silverware (silversmiths)	London	Wage increase
1761	Farming (reapers)	Ely and King's Langley	Wage increase
1762	Bakery	City of London	Sunday baking
1762	Merchant shipping	Liverpool	Wage reduction
1762	Timber (sawyers)	Liverpool	Method of wage fixing
1762	Silk weaving	Spitalfields	Wage reduction
1762	Leather (curriers)	Bristol	Earnings reduction
1762	Linen weaving	Dublin	Wage increase
1763	Haymaking	Islington	Wage increase
1763	Silverware	London	Hours of work
1763	Silk weaving	Spitalfields	Wage reduction
1763-4	Tailoring	London	Wage increase
1764	Tailoring	Aberdeen	Wage increase
1764	Coal mining	Scotland	Wage increase
1764	Weaving	Carrick	Apprenticeship
1764	Building (masons)	Edinburgh	Wage increase
1765	Timber (sawyers)	Liverpool	–
1765	Coal mining	Newcastle-upon-Tyne	Change in hiring system
1765	Tailoring	Liverpool	Employment of non-unionist
1765	Building (labourers)	Holborn	Wage increase

Year	Trade or occupation	Place(s)	Principal issue(s)
1765	Weaving	Coventry	Wage increase
1766	Haymaking	Islington	Wage increase
1766	Shoemaking	London	Apprenticeship
1767	Silk weaving	Spitalfields	Wage reduction
1767	Tailoring	London	Wage increase
1767	Bookbinding	London	–
1768	Timber (sawyers)	Limehouse	Introduction of wind-powered sawmill
1768	Merchant shipping (East India and Hudson's Bay Companies)	Deptford Pool of London	Wage increase
1768	Lighterage	London	Wage increase
1768	Cooperage	Wapping	Introduction of large vats
1768	Canal building	(Ware-Thames)	Wage increase
1768	Spectacle making (glass grinders)	Southwark	Wage increase
1768	Gardening (lawn trimmers)	Paisley	Wage increase
1768	Tailoring	London	Wage increase
1768	Hatmaking	London	Wage increase
1768	Coal trade (coalheavers)	Wapping	Wage increase
1768	Merchant shipping (West India trade)	Limehouse	Wage increase
1768	Silk weaving	Spitalfields	Wage increase
1768	Silk weaving	Manchester	Employment of non-unionists
1768	Canal building (bankers)	Boston	–
1768	Weaving	Carlisle	Wage increase
1768	Merchant shipping	Port Glasgow Greenock	Wage increase
1768	Shoemaking	London	Wage increase
1769	Merchant shipping (East India Company)	Gravesend	Wage increase
1769	Merchant shipping (Greenland trade)	Tyne	Wage increase
1769	Silk weaving	Spitalfields	Wage increase
1769	Coal mining	Newcastle-upon-Tyne	
1769	Coal trade (keelmen)	Newcastle-upon-Tyne	–

Year	Trade or occupation	Place(s)	Principal issue(s)
1769	Woolcombing	Aberdeen	Wage increase; employment of apprentices
1769	Linen weaving	Dublin	Wage increase
1769	Building (carpenters, bricklayers, masons, labourers)	London (Strand)	Dismissal of foreman
1769	Baking	Dublin	Wage increase
1769	Cooperage	Dublin	Wage increase
1770	Tailoring	City of London Westminster	Wage increase
1770	Merchant shipping (East India Company)	London Gravesend	Wage increase
1770	Hatmaking (dyers)	Southwark	Work 'under price'
1770	Woollen weaving	Leeds	Work 'under price'
1770	Leather dressing	Southwark	Work 'under price'
1771	Merchant shipping	Tyne	Wage increase
1771	Tailoring and staymaking	London	Wage increase
1771	Silk weaving	Spitalfields	Wage increase
1771	Coal trade (coalheavers)	London	Wage increase
1771	Coal trade (keelmen)	Newcastle-upon-Tyne	–
1772	Merchant shipping (East India Company)	Wapping	Wage increase
1772	Shoemaking	Manchester	Wage increase
1772	Leather dressing (curriers)	London	Wage increase
1773	Hosiery (stocking makers)	Leicester	Introduction of faster machinery
1773	Shipbuilding and repair (apprentice shipwrights)	Liverpool	–
1773	Merchant shipping	Greenock	Additional payment
1773	Merchant shipping	London	Employment of foreigners
1773	Hosiery (stocking weavers)	Nottingham	Introduction of new machinery
1773	Bargemen	Maidenhead	Introduction of horses for towing
1774	Haymaking	Hendon	Employment of

Year	Trade or occupation	Place(s)	Principal issue(s)
		Mill Hill	Irishmen 'below price'
1774	Haymaking	Islington	—
1774	Sugar-baking	Tower Hamlets	—
1775	Naval dockyards	Plymouth Portsmouth Chatham Woolwich Deptford	Wage increase; task-work
1775	Haymaking	Islington	Wage increase
1775	Merchant shipping	Liverpool	Wage reduction
1775	Troopships (sailors)	Wapping	Wage increase
1775	Building (bricklayers)	Marylebone	Wage increase
1775	Coal trade (seamen)	Shields Sunderland	—
1775	Weaving	Keighley	Wage increase
1775	Ironworks (coal miners)	Carronhill Kinnaird	Wage increase
1776	Building (carpenters)	Holborn Westminster Southwark	Wage increase
1776	Building (masons)	City of London Westminster	Wage increase
1776	Timber (sawyers)	Wapping	Work 'under price'
1776	Breeches making (leather)	London	Wage increase
1776	Bakery	Dublin	—
1776	Wool cloth manufacture	Shepton Mallet	Introduction of machinery
1777	Coal trade (seamen)	Shields Sunderland	Double wages
1777	Building (carpenters)	London	—
1777	Woolcombing	Bradford (Yorks)	Wage increase
1777	Sword-hilt making	London	Wage increase
1777	Tailoring	City of London Westminster Southwark	Wage increase

Year	Trade or occupation	Place(s)	Principal issue(s)
1777	Tailoring	Birmingham	Wages
1777	Hatmaking	London	Wage increase; apprenticeship
1777	Hatmaking	Manchester	Employment of non-unionist
1777	Shoemaking	London	Wage increase
1777	Tailoring	Leeds	Wage increase
1777	Chair-making (carvers)	Westminster	–
1778	Woollen weaving	Dublin	Imported cloth (English)
1778	Cabinet-making	Manchester	Piecework price-lists
1779	Hosiery (stocking makers)	Nottingham	Delay in Wage Regulation Bill
1779	Coal trade (coalheavers)	London	–
1779	Cotton spinning	Chorley Bolton Bury and Ratcliff Toddington Stockport Altrincham Preston	Introduction of water-powered machinery
1779	Fortifications (miners)	Plymouth	Wage increase
1780	Woollen manufacture	Hunslet	Construction of scribbling mill
1780	Hatmaking	Manchester	–
1780	Royal Navy	HMS *Invincible* and *Thunderer*	Non-payment of wages
1781	Woollen manufacture	Frome	Introduction of spinning jenny
1781	Coachbuilding (wheelwrights)	London	Wage increase
1783	Royal Navy	London	Arrears of wages and prize-money
1783	Merchant shipping	London	Employment of foreigners 'at lower wages'
1783	Hatmaking (finishers)	London	Subcontracting of work
1783	Hatmaking	Manchester	–

Year	Trade or occupation	Place(s)	Principal issue(s)
1783	Merchant shipping (West India trade)	Montego Bay (London reg?)	Extra payment for home run
1783	Cloth dressing	Ludlow	Construction of dressing-mill
1783	Shearing	West Port Edinburgh	Wage increase
1783	Hosiery (stocking makers)	Nottingham	Wage reduction
1784	Woollen weaving	Tiverton	Wage reduction
1784	Building (masons)	Manchester	—
1784	Serge making (fullers)	Exeter	Employment of non-freeman; number of apprentices
1785	Coal mining	Newcastle-upon-Tyne	Wage increase
1785	Coal trade (keelmen)	Sunderland	Wage increase
1785	Coal trade (seamen)	Shields	Wage increase and victuals when in harbour
1785	Newspaper printing (compositors)	London	Piecework prices
1785	Linen weaving	Darlington	Wage increase
1785	Hatmaking	Manchester Stockport	Employment of apprentices
1785	Building (joiners)	Liverpool	Wage increase
1785	Cabinet-making	London	Wage increase
1786	Calico printing	Manchester	Introduction of cylinder printing
1786	Check calendering	Manchester	Employment of learners
1786	Weaving	Reading	—
1786	Bookbinding	London	Hours of work
1786	Felt hatmaking	London	—
1786	Silk weaving	Manchester	Wage regulation; apprenticeship
1787	Wool sorting	Exeter	Wage increase
1787	Stocking making	Nottingham	Introduction of machine frame
1787	Stocking making (wool spinners)	Leicester	Introduction of spinning jenny

Year	Trade or occupation	Place(s)	Principal issue(s)
1787	Carpet weaving	Leeds	Wage increase
1787	Weaving	Glasgow	Wage reduction
1787	Woollen weaving	Bradford-on-Avon Trowbridge	Grouping of narrow looms in workshops
1787	Building (carpenters and joiners)	London	Wage increase
1787	Broad weavers	Dublin	Wage increase
1787	Coal trade (seamen)	Newcastle-upon-Tyne Shields	Wage increase
1787	Coachbuilding (wheel-wrights)	City of London	Apprenticeship
1787	Cutlery	Sheffield	Piece-prices (13 knives to the dozen)
1789	Coal mining	Northumberland Durham	—
1789	Papermaking	Edinburgh	Wage increase
1789	Weaving	Carlisle	—
1789	Gold and silver wire-drawing	London	Wage increase
1789	Papermaking	Kent	Wage increase
1789	Papermaking	Hatfield	Wage increase
1790	Linen manufacture	Dublin	Demarcation (employment of silk weavers)
1790	Coal trade (seamen)	Newcastle-upon-Tyne Shields	Wage reduction (withdrawal of war bonuses)
1790	Cloth manufacture	Dublin	Introduction of 'gig mill'
1790	Timber (sawyers)	Dublin	Wage increase
1790	Hosiery (framework-knitters)	Nottingham	—
1790	Scissors grinding	Sheffield	Piecework prices
1791	Wool spinning and weaving	Bradford-on-Avon	Introduction of carding machines and spinning jennies

Year	Trade or occupation	Place(s)	Principal issue(s)
1791	Cutlery	Hereford-shire	Wage increase
1791	Weaving	Carrick	Introduction of 'spring-loom'
1791	Bay weaving	Colchester	Wage increase
1791	Stocking making	Dereham Swaffham	Wage increase
1791	Hat making	Dereham Swaffham	Wage increase
1791	Hat finishing	Manchester	—
1791	Coal trade (keelmen)	Newcastle-upon-Tyne	Wage increase
1791	Wool trade (woolstapler's journeymen)	Southwark	—
1791	Coal mining	Whitehaven	—
1791	Woolcombing	Halifax	Wage increase
1791	Weaving	Kendal	Wage increase
1791	Ironworks (coal miners and foundrymen)	Colebrook-dale	Wage and hours of work
1791	Dockyard (carpenters)	Liverpool	Wages
1791	Pottery	Stoke-on-Trent	—
1792	Shoemaking	City of London Westminster	Wage increase
1792	Shoemaking	Nottingham	Wage increase
1792	Tailoring	Dublin	—
1792	Stocking weaving	Leicester	—
1792	Brass trade	Birmingham	Wage increase
1792	Woolcombing	Woodchester (Glos)	Introduction of 'scribbling machines'
1792	Coal mining	Sheffield	Wage increase
1792	Merchant shipping	Dublin	Supplementary payments ('kettle-money')
1792	Merchant shipping	Leith	Wage increase
1792	Merchant shipping	Yarmouth	Wage increase
1792	Merchant shipping	Shields	Wage increase

Year	Trade or occupation	Place(s)	Principal issue(s)
1792	Merchant shipping	Ipswich	Wage increase
1792	Woollen weaving	Trowbridge	Introduction of labour-saving machinery
1792	Coal mining	Kingswood Radstock Paulton Timsbrough (Som.)	Wage increase
1792	Coal mining	Rothwell Haigh (nr. Leeds)	Wage increase
1792	Leather dressing (curriers)	City of London Westminster Southwark	Wage increase
1792	Tailoring	Bristol	Wage increase
1792	Merchant shipping	Bristol	Wage increase
1792	Building (masons)	Bristol	Wage increase
1792	Building (bricklayers)	Bristol	Wage increase
1792	Flax dressing (hecklers)	West Ferry (Lincs)	Wage increase
1792	Pottery	Staffordshire	Wage increase
1792	Carpentry	Liverpool	Wage increase
1792	Coal trade (flat-boat men)	Liverpool	Wage increase
1792	Coal mining	Wigan	Wage increase
1792	Merchant shipping	Lynn	Wage increase
1792	Port workers	Lynn	Wage increase
1792	Merchant shipping	Aberdeen	Wage increase
1792	Scythemaking	Sheffield	Wage increase
1793	Shag weaving	Banbury	Employment of apprentice
1793	Merchant shipping (ship's carpenters)	Newcastle-upon-Tyne	Wage increase
1793	Coal mining	Washington Birtley (Northumberland)	Wage increase
1793	Coal trade (keelmen)	Sunderland	Wage increase
1793	Various occupations	Sunderland	Wage increase

Year	Trade or occupation	Place(s)	Principal issue(s)
1793	Naval dockyard (shipwrights)	Chatham	Loss of overtime
1793	Wool spinning	Gloucester-shire	Introduction of spinning jennies
1793	Naval dockyard (rope-makers)	Plymouth	Dismissal of work-man (misconduct)
1793	Canal building (bankers)	Stamford	Arrest of work-men (fighting)
1793	Nailmaking	Dudley	Wage increase
1793	Coal mining	Dudley	Wage increase
1793	Lamplighting	London	Wage increase
1793	Coal trade (carmen and coal porters)	London	Wage increase
1793	Saddlers	City of London Westminster	Hours of work
1793	Bakery	London	Sunday baking
1793	Farming (labourers)	Potton (Beds)	Wage increase
1793	Farming (labourers)	Thaxted (Essex)	Wage increase
1793	Printing (pressmen)	London	Apprenticeship
1793	Copper mining	Truro	Increased ore prices
1793	Ropemaking	Shadwell	–
1794	Hosiery (framework-knitters)	Nottingham	Wage reduction
1794	Coal trade (keelmen)	Newcastle-upon-Tyne	Introduction of 'spouts' for loading colliers
1794	Saddlery	London	–
1794	Shoemaking	Leicester	Wage increase
1794	Bookbinders	London	Working hours
1794	Papermaking	Kent	Wage increase
1795	Serge making (fullers)	Exeter	Wage increase
1795	Flourmill maintenance (millwrights)	London Bridge	Wage increase
1795	Naval dockyard (shipwrights)	Chatham	Employment of house-carpenters and joiners
1795	Coal trade (coalheavers,	London	Wage increase

Year	Trade or occupation	Place(s)	Principal issue(s)
	whippers, porters)		and payment for 'idle time'
1795	Tailoring	London	Wage increase
1795	Coal trade (keelmen)	Carlisle	Introduction of 'spouts'
1795	Dockyards (ship-riggers)	Thames	Wage increase
1795	Farming and market gardening (labourers)	Monkton Minster (Kent)	Wage increase; victuals and perquisites
1795	Bargemen	Ware (Herts)	Wage increase
1796	Building (bricklayers)	Grays Inn Lane, London	Wage increase
1796	Shoemaking	Glasgow	Wage increase
1796	Cutlery (spring- and table-knife makers)	Sheffield	Wage increase
1797	Woollen manufacture	Crossflats (Yorks)	Introduction of cloth-raising mill
1797	Royal Navy	Spithead Portsmouth Plymouth The Nore	Wage increase, provisions (initially conventional labour dispute, becoming large-scale mutiny)
1797	Papermaking	Kent	—
1798	Sugar trade (coopers)	Pool of London	Wage increase
1798	Coal mining	Dudley	Wage increase
1798	Cotton manufacture (spinners)	Manchester	Wage increase; employment 'under price'
1798	Printing (pressmen)	London	Employment of apprentices
1798	Coal trade (coalheavers)	London	—
1798	Shoemaking	London	Wage increase; employment of apprentices
1799	Flourmill maintenance (millwrights)	London Bridge	Wage increase
1799	Bakery	London	Wage increase

Year	*Trade or occupation*	*Place(s)*	*Principal issue(s)*
1799	Coal trade (seamen)	Shields	Wage increase
1799	Hatmaking	Stockport	Employment of non-unionists
1799	Shoemaking	Edinburgh	Wage increase
1799	Shoemaking	Newcastle-upon-Tyne	Wage increase
1799	Woolcombing	Darlington	Employment of non-unionist
1799	Tailoring	Edinburgh	Wage increase
1799	Shoemaking	Hull	Wage increase
1800	Cabinet-making	City of London	Wage increase
1800	Farming (labourers)	Steeple Dengie (nr Burnham-on-Crouch, Essex)	Wage increase
1800	Tailoring	City of London Westminster	Wage increase

NOTES AND REFERENCES

INTRODUCTION

1. H. Pelling, *A History of British Trade Unionism* (Harmondsworth, 1963), p. 9.
2. See W. Brown, 'A Consideration of Custom and Practice', *British Journal of Industrial Relations*, vol. X, no. 1 (1972); also M. Terry, 'The Inevitable Growth of Informality', *BJIR*, vol. XV, no. 1 (1977).
3. T.S. Ashton and Joseph Sykes, *The Coal Industry of the Eighteenth Century*, 2nd edn (Manchester, 1964), p. 133.
4. G.D.H. Cole and R. Postgate, *The Common People 1746-1946* (London, 1966 edn), pp. 169, 172.
5. Sidney and Beatrice Webb, *The History of Trade Unionism* (London, 1920 edn), pp. 46-51; F.W. Galton, *Select Documents illustrating the History of Trade Unionism: (i) The Tailoring Trade* (London, 1923 edn); George Unwin, *Industrial Organization in the Sixteenth and Seventeenth Centuries* (London, 1904).
6. H. Heaton, *The Yorkshire Woollen and Worsted Industries* (Oxford, 1920, reprinted 1965); A.P. Wadsworth and J. de L. Mann, *The Cotton Trade and Industrial Lancashire 1600-1780* (Manchester, 1831, reprinted, 1965); W.G. Hoskins, *Industry, Trade and People in Exeter*, 2nd edn (Exeter, 1968); M. Dorothy George, *London Life in the Eighteenth Century* (London, 1925).
7. Cf. M. Beer, *A History of British Socialism*, one-volume edn (London, 1948), pp. 137-8.
8. Webbs, *Trade Unionism*, pp. 22-6.
9. Arnold Toynbee, *Lectures on the Industrial Revolution of the Eighteenth Century* (London, 1919), p. 206; F. Engels, *The Condition of the Working Class in England*, trans. W.O. Henderson and W.H. Chaloner (Manchester, 1958), Ch. 9.
10. Toynbee, *Industrial Revolution*, pp. 198-9.
11. Samuel Bamford, *Early Days* (London, 1849), p. 120.
12. *Henson's History of the Framework Knitters* (1831, reprinted Newton Abbott, 1970), pp. 376-83, 418-21.
13. E.J. Hobsbawm, *Labouring Men* (London, 1964), pp. 5-17.
14. G. Rudé, *The Crowd in History* (New York, 1964), pp. 68, 77.
15. Rinaldo Rigola, cit. Hobsbawm, *Labouring Men*, p. 10.
16. Galton, *Tailoring Trade*, pp. 88-95.
17. *Lloyd's Evening Post*, 18-20 November 1761.
18. *Lloyd's Evening Post*, 18-20 November 1777.
19. *An Account of the Rise and Progress of the Dispute between Masters and Journeymen Printers* (London, 1799).
20. An 'industrial-relations system' is defined here as a set of arrangements for institutionalizing disputes over the rules of work, with a view to joint regulation. 'Industrial relations thus become the management of conflict looking towards agreement, where each party recognizes the right of the other parties to exist and the legitimacy of their claim to be heard'. Jack Barbash, 'The Elements of Industrial Relations', *BJIR*, vol. II, no. 1 (1964).
21. *Lloyd's Evening Post*, 10 January 1797.

172 Notes and References

22. Henson, *Framework Knitters*, p. 116.
23. See *Old Bailey Sessions Papers* (1771) (trial of Stroud and Campbell for the murder of Daniel Clarke), pp. 356 ff.
24. *Lloyd's Evening Post*, 9-11 May 1768.
25. See G. Rudé, *Paris and London in the Eighteenth Century* (London, 1969), p. 57.

CHAPTER 1

1. J.H. Plumb, *England in the Eighteenth Century* (Harmondsworth, 1950), p. 11.
2. K.G.J.C. Knowles, *Strikes* (Oxford, 1952), p. 2.
3. *St. James's Chronicle*, 5-7 May, 7-10 May 1768.
4. *Lloyd's Evening Post*, 26-28 March 1764; Robert Galloway, *Annals of Coal Mining and the Coal Trade* (London, 1898, reprinted Newton Abbot, 1971), p. 269.
5. *London Journal*, 11 October 1729; *Daily Advertiser*, 29 June 1731; *Lloyd's Evening Post*, 6-8 March 1771, 29-31 May 1776, 20-23 May 1785, 18-20 July 1792.
6. Lord Mulgrave, in the debate on the Navy estimates, House of Commons, 13 February 1782.
7. B. Howard (ed.), *Records of the County of Wiltshire* (Devizes, 1932), pp. 259-60.
8. William Brewer the second, who 'drove the greatest trade for medleys of any clothier in England', settled in Trowbridge about 1651. By 1674 he had recruited 'a whole colony' of Dutch workers. See J. de L. Mann, *The Cloth Industry in the West of England from 1640 to 1880* (Oxford, 1971), pp. 8, 12, 78, 116.
9. *House of Commons Journals*, vol. 15 (26 February 1706), p. 312.
10. Ibid., p. 313.
11. *Evening Post*, 19-21 November 1717.
12. Ibid., 10-12 April 1718.
13. Greater London Council Record Office, *Middlesex Sessions Book*, September 1720.
14. D.B. Horn and Mary Ransome, *English Historical Documents*, vol. X. (1714-83) (London, 1957), pp. 484-6.
15. *Daily Advertiser*, 1 March 1743.
16. *The Political State of Britain* (August 1739), p. 143.
17. *Gentleman's Magazine* (1753), pp. 342-3.
18. *Lloyd's Evening Post*, 26-28 June 1776.
19. *London Chronicle*, 17-19 September 1761.
20. *Lloyd's Evening Post*, 27-29 September 1769.
21. *St. James's Chronicle*, 18-21 May 1765; *Lloyd's Evening Post*, 26-28 July 1775.
22. Webbs, *History of Trade Unionism*, pp. 10-11.
23. Ibid., p. 10.
24. For three houses of call for journeymen carpenters and joiners, see Ch. 4. at page 53.
25. *Lloyd's Evening Post*, vol. I (1763), pp. 566, 606.
26. Ibid., vol. II (1766), pp. 509, 534.
27. Ibid., 13-15 June 1774, 31 May-2 June 1775.
28. Webbs, *History of Trade Unionism*, pp. 27-8.
29. See Christopher Lloyd, *The British Seaman* (London, 1970 edn), p. 121.

30. R. Campbell, *The London Tradesman* (London, 1747), pp. 323-4.
31. *Lloyd's Evening Post*, vol. I (1783), p. 450.
32. See George Rudé, *Wilkes and Liberty* (Oxford, 1962), pp. 103-4.
33. Lloyd, *British Seamen*, p. 183. See also G.E. Manwaring and Bonamy Dobrée, *The Floating Republic* (London, 1935), Appendix II.
34. But see A. Aspinall, *The Early English Trade Unions*, p. xi; also J.L. and Barbara Hammond, *The Town Labourer*, vol. II, p. 123, note 5: 'It seems probable that the Government were alarmed by the newly formed Association of Weavers in the north.' This is possible, although, as the Hammonds show elsewhere, there was nothing very alarming in the address of the Association sent to the Home Secretary from Wigan on 27 May, which was couched in moderate and even anti-Jacobin terms. Hammonds, *The Skilled Labourer*, pp. 58-61.
35. *Lloyd's Evening Post*, 8-10 September 1773.
36. Ibid.
37. As late at 1764, a plan to erect 'mills for sawing timber in the dockyards, the same as now used in Holland, Norway, and other parts', was 'humanely' rejected. Ibid., 17-20 February 1764.
38. *London Journal*, 27 April 1723; *Daily Journal*, 30 April 1723.
39. *General Advertiser*, 27 May, 17 October, 18 November, 5 December 1749; *London Evening Post*, 25-27 May, 16-18 November 1749.
40. *Lloyd's Evening Post*, 17-19 April 1786.
41. Or, 'a general disease' requiring 'a general remedy'. Speech by Wilberforce, House of Commons, 9 April 1799, in *Parliamentary Register*, 9 April 1799, quoted by Hammonds, *Town Labourer*, II, p. 121, note 2. Cf. *St. James's Chronicle*, 8-11 June 1799: 'Mr Wiberforce thought it worthy of the consideration of the House, whether it might not be proper to give the Bill a more extensive application than his Hon. Friend proposed.'

CHAPTER 2

1. Clark Kerr and Abraham J. Siegel, 'The Interindustry Propensity to Strike: an international comparison' (1954), in C. Kerr, *Labor and Management in Industrial Society* (New York, 1964), p. 109.
2. *Evening Post*, 20-23 June 1724; *Read's Weekly Journal*, 7 October 1752.
3. *Weekly Journal or British Gazetteer*, 31 July 1725.
4. Ibid., 16 October 1725.
5. *Daily Post* 18 October 1725.
6. *British Journal*, 19 November 1726.
7. *London Journal*, 13 September, 4, 11 October 1729; *British Journal*, 13 September, 4 October 1729, 20 June 1730.
8. *House of Commons Journals* (1726), pp. 648, 695.
9. Ibid.; D.B. Horne and Mary Ransome, *English Historical Documents*, vol. X (1714-1783) (London, 1957), pp. 484-6.
10. *British Journal*, 10 December 1726.
11. Ibid., 3 June 1727.
12. *London Journal*, 12 October 1728.
13. *London Evening Post*, 6-9 May 1738.
14. Ibid.
15. *London Evening Post*, 2-5, 5-7, 16 December 1738; *Political State*, vol. I (1739), pp. 386, 448-9, 520, 524. For the 'Essay on Riots' and a rejoinder, see *Gentleman's Magazine* (1739), pp. 7-9, 84-5, 124.
16. William Carlile, 'New Description of Paisley', *Gentleman's Magazine* (1787),

p. 465.

17. *London Journal*, 8, 15, 22 July 1727.
18. *London Evening Post*, 14-17 October 1738. There is also a brief report of the disturbances in the *Daily Gazetteer* for 17 October, which omits any reference to the wages issue.
19. *London Evening Post*, 14-17 October 1738.
20. Ibid.
21. Ibid., 14-17 October, 4-7 November 1738.
22. *Daily Gazetteer*, 7 November 1738. Sir Isaac Newton died in 1727.
23. *London Evening Post*, 11-14, 14-16 November; *Daily Gazetteer*, 14 November 1738.
24. *London Evening Post*, 2-5 December 1738. The destruction of the lock was achieved by 'cutting to pieces the four swing posts, the stems of seven lashers, the two back harrows, splitting off the two heads of the upper gates, blowing up one of the larger gates, and part of the lock wall, with gunpowder'. Ibid. Another version of the notice was given in the *Daily Gazetteer* for 28 November: 'What they had done was nothing; the Damage was to come. That at present they assembled but in a small Body; but when they came again they would be 1,000 strong. That if a Bit of Coal was carried up the River for the future, they would destroy all the Locks; for they had as good be hanged, as they and their Families to starve.'
25. *London Evening Post*, 20-23 January 1739.
26. In November, there had been comment on the effects of standing armies, following an incident involving the wife of a publican. The affair seems unconnected with the strike, as the troops allegedly involved were in Bristol for a visit by the Prince of Wales. *London Evening Post*, 18-21 November 1738.
27. *Lloyd's Evening Post*, 24-27 August, 1792.
28. Ibid.
29. Letter from Captain George Monro to Henry Dundas, dated Bristol, 9 August 1792 (PRO, HO 42/22), in Aspinall, *Early English Trade Unions*, pp. 6-7.
30. Ibid.
31. *Lloyd's Evening Post*, 5-7 July 1779.

CHAPTER 3

1. F.J. Fisher, 'The Development of London as a Centre for Conspicuous Consumption in the Sixteenth and Seventeenth Centuries', *Transactions of the Royal Historical Society*, 4th series, vol. XXX (1948); reprinted in E.M. Carus-Wilson, *Essays in Economic History*, vol. 2 (London, 1962).
2. E.A. Wrigley, 'London and the Great Leap Forward', *The Listener*, 6 July 1967.
3. Henry Robinson, *The Office of Addresses and Encounters* (London, 1650).
4. See M. Dorothy George, 'The Early History of Registry Offices', *Economic Journal (supplement)* (January 1929).
5. William Maitland, *History and Survey of London* (London, 1756), vol. II, p. 1326.
6. Ibid.
7. Ibid.
8. *Lloyd's Evening Post*, 20-23 November 1761.
9. R. Campbell, *The London Tradesman* (London, 1747), p. 193.
10. *Evening Post*, 15-17, 17-20 September 1720.

11. For hatters in the seventeenth century, see Unwin, *Industrial Organization*, pp. 213-27, and 'A Seventeenth-Century Trade Union', *Economic Journal* (1910); For the hatters' 'congresses', see 'Report relating to the internal Management of the (Hat) Trade', presented by Mr Alderman Harley, *House of Commons Journals*, vol. 36 (18 February 1777), p. 192. The Manchester master feltmakers required their journeymen to dissociate themselves in writing from 'any pretended Laws made by a Congress, Committee or any other Combination of Piece-Makers, or Journeymen'. Wadsworth and Mann, *Cotton Trade*, pp. 381-2.
12. *Daily Advertiser*, 13, 16 July 1744.
13. Ellic Howe and Harold E. Waite, *The London Society of Compositors: a Centenary History* (London, 1948), p. 69. A journeyman printer 'dropped down dead among his companions' at a club in Little Carter Lane on Tuesday 5 October 1725. *Daily Journal*, 7 October 1725.
14. A letter signed 'A Whig' refers to the case of the journeymen printers, prosecuted and successfully defended in the *North Briton* affair: 'the venal tools of the ministerial party . . . will . . . tell the Public, that, if their advocates have gained any seeming advantage, it is all owing to unlawful combinations.' *Lloyd's Evening Post*, vol. II (1763), p. 32.
15. See advertisements in *Daily Advertiser*, 9, 10, 14, 15 August; 2, 3, 4, 9, 10, 11, 13, 14, 16 September 1745.
16. *Lloyd's Evening Post*, 3-6, 6-8 July 1772; *Annual Register*, May, June, July 1772.
17. *The Grounds of Complaint against the Practice of Sunday Baking* (London, 1794).
18. *Daily Advertiser*, 21 January, 21, 30 April, 1, 2 May 1744.
19. Ibid., 10 November, 28 December 1744; 1, 6, 8, 10, 11, 12, 13, 15, 20, 23, 24, 26, 27, 31 July, 1 August 1745.
20. *Daily Advertiser*, 14 August 1745; *Grounds of Complaint*.
21. *Public Advertiser*, 31 July 1756.
22. Ibid., 11, 12, 13 August 1756.
23. W.A. Englefield, *History of the Painter-Stainers' Company* (London, 1923), p. 173; *Public Advertiser*, 12, 14 June 1756.
24. 'The private houses of call for Taylors, where the Journeymen are sent to work without the necessity of spending their money, is of great advantage to the industrious, sober men, and particularly those who have families to maintain, and is an example worthy of imitation in other trades.' *Lloyd's Evening Post*, 9-12 December 1763.
25. M. Dorothy George, 'The London Coal-heavers: attempts to regulate waterside labour in the eighteenth and nineteenth centuries', *Economic Journal* (May 1927), pp. 229-48.
26. Maitland, *History of London*, p. 1326.
27. *Daily Gazetteer*, 8 June 1736; *London Evening Post*, 5-8 June 1736.
28. House of Lords, 10 February 1737, in *Gentleman's Magazine* (1737), p. 378.
29. Wadsworth and Mann, *Cotton Trade*, pp. 342-3.
30. The masters' houses of call were: Flying Horse, Oxford Road; Feathers, Spring Gardens; Waggon and Horses, Goswell Street; Wheelwrights' Arms, East Smithfield; Sampson's Castle, Grange Yard, Southwark; The Bell, near the Glass-house, Southwark; Swan and Horseshoe, Grays Inn Lane. *Daily Advertiser*, 29, 31 August 1745. For journeymen's reply, ibid., 2 September 1745.
31. *Daily Advertiser*, 29, 31 August, 4 September 1745.
32. Ibid.
33. Cf. G.D.H. Cole, *British Trade Unionism Today* (London, 1939), pp. 33-4;

G.D.H. Cole and A.W. Filson, *British Working Class Movements: select documents 1789-1875* (London and New York, 1967), pp. 261-6.

CHAPTER 4

1. Sir William Ashley, *Surveys: Historic and Economic* (London, 1900), cit. Webbs, *Trade Unionism*, p. 13n.
2. Webbs, *Trade Unionism*, p. 3.
3. K.S. Laurie, *The History of the Guild of Saddlers of the City of London*, 3rd edn (revised) (privately circulated London, 1956), pp. 13, 28.
4. Laurie, *Guild of Saddlers*, p. 28.
5. Curriers' Company, *Fair copy extracts from Court Minute Books*, vol. 1, fo. 216-20. (Guildhall MSS 6113/1).
6. See George Unwin, *The Gilds and Companies of London*, pp. 224-9, 231, 265-6, 344-51.
7. T.F. Reddaway, *The Rebuilding of London after the Great Fire* (London, 1940), p. 113; B.W.E. Alford and T.C. Barker, *A History of the Carpenters' Company* (London, 1968), pp. 538-9.
8. Walter George Bell, *A Short History of the Worshipful Company of Tylers and Bricklayers of the City of London* (London, 1938).
9. W. Maitland, *The History and Survey of London, etc.* (London, 1756 edn), pp. 511-12.
10. Blacksmiths' Company, *Court Minute Books*, vol. 10, fo. 89 (Guildhall MSS 2881).
11. Ibid., fo. 90-1.
12. Unwin, *Gilds and Companies*, p. 349; E. Bennet, *The Worshipful Company of Wheelwrights of the City of London, 1670-1970* (David and Charles, Newton Abbott. 1970). p 51.
13. *Evening Post*, 10-13 December; *London Journal*, 10-17 December 1720.
14. Greater London Council Record Office, *Middlesex Sessions Books, Process Register of Indictments* (October 1734), no. 14, fo. 28-9.
15. Unwin, *Gilds*, p. 349; *Read's Weekly Journal*, 16 September 1732; *Daily Courant*, 18 October 1732.
16. *London Evening Post*, 12-14 April 1739.
17. *London Evening Post*, 1-3 August 1734.
18. 'An Answer to a Letter from a Citizen Retired into the Country, to his Brother in London', *General Advertiser*, 6 April 1750.
19. Ibid.
20. Ibid.
21. R. Campbell, *The London Tradesman* (London, 1747, reprinted Newton Abbot, 1969), pp. 103-4.
22. Painter-Stainers' Company. *Court Minute Book, 1649-1793*, fo. 559 (Guildhall MSS 5667).
23. *Whitehall Evening Post*, 7-9 December 1749; *London Evening Post*, 7-9 December 1749; *General Advertiser*, 8 December 1749.
24. *General Advertiser*, 12 December, 13 December 1749.
25. Ibid., 13 January 1750.
26. Ibid., 6 February 1750.
27. 'The compositors were summoned to hear counsel's report (concerning apprenticeship limitations) at the Hole-in-the-Wall on the 1st October 1787. This is the earliest evidence of the compositors meeting at that house.' Ellic Howe and Harold E. Waite, *The London Society of Compositors: A Centenary History* (London, 1948), p. 69. 'The pressmen's union met there as late as 1839.' Ibid., p. 47n.

28. *General Advertiser*, 12 February 1750.
29. Corporation of London Record Office, *Journals of the Court of Common Council*, vol. 59, fo. 254-5.
30. Ibid.
31. Ibid.
32. Ibid., fo. 256-7.
33. *The privileges of the free artificers of the City of London defended; in an appeal to the committee appointed to receive the complaints of the masters of the several manufactures in the city against their journeymen* (London, n.d.) (Guildhall Library, cat. 'FREE'; Goldsmith's Library, 8612).
34. Ibid., p. 10.
35. Ibid., p. 22.
36. Corporation of London, *Journals of the Court of Common Council*, vol. 59, fo. 254.
37. *General Advertiser*, 10 February 1750.
38. 'Report of the Committee appointed to examine the Petitions of the Masters and Journeymen Freemen', *London Magazine* (1750), pp. 282-3; *Gentleman's Magazine* (1750), pp. 271-2.
39. Abstract of the Act in *General Advertiser*, 23 November 1750.
40. Curriers' Company, *Court Minutes*, 4 October, 7 November 1760 (Guildhall MSS 6112/3).
41. Horace Stewart, *History of the Worshipful Company of Gold and Silver Wire-drawers* (London, 1891), p. 91.
42. Cordwainers' Company, *Court Minute Book, 1752-1771*, fo. 301-2, 308-9, 313 (Guildhall MSS 7353/6, Book A).
43. Cordwainers' Company, *Court Minutes*, 7, 9 March 1792, fo. 231-3. (Guildhall MSS 7353/8 book C); *Lloyd's Evening Post* 15-17, 24-27 February 1792.
44. Bennet, *Worshipful Company of Wheelwrights*, p. 52-3.
45. J.H. Hawkins, *History of the Worshipful Company of the Art or Mystery of Feltmakers of London* (London, 1917), p. 77.
46. Ibid., p. 80.
47. *Lloyd's Evening Post*, 27-29 October 1788.
48. See Chapter 9.
49. Curriers' Company, *Court Minutes*, 30 March 1793, fo. 348.
50. Edward Mayer, *The Curriers and the City of London: a history of the Worshipful Company of Curriers* (London, 1968), p. 145. *The Middlesex Sessions Book*, Tuesday 3 April 1792, no. 1435, fo. 106-12, under 'Leatherworkers', shows the following convictions quashed on the oath of masters (in columns of the MSS, given here in brackets): Matthew Cape, Dugald McDugald, Richard Sweetland, Thomas Whitaker (George Gordon), Walter Hobkirk, John Naylor (David Taylor), William Jones, Richard Masters (William Martin), Thomas Rastall, William Smedly, Benjamin Thew (Edward Rymer), John Tarbart (John Newcomb) and Thomas Brooks (John Walker).
51. Mayer, *Curriers*, p. 146.

CHAPTER 5

1. 'Report submitted by the Master Tailors' Committee (1810)', in Galton, *Tailoring Trade*, pp. 88-95. Also Brit. Mus. Place MSS 27,799 (10).
2. Henson, *Framework Knitters*, p. 380.
3. George, *London Life*, p. 211.

4. Ibid., p. 270; Galton, pp. 27-9.
5. Galton, p. xxi, note 3.
6. Francis Place, article in *Gorgon*, 3 October 1818.
7. Galton, pp. 115-21; in 1834, the chairman of the Roebuck house of call was foreman to Mr Baldwin, Cheapside, and another delegate was foreman to Mr Stafford of Smithfield. See 'The London Tailors' Strike, 1834: an account compiled from secret reports by a police informer within the Grand Lodge of Operative Tailors' (Home Office Papers, HO 64/15), Appendix 2 of my unpublished MA dissertation, 'The London Tailors 1720-1834' (Univ. of Sussex, 1967).
8. Joseph Redington, *Calendar of Home Office Papers of the Reign of George III, 1760-1765* (London, 1879), paper no. 1389.
9. 'Tailors and their Words and Phrases', *Tailor and Cutter*, 10 February 1927.
10. *Evening Post*, 13-15 October 1720.
11. See Galton, pp. 1-128, *passim*.
12. R. Leslie-Melville, *The Life and Work of Sir John Fielding* (London, 1934), p. 170.
13. Ibid.
14. *Evening Post*, 15-17 September 1720.
15. *London Journal*, 6-13 August 1720.
16. *Evening Post*, 30 August-1 September 1720.
17. *Applebee's Original Weekly Journal*, 28 January 1721. See also King *v.* Journeymen Taylors of Cambridge, King's Bench, Michaelmas Term 1721, 8 Geo. I., case 7.
18. *Evening Post*, 30 August-1 September, 6-8 September, 17-20 September 1720; *London Journal*, 26 November-8 December 1720; 14, 28 January, 18 February 1721 (printed as '1720'); *Applebee's Original Weekly Journal*, 7 January, 18 February 1721.
19. *Weekly Journal or British Gazetteer*, 29 April 1721; *Weekly Journal or Saturday's Post*, 25 March 1721; *Applebee's Original Weekly Journal*, 29 April 1721; *London Gazette*, 6-10 June 1721; *London Journal*, 10, 17 June 1721.
20. *London Journal*, 10 March 1722 (dated '1721').
21. *Daily Journal*, 11, 14, 16, 18 January 1723.
22. *London Evening Post*, 22-24 November 1737; *Country Journal, or the Craftsman*, 26 November 1737.
23. *Daily Advertiser*, 1 March 1743.
24. Ibid.
25. Ibid., 21, 23-24 July, 10 August 1744.
26. Ibid., 29 June, 7, 13, 14, 16, 23, 24, 28, 30, 31 July, 3, 6, 7, 11, 14, 18, 20, 21, 25, 27, 28 August, 1 September 1744.
27. Ibid., 2, 3, 4, 10 August 1744.
28. Ibid., 10 August 1744.
29. Ibid., 21, 22, 23 August 1744.
30. Ibid., 6 September 1744. The Savoy, between the Strand and the riverside, was a derelict medieval palace, used as a barracks and a prison. It also housed the King's printing press. See Edward Walford, *Old and New London*, vol. III (London, n.d.), pp. 95-100.
31. *Daily Advertiser*, 26 November 1744.
32. E.G. Dowdell, *A Hundred Years of Quarter Sessions: the government of Middlesex from 1660 to 1760* (Cambridge, 1932), pp. 199-200. See also Greater London Council, *Middlesex Country Records*, Process Register of Indictments no. 15, OT4 and OT23, at pp. 218-20.
33. *London Evening Post*, 24-26 January 1745; *London Daily Advertiser*, 23,

25 January 1745.

34. *London Daily Advertiser and Literary Gazette*, 18, 19 July 1751.
35. Ibid., 16 October 1751.
36. *London Gazette*, 15-19 October 1751. Galton, following *Gentleman's Magazine* (19751), pp. 473-4, refers to threatening letters but not to assaults (*Tailoring Trade*, p. xxxv).
37. *Read's Weekly Journal*, 25 November 1752.
38. Galton, pp. 45-6. For text of Middlesex Sessions order, see *London Daily Advertiser and Literary Gazette*, 18, 19 July 1751.
39. The term 'affairs of importance' appears frequently in announcements of employers' meetings, but was rarely employed by trade clubs.
40. See L. Namier, *The Structure of Politics at the Accession of George III*, second edn (1957), pp. 228, 430, 447-8. Fielding received annual allowances of £400 to pay police informers. The secret funds were also available for election expenses and 'pensions' of the King's supporters in Parliament.
41. *Public Advertiser*, 25 March, 5, 6, 7 April 1756.
42. Ibid., 21, 22, 23 April 1756.
43. Ibid., 2, 3, 5, 6 August 1756.
44. Ibid., 10, 11, 12 August 1756.
45. Ibid., 25, 26, 27 August, 7 September 1756. Summaries of the penalties under the Act of 7. Geo. I, c.13 are also given.
46. Ibid., 2, 4, 23 September, 1, 11 October 1756.
47. Ibid., 11 October 1756, 2 April 1757.
48. Summary of 'Sir John Fielding's Extracts from such of the Penal Laws as Relate to the Peace and Good Order of this Metropolis', *Lloyd's Evening Post*, vol. II (1760), p. 371. See also Leslie-Melville, *Life of Fielding*, p. 170.
49. *Old Bailey Sessions Papers* (1765), p. 173. The following committee members in office between 1762 and 1764 were indicted for conspiracy: Alexander Sparks (Brown Bear, Strand, chairman), Walter Berry (Crown, Duke's Place), John Cannon (One Ton, Strand), Joseph Carrick (Rising Sun, Blackfriars), John Dobson (to 1762), Robert Jones (India House, Fenchurch Street), *Magazine* (1751), pp. 473-4, refers to threatening letters but not to assaults William Milburn (Shepherd and Goat, Fleet Ditch). Mr Hewlate, attorney, was legal adviser to the committee.
50. *Old Bailey Sessions Papers* (1765), p. 174.
51. Ibid., p. 173.
52. Ibid.
53. *Public Advertiser*, 28 January 1764. The masters' committee members were: John Dove (chairman), William Woodley, Thomas Rackett, Isaac Pearce, Richard Elmer, John Edwards, John Jarman, John Thornthwaite, Henry Cline, William Adams, Samuel Plummer, John Seaber, John Wintle, William Fell, William Harrison, David Young, Thomas Coombe, John Holland, C. Pearce, John Priestman, Joseph Thornthwaite, Messrs Lynch, Winter and Lamb, Daniel Jennings, William Davies. *Lloyd's Evening Post*, 10-13 February 1764. The private houses of call were given as Mr Littleford's, Shepherd's Yard, Great Minories; Mr Hern's, at the Adam and Eve, New Rents, St Martins-le-Grand; Mr Richard's at the Angel Court, near Norfolk Street, Strand; Mr Pugh's, in Leg Alley, Long Acre; Mr Dilke's, Coventry Court, Haymarket; Mr Miles Hart's, next door to the Horseshoe, Labour-in-vain Court, Old Fish Street; John Quigly's, next door to the Rising Sun, Fashion Street, Spitalfields; Mr William Brown's, near the White Lion and Star, Broad Street, Old Gravel Lane, Ratcliff Highway; and Mr Holliday's, at the Blue Ball, opposite the Meeting House, St Thomas's, Southwark (ibid.).
54. *Public Advertiser*, 10 March 1764.

55. *Lloyd's Evening Post*, 4-6 April 1764.
56. *Public Advertiser*, 7 April 1764.
57. *Lloyd's Evening Post*, 6-9 April 1764; *Public Advertiser*, 19 May 1764.
58. *Lloyd's Evening Post*, 28 September 1764; cf. E.J. Hobsbawm, 'The Tramping Artisan', *Labouring Men*, p. 36.
59. *Lloyd's Evening Post*, 28 September 1764.
60. Ibid., 29 April-1 May 1765.
61. Ibid., 6-9 September 1765.
62. Ibid., 19-22 April 1765. There is a full account of the trial in *Old Bailey Sessions Papers* (1765).
63. *Lloyd's Evening Post*, 17-19 November 1766.
64. See, for example, *Lloyd's Evening Post*, vol. I (1767), p. 441.

CHAPTER 6

1. Leslie-Melville, *Life of Fielding*, pp. 131-2.
2. Namier, *Structure of Politics*, p. 228.
3. Saunders Welch, *Proposal to Remove Common Prostitutes* (London, 1753), p. 48.
4. Saunders Welch, *Observations on the Office of Constable* (London, 1758), p. 4.
5. See T.A. Critchley, *A History of Police in England and Wales, 900-1966* (London, 1967).
6. *Public Advertiser*, 24 May 1756.
7. Ibid., 27, 28 May, 1 June 1756.
8. 'Wee, the Mr. and Wardens of the Company of Carpenters, in pursuance of your lordships desire for the reducing of the excessive wages of Labourers and Workmen in these times of great plenty, we humbly conceive to be sufficient that Labourers take for wages but 16d a day only etc.' R.H. Tawney, 'The Assessment of Wages in England by the Justices of the Peace', in W.E. Minchinton (ed.), *Wage Regulation in Pre-Industrial England* (Newton Abbot, 1972), p. 54.
9. *Read's Weekly Journal, or British Gazetteer*, 16 September 1732; *Daily Courant*, 18 October, 8 November 1732; *London Gazette*, 24-28 October 1732; *Political State of Britain* (1733), p. 129.
10. Cf. letters to Peter Auber, master silk weaver of Spital Square, before an attack on his house in August 1769, reprinted in George Rudé, *Wilkes and Liberty* (Oxford, 1962), p. 205.
11. See R.K. Kelsall, 'Wage Regulations under the Statute of Artificers', in Minchinton (ed.), *Wage Regulation*, pp. 101-3.
12. *London Evening Post*, 18-20 August 1737.
13. Ibid., 20-23 August 1737.
14. Ibid., 28-30 April 1737.
15. 'The History of the last Session of Parliament', *London Magazine* (January, 1758), pp. 9-11.
16. W.E. Minchinton, 'The Beginnings of Trade Unionism in the Gloucestershire Woollen Industry', *Transactions of the Bristol and Gloucestershire Archaeological Society*, vol. 50 (1954), p. 131.
17. Ibid.
18. *Public Advertiser*, 6 May 1755.
19. Formally, representatives of masters and journeymen appeared as witnesses; informally, negotiations took place through counsel.
20. *Lloyd's Evening Post*, vol. II (1766), p. 557.

21. J.T. Smith, *Nollekens and his Times*, vol. I (London, 1828), pp. 128-9.
22. *Lloyd's Evening Post*, 18-20 November 1761.
23. *London Gazette*, 11 November 1761.
24. *Lloyd's Evening Post*, 19-21 October 1761.
25. Ibid., 25-27 November 1761.
26. Ibid.
27. *Annual Register* (1761), p. 175. The paragraph is dated '6 November'.
28. *London Chronicle*, 12-15 December 1761.
29. *Lloyd's Evening Post*, 27-29 January 1762.
30. Ibid., 1-3 July 1762.
31. Ibid., 25-27 July 1763.
32. In 1770, James Waller, Clerk to the Middlesex Sessions, was removed from office on grounds of negligence in drawing bills of indictment, resulting in miscarriages of justices. He was also accused of failing to attend Sessions or appoint proper deputies, of failing to take care of records and of taking unlawful fees. Waller denied all charges, and obtained a writ of *certiorari*, but the decision was upheld by King's Bench. He died the following year. See (Sir) Edgar Stephens, *The Clerks of the Counties 1360-1960* (Society of Clerks of the Peace of Counties and of Clerks of County Councils, 1961), p. 128.
33. Dr G. Rudé was the first historian to draw a clear distinction between the political and industrial unrest in London in May 1768. See 'Wilkes and Liberty' 1768-9', *Guildhall Miscellany*, vol. I, no. 8 (July 1957), and *Wilkes and Liberty* (Oxford, 1962), pp. 90-104. In Paris exactly two hundred years later, workpeople similarly took the opportunity of a political crisis to press their wage and other social demands; cf. Georges Séguy, *Lutter* (Paris, Stock, 1975), Ch. V; J-D. Reynaud, *Les Syndicats en France*, 2nd edn, vol. I (Paris, Seuil, 1975), pp. 111-17.
34. This speech was not reported at the time, but mentioned in *Lloyd's Evening Post*, 27-29 March 1769.
35. *London Magazine* (1763), p. 559; *London Gazette*, 4-8, 8-11 October 1763.
36. Horace Walpole, *Memoirs of the Reign of King George III*, vol. III (London, 1894), p. 144. This source is biased, but Barrington's subordination to the King is discussed in Richard Pares, *King George III and the Politicians* (Oxford, 1953), p. 144.
37. *Lloyd's Evening Post*, 29 April-2 May 1768.
38. *St James's Chronicle*, 5-7 May 1768.
39. *Lloyd's Evening Post*, 6-9 May 1768.
40. *St. James's Chronicle*, 10-12 May 1768.
41. *Lloyd's Evening Post*, 9-11 May 1768.
42. Walpole, *King George III*.
43. *Lloyd's Evening Post*, 11-13 May 1768.
44. *Public Advertiser*, 14 May 1768.
45. Ibid.
46. *Lloyd's Evening Post*, 16-18 May 1768; Rudé, *Wilkes and Liberty*, pp. 94-5.
47. J. Redington (ed.), *Calendar of Home Office Papers 1766-1769*, p. 338; Leslie-Melville, *Life of Fielding*, pp. 180-1.
48. *Lloyd's Evening Post*, 26-28 October 1768.
49. West to Newcastle, 16 May 1768, cit. Rudé, *Wilkes and Liberty*, p. 95.
50. *Public Advertiser*, 9, 16 June 1768.
51. Ibid., 16, 20 June 1768.
52. Ibid., 20 June 1768.
53. Ibid.
54. *Lloyd's Evening Post*, 1-4 July 1768.

55. Ibid., 5-7 July 1768.
56. Ibid., 11-13 July 1768.
57. *Lloyd's Evening Post*, 28-30 August 1769; for a concise account see Rudé, *Crowd in History*, pp. 73-7.
58. *Lloyd's Evening Post*, 9-11 October 1769.
59. Ibid., 13-16, 18-20 October 1769.
60. Ibid., 13-15, 27-29 November 1769.
61. Ibid., 4-6 December 1769.
62. Ibid., 18-20 December 1769.
63. Ibid., 19-22 April 1771.
64. Ibid., 15-18 November 1771.
65. Ibid., vol. I (1773), p. 127.
66. Ibid., 1-4 January 1773.
67. Ibid.
68. Ibid., *passim*, pp. 382-94.
69. Ibid.
70. Ibid., p. 394.
71. See J.L. and Barbara Hammond, *Skilled Labourer*, p. 209.
72. A.E. Bland, P.A. Brown and R.H. Tawney, *English Economic History: Select Documents* (London, 1914), p. 551.
73. J.H. Clapham, 'The Spitalfields Acts, 1773-1824', *Economic Journal*, vol. XXVI (1916).
74. *Lloyd's Evening Post*, 17-19 November 1769.
75. Ibid., 26-29 October 1772.
76. Ibid., 19-21 August 1771.
77. Ibid., vol. I (1771), p. 61.
78. Ibid.
79. *Calendar of Home Office Papers 1773-1775*, pp. 81, 83.
80. *Lloyd's Evening Post*, 6 July 1773.
81. Ibid., 15 June 1774.
82. *House of Commons Journals*, vol. 35 (1775), p. 491.
83. *Lloyd's Evening Post*, 1 June 1776.
84. Ibid., 24-26 June 1776; *Annual Register* (1776), p. 160 (entry for 8 July).
85. Ibid.
86. Ibid., 26-28 August, 19 September, 31 October 1776.
87. Ibid., 19-21 May 1777.
88. *A Practical and Eligible Plan to Secure the Rights and Privileges of Mechanics: With Proper Directions for the Journeymen, Whereby They May Get an Advancement in Their Wages Without Loss of Time or Hindrance of Business* (London, 1776) (British Library, 1029, i.6(6)).
89. Ibid.
90. *Lloyd's Evening Post*, 29-31 October 1777; *General Evening Post*, 28-30 October 1777.
91. House of Commons, 8 May 1780, in *Lloyd's Evening Post*, 8-10 May 1780.
92. Resolution of Common Council 18 November 1795; Court of Aldermen, 16 December 1795; *Lloyd's Evening Post*, 13-15 July, 14-16 December 1795.
93. Joseph Lowe, *The Present State of England in Regard to Agriculture, Trade and Finance*, 2nd edn (London, 1823), pp. 56-7.

CHAPTER 7

1. Quoted by T.S. Ashton, *An Economic History of England: The Eighteenth Century* (London, 1955), p. 113.

2. House of Commons, 10 February 1721 (1722), reported in *Evening Post*, 17-19 April 1722.

3. House of Commons, 22 March 1781, reported in *Lloyd's Evening Post and British Chronicle*, 21-23 March 1781.

4. *London Journal*, 9 December 1721.

5. 'Letter from Chatham', *Lloyd's Evening Post*, 8-11 July 1785. Sidney Pollard has noted that naval yards, 'with their discipline compounded of civil service and armed service practices, and the absence of any direct profit motive, fit badly into our concept of "management" '. *The Genesis of Modern Management* (1968 edition), p. 104n.

6. *Flying Post, or the Postmaster*, 1-4 March 1701; *The Post-Boy*, 8-11 March 1701.

7. *London Journal*, 25 November 1727.

8. *Lloyd's Evening Post*, vol. I (1774), p. 309.

9. Ibid., vol. II (1778), p. 61.

10. Extract from 'Reflections on the Domestic Policy proper to be observed on the conclusion of a Peace', *Lloyd's Evening Post*, 8-10 November 1762.

11. *Victoria County History of Kent*, vol. II (London, 1926), p. 347.

12. Ibid. See also W.T. Vincent, *The Records of the Woolwich District*, vol. I (Woolwich and London, 1890), p. 253.

13. Report by Colonel Thompson, 13 March 1649, in *House of Commons Journals*, vol. 6, pp. 381-2.

14. Vincent, *Woolwich Records*, I, p. 305.

15. *V.C.H., Kent*, II, p. 357.

16. Ibid., p. 364.

17. Vincent, *Woolwich Records*, I, pp. 305, 352.

18. Ibid.

19. *The Diary of Samuel Pepys* (Ed. Latham and Matthews), vol. III (1662) (London, 1970), pp. 200-1 (entry for 19 September).

20. *V.C.H., Kent*, II, p. 357.

21. Vincent, *Woolwich Records*, I, p. 305; *State Papers Domestic*, addenda 1660-1670, pp. 50, 139.

22. Vincent, *Woolwich Records*, pp. 307-8.

23. *V.C.H., Kent*, II, p. 352.

24. Ibid.

25. *The British Journal, or The Censor*, 9 August, 1 November, 6 December, 27 December 1729.

26. *V.C.H., Kent*, II, p. 369.

27. *London Evening Post*, 10-12 April 1739; *Daily Post*, 7 November 1739; *Daily Gazetteer*, 7 November 1739; *Political State of Britain* (1739), pp. 404, 407.

28. *Daily Gazetteer*, 8 November 1739; *Daily Post*, 7 November 1739; *London Evening Post*, 6-8 November 1739.

29. *Daily Post*, 8 November 1739.

30. Ibid., 10 November 1739.

31. *Daily Gazetteer*, 3 December 1739.

32. *V.C.H., Kent*, II, p. 374.

33. Ibid.

34. *London Magazine* (1757), p. 256.

35. Ibid.; *Gentleman's Magazine* (1757), p. 187.

36. *Lloyd's Evening Post*, 4-6 January, 26-29 May 1758.

37. Ibid., 21-24 July, 30 April 1759. Evidence that the 'flag of defiance' flown above the mill was indeed of deepest red is indirect but persuasive. Witnesses to an affray between coalheavers and seamen nine years later also 'saw a

flag of defiance hoisted as they called it'. 'I met a mob . . . they said there was a bloody flag at a mast-head; I went down to see that, I had never seen one in my life before, I saw some boats coming on shore.' 'I saw a red flag hoisted on board one of the ships.' 'Was there not a flag hung out for a signal for others to go and assist against the coal-heavers? – There was a flag out.' *Old Bailey Sessions Papers* (July 1768), trial of Murphy, Dugan, Castillo, Davis, Hammond, Henley, Doyle and Palmer for the murder of J. Beatty, pp. 266, 268, 269. On this occasion, the Red Flag was flown by strike-breakers, not the strikers.

38. 'Dialogue between an Artificer in a dockyard, and those who required his Vote in the next election for Kent', *Lloyd's Evening Post*, 18-21 July 1760.
39. Richard B. Morris, *Government and Labor in Early America*, 2nd edn (New York, 1965), p. 23.
40. *Lloyd's Evening Post*, 19-22 October 1764.
41. 'W.S.' (William Shrubsole), *A Plea in Favour of the Shipwrights belonging to the Royal Dock Yards, Humbly offering Reasons to the Public for an Addition to their Pay; With a Method to Effect it* (Rochester, 1770), p. 2.
42. *Lloyd's Evening Post*, 13-15 March 1765.
43. Ibid., 11 April 1767. After an outbreak of arson at Portsmouth, the chip-women were forbidden free access to the yard, and they rioted in protest. Ibid., 3-6 September 1771.
44. *Parliamentary Register*, vol. V, entry for 5 December 1781; Cobbett's *Parliamentary History*, vol. XXII, entry for same date.
45. *Calendar of Home Office Papers, 1773-75*, p. 1125.
46. Shrubsole, *Plea*, p. 3.
47. Ibid., p. 8.
48. Ibid., pp. 14-21.
49. Ibid., p. 21.
50. *Lloyd's Evening Post*, 26 August 1771.
51. Ibid.
52. Ibid., 18-20 December 1771.
53. *Gentleman's Magazine* (1772), p. 387.
54. *Lloyd's Evening Post* (1772), p. 162.
55. *Gentleman's Magazine* (1772), p. 434.
56. *Lloyd's Evening Post* (1773), p. 109.
57. Ibid., 20 January 1773.
58. Ibid. (1773), p. 218.
59. Ibid.
60. Ibid.
61. Ibid. (1773), p. 476.
62. Ibid., 15-17 March 1775.
63. 'Letter by a Friend to the Navy', *Lloyd's Evening Post*, 15-17 March 1775.
64. *Annual Registry* (1775), pp. 168-9.
65. *Lloyd's Evening Post*, 5-7 July 1775.
66. *Morning Post and Daily Advertiser*, 24 May 1775; *Daily Advertiser*, 23 May 1775; *London Chronicle*, 20-23 May 1775; *Lloyd's Evening Post*, 22-24 May 1775.
67. *London Chronicle*, 25-27 May; *Morning Post and Daily Advertiser*, 26 May; *Gazetteer and New Daily Advertiser*, 26 May 1775; *Lloyd's Evening Post*, 24-26 May 1775.
68. *Lloyd's Evening Post*, 5-7, 9-12, 14-16, 16-19 June 1775.
69. Ibid., 16-19, 23-26, 28-30 June 1775.
70. Ibid., 28-30 June 1775.
71. Sandwich to the King, in Sir John Fortescue (ed.), *The Correspondence*

of King George the Third from 1760 to December 1783, vol. III (July - December 1777) (London, 1928), p. 227.

72. *Lloyd's Evening Post*, 28-30 June 1775.
73. Ibid., 21-24 July 1775.
74. *The Gazetter and New Daily Advertiser*, 19, 21 July; *London Chronicle*, 18-20 July, *Morning Post and Daily Advertiser*, 19 July 1775.
75. *London Gazette*, 15-18 July 1775.
76. *Morning Post and Daily Advertiser*, 22 July 1775.
77. *Lloyd's Evening Post*, 21-24 July 1775. The men were subsequently sent to Maidstone gaol, to stand trial at the next Assizes. Twelve others were indicted *in absentia* but the Grand Jury was divided 15-10. Ibid., 9-11 August, 1775.
78. Ibid., 18-20 July; *Daily Advertiser*, 19 July; *Gazetteer and New Daily Advertiser*, 19 July 1775. There is a paragraph signed 'H. Randall' in the *Public Ledger* for 31 July: 'A noble Lord may think to frighten the shipwrights into the yard again, by talking of warrants, gaols, imprisonment, &c., but he is deceived, and the shipwrights know, that while they do nothing against the law and the constitution, they cannot come legally before a judge and jury.'
79. *London Chronicle*, 15-18 July 1775.
80. 'Letter from Portsmouth, August 11', *Lloyd's Evening Post*, 14-16 August; 'Letter from Plymouth, August 15', *Daily Advertiser*, 21 August 1775.
81. *Lloyd's Evening Post*, 21-24 July 1775.
82. *Lloyd's Evening Post*, 4-7, 24-26 August 1775.
83. *Morning Post and Daily Advertiser*, 9 August 1775.
84. *Gazetteer and New Daily Advertiser*, 17 July 1775.
85. Ibid., 18 August 1775.
86. 'Letter from Paris, June 21', *Lloyd's Evening Post*, 30 June 1781. The report says that troops had fired, and several workmen were killed or injured, but 'the happy arrival of M. d'Estaing (Admiral Jean-Baptiste, Comte d'Estaing) from Brest may put an end to it sooner than expected'.
87. Fortescue, *George III Correspondence*, vol III, p. 245.
88. 'Letter from Plymouth', *Daily Advertiser*, 21 August 1775.
89. *Lloyd's Evening Post*, 14-16, 21-23 August 1775.
90. *Lloyd's Evening Post*, 30 August-1 September; *Morning Chronicle and London Advertiser*, 31 August; *London Chronicle*, 29-31 August 1775.
91. *House of Commons Journals* (1972), p. 279.
92. *Daily Advertiser*, 21 August; *London Chronicle*, 17-19 August 1775.
93. *Lloyd's Evening Post*, 4-7 August 1775.
94. Ibid., 14-16 August 1775.
95. 'Letter from Plymouth, August 27', *Lloyd's Evening Post*, 30 August- 1 September 1775.

APPENDIX

1. *Debrett's Parliamentary Debates* (1781), pp. 312-13.

CHAPTER 8

1. 'To the Ministry', *Lloyd's Evening Post*, vol. I (1774), p. 97. The paragraph is initialled 'M'.
2. *Lloyd's Evening Post*, 29-31 December 1783.
3. *Public Advertiser*, 24 June 1768.
4. *Lloyd's Evening Post*, 16-19 October 1772.

5. Ibid.
6. Letter to *Lloyd's Evening Post*, 30 September-3 October 1763.
7. Ibid.
8. *Lloyd's Evening Post*, vol. I (1766), pp. 574, 582, 590; vol. II (1766), pp. 129, 161, 254, *passim*.
9. Bakers' Company, Petition read and agreed at a Special Court of Assistants, 15 March 1779, in *Court Minutes*, vol. 10 (Guildhall MSS 5177).
10. *Lloyd's Evening Post*, 23-25 October 1780, 16-19 October 1789.
11. When candles increased from 6s 8d to 7s 6d per dozen, there were several prosecutions of 'tallow forestallers'. Ibid., vol. I (1762), pp. 101, 339, 351, 359; vol. II (1762), pp. 485, 573, *passim*.
12. Advertisement in *Daily Post*, 11 September 1724.
13. 'Letter from Edinburgh, January 7', *Lloyd's Evening Post*, 13-16 January 1769.
14. E.P. Thompson, 'The Moral Economy of the English Crowd in the Eighteenth Century', *Past and Present* (February 1971), p. 79.
15. Galton, *Tailoring Trade*, pp. 31 ff.
16. Greater London Council, *Middlesex County Records* (MJ/SB 1303, pp. 79-86).
17. Englefield, *Painter-Stainers' Company*, p. 183.
18. Particularly when paid partially in kind, as were farm labourers and some miners.
19. *Lloyd's Evening Post* (1761), p. 541.
20. Ibid., 2-4 May 1763.
21. Ibid. Christopher Hill mentions two attacks on sawmills, in 1763 and 1767, *Reformation to Industrial Revolution* (Pelican edn, 1969), p. 265.
22. *Old Bailey Sessions Papers* (1768), case no. 468, indictment of Edward Castles, p. 256. See also Rudé, *Wilkes and Liberty*, pp. 93-4, and, for the full quotation, *London and Paris*, p. 250. Castles pleaded mistaken identity and was acquitted.
23. *Lloyd's Evening Post*, 25-28 November, 30 November-2 December 1768.
24. J. de L. Mann, *The Cloth Industry in the West of England from 1640 to 1880* (Oxford, 1971), p. 123.
25. Ibid., p. 124.
26. *Lloyd's Evening Post*, vol. III (1792), pp. 467, 488, 506, 514.
27. Ibid., II (1792), p. 520.
28. Ibid., pp. 514, 522.
29. Ibid., p. 544.
30. A.F.J. Brown, *Essex at Work 1700-1815* (Chelmsford, 1969).
31. *Lloyd's Evening Post*, vol. I (1793), p. 384.
32. Ibid., vol. II (1795), p. 536.
33. *Debrett's Parliamentary Debates, House of Commons*, vol 44 (12 February 1796), pp. 19-21.
34. Ibid.
35. *Lloyd's Evening Post*, II (1765), p. 349.
36. To prevent 'any studied delay of supply', the Bill of 1780 provided that, 'as soon as a collier hath entered past the Nore, he will be deemed to be in the port of London'. Ibid., 23-25 October 1780.
37. Ibid., 1-3 August 1785.
38. *The Times*, 24 December 1800. Keynes made the same point in the 1930s: 'A movement by employers to revise money-wage bargains downward will be much more strongly resisted than a gradual and automatic lowering of real wages as a result of rising prices.' *The General Theory of Employment, Interest and Money* (London, 1936), p. 264.

39. Act of 22 November 1750.
40. *Grounds of Complaint against the Practice of Sunday Baking* (London, 1794).
41. *Lloyd's Evening Post*, 28-30 October 1793.
42. Ibid.
43. Corporation of London Record Office, *Journals of the Court of Common Council*, vol. 73, entry for 31 October 1793.
44. King *v*. Younger, King's Bench, 23 November 1793.

CHAPTER 9

1. See K.W. Wedderburn, *The Worker and the Law* (Harmondsworth, 1965), p. 216; J.L. and Barbara Hammond, *The Town Labourer*, vol. 1 (London, 1949), p. 118; M. Dorothy George, 'The Combination Laws Reconsidered', *Economic History*, vol. I (1927); A. Aspinall, *The Early English Trade Unions* (London, 1949); W. Milne Bailey, *Trade Union Documents* (London, 1929), p. 14; Henry Pelling, *A History of British Trade Unionism* (Harmondsworth, 1963), pp. 25-6; E.P. Thompson, *The Making of the English Working Class* (London, 1963), p. 504.
2. Sidney and Beatrice Webb, *History of Trade Unionism* (1950 edn), p. 65.
3. M.D. George, 'Revisions in Economic History. The Combination Laws', *Economic History Review*, vol. VI (1936), p. 172 ff.
4. Webbs, *History of Trade Unionism*, pp. 74-5.
5. See E.P. Thompson, *The Making of the English Working Class* (London, 1863), pp. 500-21.
6. Ibid., p. 504.
7. Ibid., p. 515-21. See also Graham Wallas, *The Life of Francis Place 1771-1854* (London, 1925), p. 217.
8. Sir Otto Kahn-Freund, 'Industrial Relations and the Law: Retrospect and Prospect', *British Journal of Industrial Relations*, vol. III, no. 3 (November 1969), p. 304.
9. E.P. Thompson, *English Working Class*, p. 198.
10. 39 Geo. III, c.79. Two named societies were suppressed as 'unlawful Combinations and Confederacies against the Government of our Sovereign Lord the King, and against the Peace and Security of His Majesty's liege subjects'.
11. *Whitehall Evening Post*, 3-5 May 1750; *General Advertiser*, 5 May 1750.
12. *Public Advertiser*, 23 June 1768.
13. But cf. Rudé, *The Crowd in History*, pp. 108-34.
14. J.L. and Barbara Hammond, *The Town Labourer 1760-1832*, vol. I, (1949 edn), pp. 122-3.
15. *House of Commons Journals* (28 April 1796), p. 631.
16. Ibid.
17. Phipps *v*. Burgess, King's Bench, Trinity Term 1790, case no 9.
18. Galton, *Tailoring Trade*, pp. 61-3.
19. *Lloyd's Evening Post*, vol. I (1769), p. 454.
20. Ibid., 29 April – 1 May 1772.
21. Ibid., 16-18 April 1777.
22. Ibid., vol. I (1777), p. 411.
23. Ibid., pp. 420, 498.
24. Ibid., p. 396.
25. Ibid., vol. I (1778), p. 242.
26. 'The Petition of the Master Taylors of London, 1778', the report of a House of Commons committee, and a counter-petition by other master tailors, in

Galton, *Tailoring Trade*, pp. 75-80.

27. *Lloyd's Evening Post*, 24-27 April 1778.
28. *Gentleman's Magazine* (1801), p. 80.
29. E.G. Dowdell, *A Hundred Years of Quarter Sessions: the government of Middlesex from 1660 to 1760* (Cambridge, 1932), pp. 154-5.
30. S. and B. Webb, *Trade Unionism*, p. 67.
31. *Middlesex Sessions Books* (1720), no 786; *Process Register of Indictments* (July 1720), no. 11, pp. 766-7.
32. Dowdell, *Hundred Years*, p. 155n.
33. 'King *v*. Armstrong', *Lloyd's Evening Post*, 12-14 July, 29 November- 2 December 1786; 7-9 May 1787.
34. Ibid., vol. II (1788), p. 5.
35. (Edward Atkinson), *An Account of the Rise and Progress of the Dispute between Masters and Journeymen Printers* (London, 1799).
36. George W. Daniels, *The Early English Cotton Industry* (Manchester, 1920), p. 52.
37. Wadworth and Mann, *Cotton Trade*, p. 367.
38. *Old Bailey Sessions Papers 1772-1773*, p. 68.
39. *Middlesex Sessions Books*, nos. 1345, 1346; *Lloyd's Evening Post*, vol. II (1788), p. 410.
40. King *v*. Armstrong, King's Bench, 13 July, 30 November 1786, 8 May 1787. John Child, *Industrial Relations in the British Printing Industry* (London, 1967), p. 62; *Lloyd's Evening Post*, 12-14 July, 29 November- 2 December 1786; 7-9 May 1787, 30 June-2 July 1788.
41. William Le Hardy (ed.), *Calendar to the Sessions Books . . . 1752-1799*, vol. VIII (Hertford, 1935), p. 399.
42. Ibid., p. 458.
43. Ibid., p. 477.
44. *Grounds of Complaint . . . against Sunday Baking*, p. 29n.
45. 'Law Intelligence', *Lloyd's Evening Post*, vol. II (1788), pp. 424-5.
46. Ibid.
47. Ibid.
48. G. White (ed.), *Digest of the Minutes of Evidence taken before the Committee on Artisans and Machinery* (London, 1834), p. 121.
49. King *v*. Bunce and others, King's Bench, 1788.
50. King *v*. Cockburn and others, King's Bench, 1793.
51. *Lloyd's Evening Post*, 17-20 October 1794.
52. *Prices to be Paid to Journeymen and Regulations agreed upon by the Master Wheelwrights at a General Meeting held November 1795*, pp. 64-5 (catalogued at British Museum under 'Wheelwrights', BM bb.18. 8275). Fifty-nine names are printed at the end of the regulations, including the committee: Messrs Gill, Harris, Wrightson, Worthy, Taylor, Bartlett, Green, Moorman, Smith, Roake, Perrin and Edmonds.
53. *At a General Meeting of the Master Plasterers, convened to receive the Report of their Committee, at the White Hart Tavern, High Holborn, March 17 and May 19, 1796* (catalogued at British Museum under 'Plasterers', BM. 1029 k.14). The chairman was William Roberts.
54. Atkinson, *Dispute between Masters and Journeyman Printers*.
55. Ibid.
56. Ibid.
57. Ibid.
58. Ibid.
59. *Lloyd's Evening Post*, vol. I (1799), p. 172.
60. Ibid.

61. Ibid.
62. Ibid.
63. Ibid.
64. Ibid.
65. Ibid.
66. Ibid.
67. Ibid.
68. 'The Proprietors resisted the demand, and all their employers have properly determined to *put a spoke in their wheel.*' *The Times*, 16 July 1795.
69. *St. James's Chronicle*, 10-12 April 1799.
70. *London Chronicle*, 20-23 April, 30 April-2 May, 4-7, 9-11 May 1799; *True Briton*, 20, 26 April, 1, 7, 11 May 1799.
71. *Lloyd's Evening Post*, 10-12 June; *St. James's Chronicle*, 8-11 June; *London Chronicle*, 8-11 June 1799.
72. *St. James's Chronicle*, 15-18 June; *Lloyd's Evening Post*, 17-19 June 1799.
73. Hammonds, *Town Labourer* (Guild Books edn, 1949), p. 128.
74. *Lloyd's Evening Post*, 25-27 November 1795.
75. Ibid., 3-6 March, 12-14 April 1780.
76. Lord Gordon addressed a mass meeting in St George's Fields on 2 June 1780. A week of rioting followed. Rudé, *Crowd in History*, pp. 57-9.
77. 'Letter from Dublin, June 17', *Lloyd's Evening Post*, 23-26 June 1780.
78. Evidence of Mr Patrick Farrell, Dublin Carpenters' Society, in White, *Artisans and Machinery*, p. 359; cf. *Lloyd's Evening Post*, 26-28 March 1792. Mr Farrell momentarily confused the event with the French Revolution, giving the year as 1789, but otherwise his memory was excellent.
79. For the debates and petitions, see *English Historical Documents 1714-1783*, vol. X, pp. 746-61; Hammonds, *Town Labourer*, vol. I, pp. 120-30.
80. Englefield, *Painter-Stainers' Company*, pp. 84-5.
81. Evidence given at Mansion House on 3 October 1799, as reported in *Lloyd's Evening Post*, vol. II (1799), p. 336.
82. Bakers' Company, *Minutes of a special Court of the Worshipful Company of Bakers held at their Hall on Tuesday the 1st Day of October 1799* (Guildhall MSS 5177).
83. *Lloyd's Evening Post*, vol. II (1799), p. 336.
84. Ibid., pp. 347, 352, 404, 476, 500, 523, 540.
85. Ibid., p. 552.
86. 'Corporations' were dissolved under Allarde's Bill of 2 March 1791, and workers' 'coalitions' by Le Chapelier's two Bills on 22 May. Michel Vovelle, *La Chute de la Monarchie* (Paris, 1972), pp. 174, 189. For the ideological rationalisation, see Jean-Daniel Reynaud, *Les Syndicats en France*, 3rd edn, vol. I (Paris, 1975), pp. 6-8; and for the *maximum général* and its totalitarian corollary, Marc Bouloiseau, *La République Jacobine* (Paris, 1972), pp. 93, 118; also Rudé, *Crowd in History*, pp. 120-2, 131-2.
87. *Lloyd's Evening Post*, vol. II (1799), p. 125.
88. *The Times*, 28 January 1800.
89. Ibid.
90. Ibid., 11 February 1800. The punishment was for contempt of court, and the *Leeds Intelligencer* report quoted by Dr Wearmouth was misleading; cf. Robert E. Wearmouth, *Methodism and the Common People of the Eighteenth Century* (London, 1945), p. 90.
91. *The Times*, 28 January 1800. From this date onwards, radicals, Jacobins and plain-clothes policemen took an active interest in trade union affairs.
92. *St. James's Chronicle*, 22-24 October 1799.
93. *Lloyd's Evening Post*, 7-10 March 1800.

94. Ibid., 1-3 January, 25-27 August, 1-3, 8-10 September 1800, *passim*.
95. Ibid.
96. Ibid.
97. Ibid., 10-12 February 1800.
98. King *v.* Waddington, 'King's Bench, May 16, Criminal Information', in *The Times*, 17 May 1800.
99. *St. James's Chronicle*, 2-5 August 1800.
100. *The Times*, 9 August 1800. Another report said that 'when they became 200 strong, they were to take the horses from the ploughs, and have everything their own way, but in effecting this, they would neither *kill* nor *slay*': *St. James's Chronicle*, 2-5 August 1800.
101. *The Times*, 9 August 1800.
102. Ibid.
103. Ibid., 19 December 1800.
104. Historical Manuscripts Commission, *Fourteenth Report, Appendix, part IV., The Manuscripts of Lord Kenyon* (London, 1894), p. 554. The letter is dated 15 October 1800. Kenyon died the following year.
105. *St. James's Chronicle*, 2-5 August 1800.
106. *Newcastle Courant*, circ. March 1800.
107. *Lloyd's Evening Post*, 1-3, 4-7 September 1800.
108. Ibid., 28-30 April, 12-15 September 1800.
109. Burdett had changed his name to inherit from his grandfather. Ibid., 18-21 April 1800.
110. 39 and 40 Geo. III, c. 100. See G.D.H. Cole and A.W. Filson, *British Working Class Movements: select documents 1789-1875*, pp. 90-3.
111. Hammonds, *Town Labourer*, I, p. 129.
112. *Lloyd's Evening Post*, 4-6 August 1800.
113. *Second Report from the Committee of Secrecy*, 15 May 1801. Appendix (A); reprinted in *Reports from Committees of the House of Commons*, vol. X (London, 1803), p. 836.
114. *Morning Post and Gazetteer*, 10 November 1800; *St. James's Chronicle*, 8-11 November 1800; *Porcupine*, 10 November 1800.
115. *St. James's Chronicle*, 11-13 December 1800.
116. Ibid., 8-11 November 1800.
117. *The Times*, 23 December 1800.
118. Ibid., 17 December 1800.
119. Galton, *Tailoring Trade*, p. 79; *House of Commons Journals*, xxxvi, p. 881.
120. Aspinall, *Early English Trade Unions*, p. 35n.; cf. Ogilvie (1926): 'We can wait for so long for new clothes that we can let a trade dispute settle itself . . . On the other hand, when . . . food may run short and turbulence may begin, the Government is involved.' Quoted by Knowles, *Strikes*, p. 293.

CHAPTER 10

1. Pelling, *British Trade Unionism*, p. 9.
2. Morris, *Government and Labor*, pp. 193-207. See also the selection of essays in David Brody (ed.), *The American Labor Movement* (New York, 1971).
3. M. Oakeshott, *Political Education* (inaugural lecture, London School of Economics and Political Science, 1951).
4. Walter Galenson (ed.), *Labor in Developing Economies* (Berkeley and Los Angeles, 1962).

SELECT BIBLIOGRAPHY

Manuscript Sources

Corporation of London Record Office

Journals of the Court of Common Council

Guildhall Library

Bakers' Company: Court Minute Books, 1739-1808, MSS 5177/9-10
Bakers' Company: Rough Court Minute Books, MSS 5178/7
Barber-Surgeons' Company: Court Minute Book, 1743-63, MS 5275/9
Barbers' Company: Court Minute Book, 1778-1803, MSS 5257/11
Barbers' Company: Rough Court Minute Book, 1780-1804, MSS 5258/9
Blacksmiths' Company: Court Minute Book, 1705-21, MSS 2881/10
Carpenters' Company: Court Minute Books (Rough and Fair) 1757-1824, MS 4329/19-21
Cordwainers' Company: Court Minute Book, 1752-71 ('Book A'), MSS 7353/6; 1787-98 ('Book C'), MSS 7353/8; 1798-1809 ('Book D'), MSS 7353/9
Curriers' Company: Fair copy extracts from Court Minutes, 1689-1730, MSS 6113/1
Curriers' Company: Court Minute Book, 1760, MSS 6112/3
Farriers' Company: Court Minute Books, 1747-1800, 3 vols, MSS 5523/2-4
Masons' Company: Court Minute Books, 1722-96, 2 vols, MSS 5304/3-4
Painter-Stainers' Company: Court Minute Books, 1649-1793, MSS 5667/2

Middlesex Records, Greater London Council Record Office

Middlesex Sessions: Process Register of Indictments, vols 15, 17 (covering October 1744 - April 1745 and January - April 1762)
Middlesex Sessions: Books nos. 1086 (1751), 1129 (1756), 1193, 1195 (1763), 1197 (1764), 1425 (1792)
Sessions Rolls for 1744
Sessions Papers for October 1756, October 1763 and January 1764

Printed Documents and Collections

A. Aspinall, *The Early English Trade Unions, Documents from the Home Office Papers in the Public Record Office* (London, Batchworth Press, 1949)

Edward Atkinson, *An Account of the Rise and Progress of the Dispute between Masters and Journeymen Printers, exemplified in the Trial at Large* (London, J. Ridgway, 1799)

Barbers' Company, *A Translation of the Charter from the Latin, Granted by King Henry VIII* (London, 1785)

F. Beckwith, *Extracts from The Leeds Intelligencer and The Leeds Mercury, 1777-1782* (Leeds, The Thoresby Society, 1955)

A.E. Bland, P.A. Brown and R.H. Tawney, *English Economic History: Selected Documents* (London, G. Bell and Sons, 1914)

A Brief State of the Inland or Home Trade of England; and of the Oppression it Suffers (London, 1730)

A.F.J. Brown, *Essex at Work, 1700-1815* (Chelmsford, Essex County Records Office, 1969)

Richard Burn, *The Justice of the Peace and Parish Officer* (London, 4th edn, 1755; 16th edn, 1788, by John Burn)

R. Campbell, *The London Tradesman* (London, 1747, reprinted Newton Abbot, David and Charles, 1969)

The Case of the Master Taylors Within the Cities of London and Westminster (1720)

The Case of Mr. R(eynold)s, Fairly Stated by an Impartial By-Stander (London, 1753. Guildhall, Pam. 2534)

The Clerks of Counties, 1360-1960 (compiled by Sir Edgar Stephens, Society of Clerks of the Peace of Counties and of Clerks of County Councils, 1961)

Cobbett's Parliamentary History

G.D.H. Cole and Andrew Filson, *British Working Class Movements, Select Documents 1789-1875* (London, Macmillan, 1951, reprinted 1967)

Collection of documents relating to the trade clubs of builders, shoemakers, smiths, tailors and weavers in Dublin, *circa* 1720 (British Museum, 1890. e.5)

John Comyns (Sir), *Reports of Cases in the Courts of King's Bench, Common Pleas and Exchequer, 1695-1740* (London, n.d.)

The Correspondence of King George the Third from 1760 to December 1783, ed. Sir John Fortescue (6 vols, London, 1927-28: vol. II, January 1768 – June 1773, vol. III, July 1773 – December 1777)

Debrett's Parliamentary Register

Digest of the Minutes of Evidence taken before the Committee on Artisans and Machinery, ed. George White (London, 1834)

E.G. Dowdell, *A Hundred Years of Quarter Sessions: The Government of Middlesex from 1660 to 1760* (Cambridge University Press, 1832)

F.W. Galton, *Select Documents Illustrating the History of Trade Unionism, (i) The Tailoring Trade* (London, P.S. King 1896, reprinted 1923)

Jean Grosley, *Londres*, vol. I (Lausanne, 1770, revised edn 1774)

The Grounds of Complaint Against the Practice of Sunday Baking, by the Master and Journeymen Bakers of London, Westminster and the Borough of Southwark (London, 1794. Guildhall, Pam. 1093)

W. Hawkins, *A Treatise of the Pleas of the Crown* (London, 1716)

Hertfordshire County Records, *Calendar to the Sessions Books, Minute Books and Other Sessions Records, 1752-1799*, vol. III, ed. William LeHardy (London, 1935)

D.B. Horne and Mary Ransome, *English Historical Documents, 1714-1783*, vol. X (London, Eyre and Spottiswood, 1957)

Ellic Howe, *The London Compositor: Documents Relating to Wages, Working Conditions and Customs of the London Printing Trade, 1785-1900* (London, 1947)

Journals of the House of Commons

Kenyon (Lord), *Notes of Cases ... in the Court of King's Bench* (London, n.d.)

Thomas Leach, *Modern Reports, or Select Cases Adjudged in ... the King's Bench* (London, 1720-21)

Joseph Lowe, *The Present State of England in Regard to Agriculture, Trade and Finance* (second edn, 1823)

William Maitland, *The History and Survey of London from Its Foundation to the Present Time*, 2 vols (London, 1756)

James Montague, *The Old Bailey Chronicle*, 4 vols (1700-84)

John Northouck, *A New History of London Including Westminster and Southwark* (London, 1773)

Old Bailey Sessions Papers: The Whole Proceedings Upon The King's Commission of Oyer and Terminer and Gaol Delivery for the City of London

Samuel Pepys, *The Diary of Samuel Pepys*, ed. Robert Latham and William Matthew, vol. iii: 1662 (London, G. Bell and Sons Ltd, 1970)

A Practical and Eligible Plan to Secure the Rights and Privileges of Mechanics: With Proper Directions for the Journeymen, Whereby

They May Get An Advancement in Their Wages Without Loss of Time or Hindrance of Business (London, 1776. British Museum, 1029. i.6(6)

Prices to be Paid to Journeyman and Regulations agreed upon by the Master Wheelwrights at a General Meeting held November 1795 (London, 1795. British Museum, 8275. bb. 18)

The Privileges of the Free Artificers of the City of London Defended: In an appeal to the Committee appointed to receive the complaints of the masters of the several manufactures in the City against their Journeymen (London, T. Howard, n.d., circa 1750. Copies in Guildhall and Goldsmiths' Libraries)

Robert Raymond (Sir), *Reports of Cases . . . in the Courts of King's Bench and Common Pleas* (London, 1694-1732)

Records of the County of Wilts(hire), being Extracts from the Quarter Sessions Great Rolls of the Seventeenth Century, extracted and edited by B. Howard Cunningham (Devizes, George Simpson and Co., 1932)

Joseph Redington, *Calendar of Home Office Papers of the Reign of George III, 1766-1769* (London, 1879)

Richard Arthur Roberts, *Calendar of Home Office Papers, 1773-1775* (London, 1899)

Henry Robinson, *The Office of Addresses and Encounters* (London, 1650. Guildhall, A.4.4. no. 35)

Senator (House of Commons Reports) (1794)

A. Francis Stewart, *The Last Journals of Horace Walpole during the Reign of George III from 1771-1783*, vol. I (London, 1910)

John Strange (Sir), *Reports . . . in the Courts of Chancery, King's Bench, Common Pleas and Exchequer*, 1716-47, 3rd edn by Michael Nolan (n.d.)

W.T. Vincent, *The Records of the Woolwich District*, 2 vols (J.S. Virtue and Co., 1890)

T. Waller, *A General Description of All Trades* (London, 1747)

Horace Walpole, *Memoirs of the Reign of King George the Third*, ed. G.F. Russell Barker, vol. III (London, 1894)

George White, *A Digest of the Minutes of Evidence taken before the Committee on Artisans and Machinery* (London, 1824)

George Wilson, *Reports of Cases . . . in the King's Courts at Westminster, 1742-1774* (3rd edn, 1799)

Woodfall's House of Commons Reports (1794)

Newspapers and Periodicals

Annual Register
Applebee's Original Weekly Journal
British Journal
Country Journal, or the Craftsman
Daily Advertiser
Daily Courant
Daily Gazetteer
Daily Journal
Daily Post
Dublin Journal
Evening Post
Flying Post, or The Postmaster
General Advertiser
General Evening Post (London)
Gentleman's Magazine
Leeds Mercury
Lloyd's Evening Post
London Chronicle
London Daily Advertiser and Literary Gazette
London Evening Post
London Gazette
London Journal
London Magazine
The Political State of Britain
The Post-Boy
Public Advertiser
Read's Weekly Journal, or British Gazetteer
St. James's Chronicle
The Times
Weekly Journal, or British Gazetteer
Weekly Journal, or Saturday's Post
Whitehall Evening Post

Secondary Sources

B.W.E. Alford and T.C. Barker, *A History of the Carpenters' Company* (London, George Allen and Unwin, 1968)

T.S. Ashton and Joseph Sykes, *The Coal Industry of the Eighteenth Century* (Manchester University Press, 1929; 2nd edn 1964)

Frank Burchill and R. Ross, *A History of the Potters' Union* (Hanley, Stoke-on-Trent, Ceramic and Allied Trades Union, 1977)

R.H. Campbell, *Carron Company* (Edinburgh and London, Oliver and Boyd, 1961)

George W. Daniels, *The Early English Cotton Industry* (Manchester University Press, 1920)

Ralph Davis, *The Rise of the English Shipping Industry in the Seventeenth and Eighteenth Centuries* (London, Macmillan and Co., 1962)

W.A.D. Englefield, *The History of the Painter-Stainers' Company of London* (London, Chapman and Dodd, 1923)

Robert Galloway, *Annals of Coal Mining and the Coal Trade* (London, Colliery Guardian Company, 1898; reprinted with a new introduction and bibliography by Baron F. Duckham, Newton Abbot, David and Charles, 1971)

M. Dorothy George, *London Life in the Eighteenth Century* (London, Kegan Paul, Trench, Trubner and Company, 1925; reprinted London School of Economics and Political Science, 1951)

Elizabeth Waterman Gilboy, *Wages in Eighteenth Century England* (Cambridge, Mass., Harvard University Press, 1934)

J.L. and Barbara Hammond, *The Town Labourer, 1760-1832* (London, 1917; reprinted Longmans Green (Guild Books), 1949)

—— *The Skilled Labourer 1760-1832* (London, Longmans Green, 1919; reprinted New York, Augustus M. Kelley, 1967)

J.H. Hawkins, *History of the Worshipful Company of the Art or Mystery of Feltmakers of London* (London, Crowther and Goodman, 1917)

Herbert Heaton, *The Yorkshire Woollen and Worsted Industries from the earliest times up to the Industrial Revolution* (Oxford, 1920: second edn, Clarendon Press, 1965)

Gravenor Henson, *History of the Framework Knitters* (Nottingham, 1831; reprinted with an introduction by Stanley D. Chapman, Newton Abbot, David and Charles, 1970)

E.J. Hobsbawm, *Labouring Men: studies in the history of Labour* (London, Weidenfeld, 1964)

W.G. Hoskins, *Industry, Trade and People in Exeter* (1935; 2nd edn, Exeter University, 1968)

George Howell, *The Conflicts of Labour and Capital* (London, Chatto and Windus, 1878)

R. Leslie-Melville, *The Life and Work of Sir John Fielding* (London, Lincoln Williams, 1934)

J. Lindsay, *1764: the Diary of a Year* (London, Frederick Muller, 1959)

Christopher Lloyd, *The British Seaman, 1200-1860* (London, Collins,

1968, reprinted Granada Publishing (Paladin), 1970)

G.I.H. Lloyd, *The Cutlery Trades: an historical essay in the econo-mics of small-scale production* (first edn, 1913; new impression, London, Frank Cass and Company, 1968)

C.H. Waterland Mander, *A Descriptive and Historical Account of the Guild of Cordwainers in the City of London* (London, privately circulated, 1931)

Paul Mantoux, *The Industrial Revolution in the Eighteenth Century* (1928; ninth impression, London, Macmillan, 1957)

L. Namier, *The Structure of Politics at the Accession of George III* (2nd edn, London, Macmillan, 1957)

J.U. Nef, *The Rise of the British Coal Industry* (London, George Routledge and Sons Limited, 1932)

Richard Pares, *King George III and the Politicians* (Oxford, 1953)

Alfred Plummer and Richard E. Early, *The Blanket Makers 1669-1969: A history of Charles Early and Marriott (Witney) Ltd* (London, Routledge and Kegan Paul, 1969)

T.F. Reddaway, *The Rebuilding of London after the Great Fire* (London, Jonathan Cape, 1940)

George Rudé, *Wilkes and Liberty, a social study of 1763 to 1774* (Oxford, Clarendon Press, 1962)

— *The Crowd in History, a study of popular disturbance in France and England, 1730-1848* (New York, John Wiley and Sons, 1964)

— *Paris and London in the Eighteenth Century* (London, Fontana, 1969)

John Thomas Smith, *Nollekens and his Times*, 2 vols (London, 1828)

Horace Stewart, *History of the Worshipful Company of Gold and Silver Wire-drawers* (London, 1891)

E.P. Thompson, *The Making of the English Working Class* (London, Victor Gollancz, 1963; 3rd impression, 1965)

Sylvia Thrupp, *A Short History of the Worshipful Company of Bakers of London* (London, Worshipful Company of Bakers, 1933)

Arnold Toynbee, *Lectures on the Industrial Revolution of the Eighteenth Century in England* (London, Longmans Green, 1919)

George Unwin, *Industrial Organization in the Sixteenth and Seventeenth Centuries* (Oxford, Clarendon Press, 1904; 2nd edn 1957; new impression with a new introduction by T.S. Ashton, London, Frank Cass and Company Ltd, 1963)

— *The Gilds and Companies of London* (London, 1908; 4th (1963) edn reprinted London, Frank Cass and Company, 1966)

A.P. Wadsworth and J. de L. Mann, *The Cotton Trade and Industrial*

Lancashire (Manchester University Press, 1931; reprinted, 1965)

Harold E. Waite, *The London Society of Compositors: a Centenary history* (London, Cassell, 1948)

Horace Walpole, *Memoirs of the Reign of King George III*, ed. Russell Barker, vol. III of 4 vols (London, 1894)

Sidney and Beatrice Webb, *The History of Trade Unionism* (London, 1894; new edn, 1920; reprinted London, Longmans Green, 1950)

Wheelwrights, *History of the Worshipful Company of Wheelwrights* (London, n.d.)

tailors 62, 85; weavers 19, 32
proclamation 83, 110, 144, 148
profits 114-15, 119, 136
proprietors: coal mines 36; cornmills 189
prosecution 56, 73, 121, 125, 132-3, 137-8
protection of strike-breakers 107
protectionism 41
Protectorate 19, 96
provisions 103, 113, 118, 145-6
public 69, 137; interest 113, 139; justice 131;
  opinion 78, 126, 146; order 112, 123, 142;
  service 107; tranquility 142
Public Advertiser 66-8
public houses 25, 38, 85; Alfriston 116-17;
  Woolwich 107, *see also* house of call
publicans 68, 89, 142; licences stopped 90;
  prosecuted 62, 78; warned 74-5, 86
Purnel, Roger, lighterman 35

quarterage 48-9
quartern loaf *see* bread, Assize of Bread
Quarter Sessions 68, 72, 76, 84, 124-5, 142, 149;
  City of London 85; Kent 98; Middlesex 66,
  85
'Queen's Arms' 70
Queen's Palace 87

radicalism 27
Radstock 36, 167
Randall, Edward, shipwright 108, 185
Rastall, Thomas, currier 177
Ratcliff Cross 85
Ratcliff Highway 85
Read, Mr, JP 84
Reading 62, 155, 164
reapers 157, 159 *see also* haymakers
Reasons lock 131
Rebuilding Act 48
recognition 47, 124
recognizances 129, 143, 146
Recorder of London 55, 58, 124, 129
'Red Cow' 44
Red Flag 183-4; Woolwich 98
registry office 82
Regnier and Son 73, 124
regrating 67, 131, 144
regulation 97, 102-3, 133
relativities 100, 113
Renfrewshire 33, 114, 122, 158, 160-1
rent 112-13
Renter Warden 130
'revolution in manufactures' 33
reward 97
Riddle, George, collier 35
riggers 93
'right' and 'left' shoes 136
ringleaders 130, 145; impressed 98
Riot Act 32-3, 85
riotous assembly 85, 131
riots 30-2, 45, 56, 62, 65, 74, 81, 83, 86,
  112, 131, 144-5

rising prices 27, 29, 103, 112, 114, 144
'Rising Sun' 179
roads 112
Roads, Mr, farmer 23
Roberts, Mr, master blacksmith 49
Robinson, Henry, registry-office keeper 38
Rochford, Lord 41
Roebuck 106, 108
'Roebuck' 178
ropemakers 24, 44, 96-7, 154, 168
Ross, journeyman baker 142
Rotherhithe 45, 85
Rothwell Haigh 167
Rowe, Joseph, master painter 51
Royal Exchange 23, 41, 82; Dublin 140
Royal Navy 157, 163, 169, *see also* Admiralty
  Board, Navy Board
Royal Pardon 76
Rudé, George 18, 30, 181
rulebook 132
rules: friendly society 45; House of Commons
  139; journeymen shoemakers 136; journey-
  men tailors 60-1
rules of work 171
Rusholme 158
Russell, Mr, agent 82
Russell, William, tailor 128
Russians, in Dutch shipyards 99
rye-meal 84
Rymer, Edward, master currier 177

saddlers 44, 47, 91, 115, 128, 133, 168
sailmakers 24, 102, 154
sailors *see* seamen
St Clement Danes 68
St Giles 22
St James's 82-3, 89; Park 98
St Malo 109, 185
St Martin's Lane 67
St Mary le Strand 68
St Paul's 76
Salford 142, 158
Salisbury 32-3
'Sampson's Castle' 175
Sanders, Mr, master tailor 124
Sandwich, Lord 102-6, 109
Savile, Sir George 81
Savoy barracks 64, 178
Sawbridge, John, JP 86-7
sawmills 27, 115-16, 160, 173, 186
sawyers 43, 78, 90, 93; *disputes* 157, 159-60,
  162, 165
Sayer, Mr, JP 84
scarcity of provisions 103, 145-6
scavengers 46
scissor-grinders 165, *see also* cutlery
Scotland 26, 33, 114, 122, 139; *disputes* 157-62,
  164-7, 169-70
scythemakers 167
seamen 24, 27, 30, 45, 110, 112; coal vend 82,
  118; *disputes* 156-7, 159-64, 166-7, 169-70;

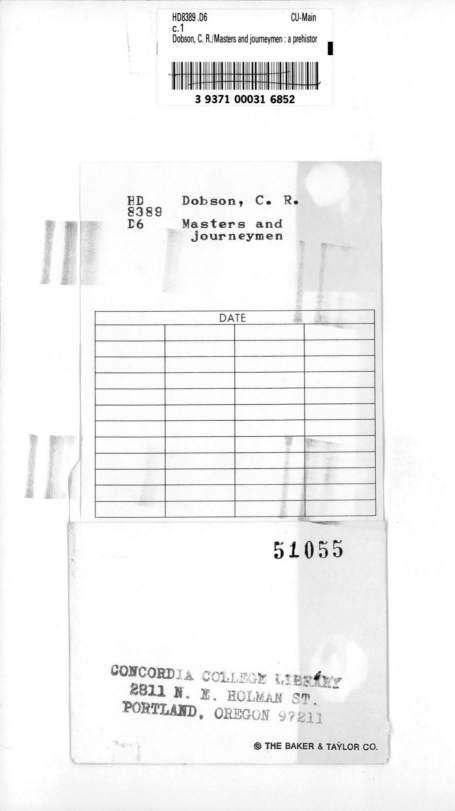

DATE			